W0259815

BASU CHATTERJI

ADVANCE PRAISE FOR THE BOOK

'This is a book which was long overdue. Anirudha Bhattacharjee writes with compassion about India's most underrated director. The harbinger of new-wave cinema, Basu-da went on to make some of the best cinema of the '70s and '80s. He worked with the biggest stars (Ashok Kumar, Dev Anand, Dharmendra, Amitabh Bachchan, Hema Malini, Jaya Bhaduri, Moushumi Chatterjee, Vidya Sinha, Shabana Azmi, Tina Munim, Neetu Kapoor) and with actors like Amol Palekar, Naseeruddin Shah, Om Puri, Pankaj Kapoor and Anupam Kher. His oeuvre is a remarkable representation of Indian cinema. I had the fortune of producing two films (*Man Pasand* and *Gudgudee*) and writing lyrics for several of Basu-da's films'—Amit Khanna, film producer, director, writer, lyricist and journalist

'There has been a visible void waiting to be captured about the cinema of Basu Chatterji, who gave Hindi cinema its common man and gave me one of my loveliest films, *Khatta Meetha*. Anirudha Bhattacharjee has done it with his meticulously researched and almost visually narrated book'—Bindiya Goswami, actress and costume designer

'The middle/parallel cinema, in which Basu Chatterji played a key role, is often overlooked today, despite its critical and commercial success and its role in the history of Hindi cinema. Anirudha Bhattacharjee's method of collecting oral histories, making connections between people and films while digging out gems of information makes his book an invaluable resource for fans, scholars and anyone interested in Indian cinema'—Rachel Dwyer, Professor Emerita of Indian Cultures and Cinema, SOAS University of London

BASU CHATTERJI

And Middle-of-the-Road Cinema

ANIRUDHA BHATTACHARJEE

VINTAGE
An imprint of Penguin Random House

VINTAGE

USA | Canada | UK | Ireland | Australia
New Zealand | India | South Africa | China | Singapore

Vintage is part of the Penguin Random House group of companies whose addresses can be found at global.penguinrandomhouse.com

Published by Penguin Random House India Pvt. Ltd
4th Floor, Capital Tower 1, MG Road,
Gurugram 122 002, Haryana, India

First published in Vintage by Penguin Random House India 2023

10 9 8 7 6 5 4 3 2

ISBN 9780670096251

Typeset in Bembo by MAP Systems, Bengaluru, India
Printed at Replika Press Pvt. Ltd, India

www.penguin.co.in

Kewal Krishna Mahajan, Bansi Chandragupta and Salil Chowdhury

Wish you were here . . .

—Artwork by Indro Ganguli

Contents

Foreword

R.D. Burman: The Man, The Music, Anirudha Bhattacharjee and Balaji Vittal's biography of the music maestro, had captivated me from the very first page. Simple in style, the book was a treasure trove of interesting anecdotes. It was quite a page-turner, and richly deserved that year's National Award for best book on Indian cinema. Anirudha had, in turn, seen my films, and was vocal in his appreciation of them, both the writing and the direction. So, you may say that an informal mutual admiration society was formed. It seemed quite befitting, therefore, that he should ask and I should agree to write the foreword of his new book. That this book was on the work of a film-maker whom I greatly admired was the icing on the cake.

I had met Basu Chatterji a number of times. Both of us being makers of parallel cinema, or the so-called 'good cinema', it was inevitable that we bumped into each other fairly often at seminars, film festivals, special screenings, soirees and so on. We were both on the National Awards jury at one time and mostly agreed on the choice of worthy films. We were also members of a newly-formed association of film-makers who championed the cause of meaningful cinema. Alas, this venture, like so many well-intended but overreaching projects, was short-lived. I do remember, however, a charming episode connected with our very first meeting at Kantilal Rathod's bungalow in Pali Hill.

In attendance were luminaries such as Mani Kaul, Saeed Mirza, Ketan Mehta and Kundan Shah. After the meeting, Basu offered to give Virendra Saini a lift home as he lived in the same area.

Saini was a cinematographer who had done camerawork for Saeed's *Arvind Desai Ki Ajeeb Dastaan* and my movie *Sparsh*. He happily accepted Basu's offer. As they were rolling along, Basu suggested that Saini stop over for a drink. 'Oh, but I don't drink,' said Saini virtuously, whereupon Basu slammed on the brakes, bringing the car to a screeching halt. 'Don't drink?!' Basu spluttered. 'Then you are a very undesirable character. What are you doing in my car? Get down. Down!' Of course, this was all in jest, and I think it throws light on an endearing facet of his character.

Basu Chatterji was a reserved, rather shy person, and I cannot claim to have been a friend or even a close associate. He did not speak much in social gatherings and was usually a silent spectator. But his films spoke volumes, and made up for his reticence. They reached out in a big way. The film society movement had taken roots in India with the forming of the Calcutta Film Society in 1947. Basu developed an insatiable appetite for world-class cinema, starting with De Sica's *Bicycle Thieves*. This new genre of realistic cinema captivated him.

His very first film, *Sara Aakash,* captured an eloquent chapter of our social history some decades ago when women were mostly the invisible sex. I will never forget the delightful scene where the husband and wife go to see a film together. Walking along the road, the wife trails well behind her lord and master, in the proper time-honoured tradition. This scene, and in fact the whole film, exudes the charm, wit, and the insight that would come to define Basu's work. He had put his own hard-earned money into the making of his first film, and funds had to be handled with great care. Moreover, Basu was depicting moderate-income group characters in the film, and being a film realist, he would allow no frills and ribbons for his simple characters. The actors' clothes were pressed under mattresses to crease them, and the women wore simple blouses stitched by some local tailor at 25 paise per blouse. The film was shot in Agra, and yet Basu refrained from showcasing the proud symbol of the town—the Taj Mahal. The famous monument merited nearly still photographs that were used in the title sequence.

Sara Aakash was not an instant hit, but slowly word of mouth, 'from the simple tongawalla to the snobby intellectual', spread and Regal Cinema in Delhi happily flashed 'House Full' signs for a long time.

Variety, the well-known Hollywood film trade journal, called it 'one of the rare Indian films.' It was also one of the first films to earn recognition as an 'offbeat art film'. Basu went on to make nearly 40 feature films. *Sara Aakash* remains my firm favourite from his entire body of work. In fact, it is one of my top five Indian films. Period.

Basu was born in Ajmer, Rajasthan in 1927. The family shifted to Mathura when he was four. His father, who worked for the Railways, was given a bungalow in the staff quarters. Basu soon became proficient in Hindi, Urdu, and Braj Bhasha, which were the languages spoken in the small town. His mother, an intelligent and well-read woman, groomed her son in Bengali, their mother tongue. Education was of prime importance in the Chatterji household, and Basu was a good student. His main interest, however, was in fine arts/drawing. He also loved flying kites from the terrace of his house. Perhaps this colourful pastime helped nurture his later flights of fancy.

At the tender age of fifteen, due to unforeseen family problems, Basu had to become the 'man of the house', the only earning member, who manned various jobs to keep the home fires burning. This greatly interfered with his education and much to his lifelong sorrow, he could never graduate.

He landed a job as a librarian at a military library in Bombay. With much spare time on his hands, he started drawing political cartoons for the weekly *Current*, and then joined the Hindi division of another journal *Blitz*, where he earned Rs 10 per cartoon.

Anirudha deftly steers readers through Basu's personal and creative journey to prepare them to better appreciate Basu's staggering output. The tight narrative does a splendid job of keeping the readers engrossed. A phenomenal amount of research has gone into the making of this biography. The writer has interviewed more than a hundred persons to cull precious insights that would embellish his work—*Cinesavants*, fans, and those who have been associated with the actual making of his films. These good people have given unstintingly of both their time and their experiences, thereby enriching the content enormously. Anirudha's love and reverence for his subject shines through every page and yet, when he dons the mantle of critic, he does not overlook or condone the film-maker's slips or lapses. He is generous in his praise but equally severe in his criticism. Basu's scant regard for the continuity of characters' clothes or footwear, his disregard for historical accuracy—showing Maruti cars plying on the road in an era when they were yet to be manufactured, or flaunting posters of films that were yet to be conceived—are examples of his careless lapses.

Basu's films mainly dealt with the travails of the common man. He empathized with the have-nots and sketched stories of their unending struggle in a city rife with problems, challenges and shortages. However, despite dealing with the downside of a tough life, Basu never lost his positive attitude. He told his tale with dollops of humour and great humanity. He saw life sunny side up and for him, the glass was always half full, never half empty.

A Chatterji film was different from the run-of-the-mill Bollywood film. He believed in showing more than telling. The ploys he used to spruce up his narrative were refreshingly charming and struck a chord with the viewers. His use of cricket commentary, familiar film songs for the background score, endless travel on local trains, and of course the glory and fury of incessant rain—these were recurring motifs in his films.

The biographer describes the making of Basu's films in great detail. Many vivid images spring to life from this biography. Basu in his *baniyan*, squatting on the floor in the early dawn, bent over his mini desk and filling page after page with dialogue; Basu on the studio floor chewing his handkerchief as the camera absorbs the action unravelling on the set; K.K. Mahajan nonchalantly shooting an important sequence on a busy street with a handheld camera; art director Bansi Chandragupta exchanging authentic old furniture from a low-key Dadar flat with brand new sofas and chairs—these are many such endearing images that add flavour to the Basu saga.

Almost every person involved in the making of his films has avowed that being part of the exciting process was just like being on an unending picnic. Of the forty or so films made by the director, many have been singled out for their fresh approach and the original style of handling social problems. They remain unique. *Piya Ka Ghar* showed the city in a new light; *Rajnigandha* in a subtle manner championed a woman's prerogative; *Chhoti Si Baat* and *Chitchor* were embraced by the public for their delightful comedy; *Khatta Meetha* was in a class by itself, while *Swami* had a serious nostalgic appeal. It is tempting to go on and on but Anirudha has analysed each Basu Chatterji film with such application and finesse that it is perhaps futile for me to conduct a parallel exercise. He has also provided a very in-depth study of Basu's television work. The phenomenal *Rajani* and the popular serial depicting the exploits of detective Byomkesh Bakshi are landmarks in Indian television. The book *Basu Chatterji: And Middle-of-the-Road Cinema* is Anirudha Bhattacharjee's gift to all lovers of good cinema in general, and to fans of films bearing Basu Chatterji's signature in particular. I thank the writer on behalf of the loyal legion of Basu fans. This gift will be cherished.

Sai Paranjpye

(Illustration by Indro Ganguli)

Author's Note

During my preteens, when my friends were heavily into films of the *dishum-dishum* variety, my parents decided that film education was a mandate for their eldest child. So, I was taken to see Hrishikesh Mukherjee's *Namak Haraam* when I was ten, and Gulzar's *Mausam* when I was twelve. By the time I saw *Chitchor* (1976), I was made aware of the term 'middle-of-the-road'. And one more name. Basu Chatterji.

Within the next 3–4 years, I saw almost all the films of Basu which were screened in Patna. *Chhoti Si Baat*, *Swami*, *Khatta Meetha*, *Baton Baton Mein*, *Apne Paraye, Rajnigandha* . . . you name it. But my real interest in Basu grew when I read Rajendra Yadav's *Sara Aakash*. It was a prescribed textbook during my Plus Two course. And it was with great difficulty that I could locate a VHS print some five years later. Twenty-something viewings and twenty-five years henceforth, when I was reading all sorts of books on cinema, I knew enough of both Hrishikesh and Gulzar. The press was kind to them. But somehow, I struggled to find comprehensive stories on the cinema of Basu.

And the thought occurred: Why don't I write one?

The book would not have happened without Rupali Guha, daughter of Basu Chatterji. Being inordinately shy, I did not have the nerve to call Basu, and sheepishly approached Rupali who was happy that someone had at least thought of writing something on her father's work.

My first interview with Basu Chatterji happened in 2014. My last and final one was in 2015. I wanted to close the manuscript by 2019, but no publisher was willing to buy the idea. Thankfully, Elizabeth Kuruvilla of Penguin Random House thought otherwise. Shantanu Ray Chaudhuri of Om books had also expressed interest, but the contract with Penguin had already been signed.

Unfortunately, due to a multitude of reasons, I could write the book only during the second phase of the COVID-induced lockdown. Basu-da had left us by then, five days after my mother passed away.

Technically, I should have used the term 'Late' with reference to Basu Chatterji, but someone who made films that are viewed with the same passion they were some fifty years ago cannot have 'Late' as the prefix to his name. His memories of the Bombay film world comprise a major part of the manuscript.

To be honest, this is not a biography. This is something many of my like-minded friends and I have always wanted to know. Behind-the-scenes stories of the films that we have loved so much.

Major portions of the book were written based on telephonic interviews, and I would like to acknowledge the film personalities who helped—in alphabetical order. But first, I would like to mention four lovely ladies from the fraternity. To start with, Sai Paranjpye. Not only did she agree to write the preface, but she was also a friend for all seasons, even facilitating my stay at the FTII. Coming to the issue of forging friendships, I was extremely lucky to befriend the talented but reticent actress Madhuchhanda Chakrabarty. She worked in *Sara Aakash* in 1969, but her memories of the film remain as good as new. In this context, I would also like to mention Praba Mahajan, who would follow up on the progress of the book from time to time. And I would often receive photos of speciality dishes made by Panchali Thakur, daughter of actress Nandita Thakur, with a promise to be served the best when we meet in Bombay.

And now the other film personalities.

Ajay Prabhakar, Akhil Mishra, Amit Khanna, Amol Palekar, Anil Dhawan, Apurba Kishore Bir, Archana Shourie, Arun Chakravorty, Arunaraje Patil, Arup Kumar Gangoly, Arvind Haldipur, Asha Sachdev, Asim Bose, Bharti Achrekar, Bindiya Goswami, Deepak Qazir Kejriwal, Dheeraj Kumar, Dinesh Shankar Shailendra, D.N. Joshi, Ferdous, Gautam Banerjee, Indraneel Kaul, Indra Kumar Bahl, Indrani Halder, Javed Akhtar, Kiran Vairale-Mumtaz, Kumar Shahani, Moushumi Chatterjee, Nandita Thakur, Narinder Singh, Nirmal Mukherjee, Pradip Acharya, Rajesh Roshan, Rajit Kapur, Rakesh Pandey, Rakesh Roshan, Ramesh Gupta, Rameshwari Seth, Ranjit Kapoor, Ravindra Singh, Saikat Mitra, Samir Samanta, Sanjoy Chowdhury, Shabana Azmi, Sukanya Kulkarni, Suresh Jindal, Syed Siraj, Tariq Khan, Tinnu Anand, Uday Chandra, Vikash Desai, Vikram, Vinay Shukla, Yogesh and Zarina Wahab.

For invaluable help with archival material, I am thankful to Saktidas Roy of Ananda Bazaar Patrika Group, Dubai-based film lover Kaustubh C. Pingle, US-based retired Dr (Professor) Surjit Singh, Bombay-based archivist S.M.M. Ausaja, and Calcutta-based collectors Mithun Pal, Sounak Chacraverti and Sudarshan Talwar.

The artistic skills of Anuvab Ojha, Indro Ganguli, Dr Jayati Sengupta, and Mehnaaz Husain were real value-adds in enriching the book. Also thanking Debkumar Mitra for getting me connected to Mehnaaz.

This book would have remained incomplete without the help of the friends and families of Basu Chatterji, his cast, and his crew. A few of them I recall are—Aditya Chakrabarty, Aloka Nanjappa, Arati Mukherjee Sen, Atima Haranahalli, Banya Barua, Bharti Gangoly, Bishnupriya Dutt, Jayanta Gupta, Kajol Majumdar, Mihir Gangoly, Panchali Thakur, Preeta Mathur, Putul Guha, Rachana Yadav, Raell Padamsee, Ranjeet Bhattacharya, Rajeev Bhattacharya, Sabita Bose, Shibani Ghosh Roy, and Viraj Dixit.

There were friends not connected with the film fraternity too who helped with contacts, suggestions and stories, and the list includes, among others, the following: Amber Banerjee, Arindam Majumdar,

Arnab Banerjee, Bhaskar Bose, Bhaskar Thakur, Biswajit Mitra, Deepanjan Deb, Dilip Raghuvanshi, Diptendu Bhattacharya, Gourab Roy Chowdhury, H. Narayan, Hetal Rao, Jaideep Mukherjee, Juhi Lahiri Adesara, Krittibas Dasgupta, Mithun Pal, Mousumi Sengupta, Nirupama Kortu, Ochintya Sharma, Samik K. Rakshit, Saptrishi Ghosh, Somraj Dutta, Sounak Chakrabarti, Pandit Subir Chakrabarty, Subrata Mitra, Sukanya Sen, Tathagata Chatterjee, Vishwanidhi Mishra, Vivek Kumar and Yasir Abbasi. Gautam Choudhury for sharing rare films like *Mere Bhaiya*, which, though not connected with Basu, had overlaps in the music. And Priyanka Bhatt for working as a research assistant. And most of all, to Balaji Vittal, who provided invaluable input and took a few major interviews.

A shout-out to authors, scribes, media professionals and film personalities who also wrote is a must in any biographical work. This book was no exception, and I thank the following for adding value: Abir Bhattacharya, Akhil Singh, Amrit Gangar, Ananth Mahadevan, Anupama Chopra, Apurba Chattopadhyay, Bidisha Ganguly Srivastava, B.K. Adarsh, B.K. Karanjia, Dayawanti Gurrung, Deepa Gahlot, Devdan Mitra, Dhruv Somani, Gautam Kaul, Girish Karnad, H.N. Narahari Rao, Indranil Mukherjee, Jai Arjun Singh, Khalid Mohamed, Mahuya Paul, Maithili Rao, Mannu Bhandari, Meena Iyer, Monojit Lahiri, Moushumi Biswas, Mrinal Sen, Nasreen Munni Kabir, Naseeruddin Shah, N. Bharathi, Pallab Chattopadhyay, Pearl Padamsee, Pinaki Chatterjee, Pritha Sarbadhikari, Raaj Grover, Rajendra Yadav, Rishi Kapoor, Rita Mehta, Roshmila Bhattacharya, Sandipan Deb, Sonal Pandya, Sourav Majumdar, Sriprakash Menon, Sulagna Biswas and Sumant Batra.

To Kanishka Gupta for getting me the contract with Penguin Random House. Many thanks to Elizabeth Kuruvilla of Penguin Random House, my editor-cum-publisher on this assignment. Also thankful to editors Saksham Garg and Vineet Gill for their fast turnarounds.

To Abhra Das, Leena Khobragade, Mayur Patel and R. Harish for sharing details of NFDC.

To Chhaya Ganguli and Juri Pandey, ex-officials of Prasar Bharti, for passing on details of DD serials.

To Suchismita Dasgupta, the well-known costume designer, for meticulously noting down details of the costumes in *Rajnigandha*, *Chhoti Si Baat* and *Chitchor*.

To Biswabijoy Sen for helping in the translation from Hindi to English.

To Swarup Bhattacharyya for providing details of the boats used in the film *Apne Paraye*.

To Dr Chandrashekhar Rao and Dr (PhD) Tanuka Ghoshal, the first readers of the manuscript.

The visit to the FTII and NFAI was like the pilgrim's visit to the holy land. Thanks to Bhupendra Kainthola (Director FTII), Prakash Magdum (Director NFAI), Sayyid Rabeehashmi (Registrar FTII), Sandeep Baid (Caretaker, FTII Guest house), and the staff of the NFAI, namely Arti Karkhanis, Dipak Kokane, Nazmin Pathan, Nilofer Nishat and Pooja Shinde. And Swapnil Joshi, my man Friday in Pune. Without him, I was like a blind man in a rainforest. Especially thankful to Shampa Das, my 'classmate-twin', for the lovely meals at her place, and to Anjana Lahiri for the dinner which reminded me of China Town in Calcutta.

To my wife, Sudipta, for reading the original stories behind many of Basu's films and discussing the same to help appreciate the connect between cinema and literature. And my sons Aritra and Shaunak, and daughter-in-law Amrita for running errands during times when the lockdown was at its worst phase.

I would also like to thank a few who I reached out to for help—often multiple times—but was turned down, their silence speaking for them. Their denial forced me to look for other avenues which added value to my work.

I have a confession to make. I have only held a film camera once, that too in order to pose with a Mitchell at the FTII. My technical knowledge of lenses and colour is limited to what I have read in physics at the Plus Two level. Whatever I know of cinema is by seeing films, at times three shows a day. And reading a lot on the subject. Hence, this book is by no means of academic interest. Don't look for highbrow interpretations. Like Basu Chatterji, it attempts to be simple, something that would leave you with a song in your heart, a smile on your lips and a twinkle in the eye.

Prologue

Agra, 1940

In early 1940, as the winter gradually eased out into a more colourful spring, ten-year-old Pratibha Mishra of Salempur was married to teenager Ram Prakash Dixit in Nagla Bariyaar, a small village in the United Provinces. The couple moved to Agra after a few days. Prakash—as addressed by his friends—went back to his study routine. Pratibha landed herself a round-the-clock job in the kitchen. Very soon, two contrasting philosophies—*Chhayavadi* poetry and the ideology of Swami Vivekananda, Subhas Chandra Bose and Bhagat Singh—would influence Prakash's thinking. These resulted in his long hair, and a stark nationalist attitude which found him throwing a rock at a British officer, only to flee the scene to escape getting locked up. Unfortunately, his romantic illusions were limited to the world of literature and the nation's demand on young, virile souls, and he remained oblivious to the happenings within his house. Unwilling to marry in the first place, his compulsive inhibition mutated into utter indifference towards his wife.

The Taj Mahal and its stories in Hindi cinema have essentially mandated a middle-aged Shah Jahan romancing his wife Mumtaz in the gardens in and around Agra; unfortunately, the post-Mughal times were probably very different. The child bride was considered another household help, old enough to carry out the responsibilities of a joint family, yet too young to romance her husband until puberty added the task of bearing children.

For Pratibha, things took an unfavourable turn when the elder sister-in-law made a ritual of poisoning the ears of the elders in the family. Starting with doctoring the *dal* to spreading rumours of an alleged affair, she played it with a fair degree of success, with the result that Prakash, already nursing a grudge, did not talk to his wife, and the marriage remained unconsummated for years.

24 October 1969

7.30 p.m. It was a normal evening at Adda, the ever-busy tea outlet outside Lady Lyall hospital in Raja ki Mandi. There was little change in the routine of the cognoscenti which had assembled, except for the fact that most had let go of *bedei*, the evening snack which they had with piping hot tea in earthen cups. It was the day of Kojagari Purnima, the Bengali Laxmi Puja, and there were invitations for prasad at Bengali households. Scribes from *Sainik Samachar* and *Amar Ujala* who had gathered had nothing new to report, apart from discussing the chaos which had to be handled during the shoot of a film at the university grounds. Little did they know that the public response to a film on that day in Delhi would change a few equations. *Aradhana* was released that day.

Oblivious to the handover in stardom which was taking place, a few of the cast and crew from the feature which was being shot in Agra had come down for a visit to the Taj, which supposedly looked its loveliest in the evening on this day of the year.

Filming the contrast of light-bluish white marble against the blue-black background with a handheld Arriflex was a young cameraman named K.K. Mahajan.

And calling 'Cut!' was someone who had risked his job and his finances, and had come to Agra to film Pratibha's story under his production company which he called Cineye Films—a man named Basu Chatterji.

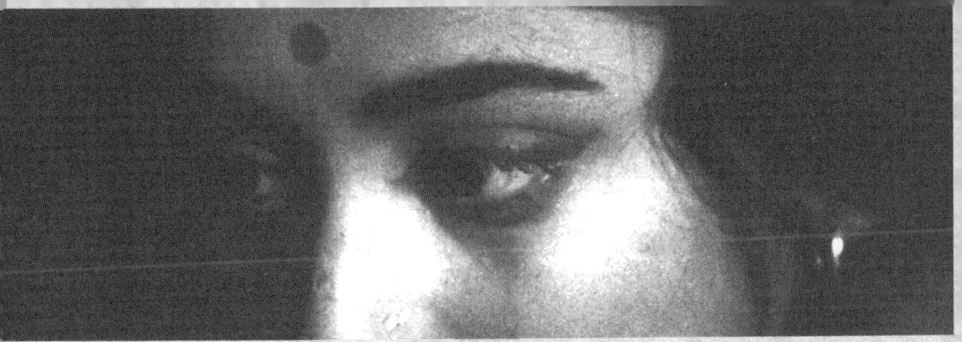

BOOK 1

Morning

'In Mathura, everything was so placid—
the Yamuna, trains on the level crossing, chaubes sitting and praying—there was absolutely no urgency in life.'
Basu Chatterji, *Filmfare*, 16–30 April 1979

Mathura

Kali Charan Chatterji was one of the first graduates of Billagram, a village in the Krishnanagar subdivision in West Bengal. A job with the government brought him to Allahabad in the later part of the nineteenth century. His son, Saroj Kumar Chatterji, born in 1886, found employment with the Bombay, Baroda and Central India Railway company and was married to the 1900-born Sushama Mukherjee in the early 1910s. Work brought him to Ajmer, Rajasthan, where his fourth child and third son Basudeb, aka Naku, was born on 10 January 1927. Basudeb's younger sister was born in 1929. The family shifted to Abu Road for a short period, and then to Mathura when Basudeb was four years old. Subsequently, there were three more additions to the family of which Bina, a girl child, passed away in infancy. The Chatterjis, who had initially put up in a railway quarter which had a big living room, shifted to a three-storeyed house in Balla Gali after a short transition at Dalpat Khidki area nearby.

> The house had many rooms. Mathura had extreme climate. During the winter we would all shift to the second floor.

> Summertime found us returning to the ground floor. We did not have electricity; there was a small room in front where the coal and cow dung cakes would be stored.[1]

The name Basu is Bengali. In any other part of India other than the east, it normally gets interpreted as Vasu. Mathura, with a limited Bengali population as compared to places like Lucknow or Varanasi in the United Provinces, was a small town where the main languages were Hindi, Urdu, and Braj Bhasha. In no time, Basudeb became Vasudev, or Basdeo, to his friends. While the spelling at the Government High School where he and his brothers studied remained Basudeb, the surname Chatterji would undergo random changeovers from time to time. Chatterjee, the majorly followed one, and Chatterji, the surname which would get the official insignia.

The brothers were named Jaideb, Bhudeb, Basudeb, Buddhadeb, and Sukhdeb. The sisters were Roma and Savita, aka Tatu.

Education held paramount importance in the Chatterji household. Saroj Kumar Chatterji knew multiple languages, and his duties included Persian-English translation. He was meant to travel to the UK for higher education, only to succumb to the norms of orthodoxy lest he be named an outcast. Subsequently, an opportunity at Grant Medical College in Bombay failed to fructify as a plague broke out at that time. His son Basu, apart from being a reasonably good student, was more than a capable sportsman representing his school in hockey and football at the district and state levels. However, his main interests were in geography and drawing. Fine Arts was one of the electives at that time, something which helped Basu excel in school. As per his younger brother Buddhadeb's memoirs, a young Basu's sketch-pen portrait of Jawaharlal Nehru would adorn the drawing hall of a certain Rai Bahadur Ganguly's kothi in Mathura for many years.

The family subscribed to the *Hindustan Times*. Kesava Shankar Pillai, aka Shankar, was the cartoonist there, whose artwork and biting humour was also one of the reasons behind Basu's love for satire in art.[2]

★ ★ ★

Compared to the Calcutta-based Bengali of the early twentieth century, the average *probashi* was brought up differently. People who had migrated to the west and north were mostly lawyers who settled in not-so-happening places where the impact of colonialism was low, to the extent that Hindi, and not Bengali or English, would often be the language they would be comfortable with. Young Basu studied in the Hindi medium and had a good understanding of Hindi literature as well. Work-related tours kept Saroj Chatterji busy and often away from home, and Sushama Chatterji took it upon herself to teach the children Bengali. She was extremely intelligent and well-read, but was unable to pursue higher education due to her early marriage. As a schoolgirl, she had received a special award—a glass doll from one of the nobles of Ajmer—for excelling in mathematics in the state exam. Her parents, Mukherjees from Khidirpore in Calcutta, were erudite and fond of contemporary Bengali literature. Sushama grew up to be a bookworm, either reading a book out to her children or asking them to read a few. In spite of staying in Ajmer and Mathura, places whose demographic profile was anything but Bengali, she would make it a point to read Bengali stories.[3]

Basu's impression of his mother was reproduced in his brother Buddhadeb's memoirs:

> Mother was very talkative. Stories, songs, anecdotes—she used to render them all. I do not remember any story now but I remember the song '*Dhono dhannyo pushpe bhora, amader ei boshundhora'* (a song written and composed by D.L. Roy and popular during the Nationalist movement in United Bengal). Her greatest contribution to my life was that she taught me Bengali—to read, write, and speak.

His take on Bengali culture was also noteworthy:

> Even though we were just five Bengali families in Mathura, we had a strong cultural link, celebrating Durga Puja, Kali Puja, and Saraswati Puja together. In those days, Bengalis were a respected class in Uttar Pradesh [United Provinces]. Naturally, we felt proud to be [a] Bengali. I used to read Bengali literature from [my] childhood. At that time, I liked the novels of Sarat Chandra Chatterjee.

It was probably courtesy of Sushama's strict upbringing that the children remained grounded throughout their lives. Bengali customs, like touching the feet of elders, and evening rituals like sprinkling water on the doorstep, watering the plants, blowing the conch shell, lighting a lamp followed by circumambulation of a potted basil tree in the courtyard, etc., came naturally to them. Buddhadeb goes on to mention:

> The old house of Balla Gali where Basu-da lived for about fifteen years or more had Rajasthani motifs at the main door and eaves. The neighbourhood was dominated by middle-class *Braj-basis* (natives of the Braj area) who had practices like spinning the charkha and hand-grinding of grains early in the morning, and celebrating Dussehra, Ram Lila, Holi, and Lord Krishna's festivals like Janmashtami. It was the blending of two regional languages, cultures, and traditions in which Basu-da grew up and spent 18–20 years of his early life.

The trade-off from the blending of cultures can backfire if it extends to culinary preferences. The Chatterjis were vegetarians; not by choice, but by design. The entry of the house was through a temple (Dauji ka Mandir); consequently, the house would fall under the periphery of the temple leading to restrictions, forcing the lady of the house not to cook non-vegetarian food.[4] Fish, a staple food of Bengalis, would normally be consumed when the children would catch them at the Raya Canal on the Jamuna during picnics. Mutton kofta would have to be bought from a small Muslim shop from a nearby locality called Holi Darwaza. Sushama was also a stickler for cleanliness; a bath in the courtyard was often a prerequisite for any child coming from outside. Her indulgence in orthodox rituals was also a cause for major irritation among the kids. Even when Lux, Margo or Hamam were household names, she would prefer to use Multani mitti (Fuller's earth) during cleaning/bathing sessions which happened with prodigious regularity.

Along with managing the house, Sushama would get the children to buy essentials. Later in the day, she would take up the onerous task of stitching garments for everyone in the family. A Singer sewing machine had its place of pride in the anteroom. The size and shape of the garments were immaterial as long as they were wearable.

While Sushama's persona was marked by a strong sense of discipline, she also had a self-deprecating sense of humour. Basu probably inherited this trait from his mother.

The Chatterjis were a well-knit unit. Life in the Chatterji household was a microcosm of the modest temple town where the art of survival was through loving and giving, where people prayed and sang with enthusiasm, albeit not always in tune. The seeds of an uncomplicated outlook were sown in Basu's mind during his pre-teen days courtesy his humble and unsophisticated upbringing. The third storey of the house at Balla Gali had a terrace, where the brothers would fly kites during the summer and on special occasions. Perhaps this is something that helped Basu to dream beyond the ordinary. Tatu, his sister, was his shadow, helping him and Buddhadeb manage the flight of the handmade multi-coloured paper quadrilaterals.

★ ★ ★

Happiness is often short-lived. Around the mid-1930s, Jaideb travelled to Moradabad for his graduation, following which he got a government job in 1938. The same year, Roma, the second child of the family, was married to Shubham Bhattacharya who was then working in Jaipur. Life was taking its normal course when Bhudeb, the third child of the family, passed away due to cholera. This was in 1940, a year after Saroj Chatterji had left the Railways. Roma was a livewire; her absence and subsequently Bhudeb's death dampened the spirit of the family considerably. Jaideb's marriage in 1942, followed by his opting out of the joint family system a year later landed the Chatterjis in financial difficulty. Suddenly, Basu was the senior-most 'young man' in the house. He was 15.

Adversity probably draws the best out of individuals, and this was the time when the generally reticent child began to exhibit leadership qualities.

On 9 August 1942, the first day of the Quit India movement, Basu was in class when a procession from a nearby college entered the premises of the Government High School. The young turks were shouting slogans and demanding that the school be closed as all private schools and colleges in the town had already done so. Basu, sympathetic to their cause, joined the procession and started chanting slogans. To avoid any more chaos, Umesh Chandra Dutt, the school principal, declared an unscheduled holiday but sensing danger, detained the students of the lower classes, waiting for their parents to take them home.

Basu, in the meantime, was taken to the police station. Considering his age, he was let off. It was a disappointment, as he felt that there was a sense of pride in getting arrested.

However, once he was told that 10-year-old Buddhadeb was serving detention, he rushed back to school and did a rescue act by escorting his brother through an alternate route back home. For once, there was violence on the main roads of this otherwise peaceful temple town. Confronted with a task daunting for his age, Basu's understanding of the bigger picture saved the day both for him and his brother.

By then, Basu had a companion for life: spectacles. He had started suffering from myopia.

* * *

On 9 August 1942, the war cry of the fifteen-year-old was *karenge ya marange* (do or die). On other days, his war cries would echo the verbose dialogues of the protagonist knocking the daylights out of the villain during the climax of films made by Wadia Movietone. Mathura had two cinema halls, where films would run for a maximum of one week before being replaced by another. Needless to say, Basu was the school kid every usher and booking clerk knew at Novelty and Laxmi Cinema. Said Basu:

> I saw all films that came to Mathura. In those days, films would be advertised on rickshaws or via posters carried by people on foot. I would also go to Agra just to see the latest films when there was no school. It was the largest town in the area and boasted of many cinema halls. Offhand, I remember two, Bharat and Jaswant. A two-hour-long train journey was fine with me as I never had to buy a ticket. My father was a railway employee; we had a pass. And incidentally, no TTE ever asked me for the ticket. I also maintained a diary where I noted down the names of the films I watched.
>
> There were no favourites. I loved action movies, colloquially known as stunt pictures. I think I had seen films from all major studios then. I also loved the songs in the films of New Theatres. Much later, when I had outgrown my childhood fantasies, I started liking films by European directors.[5]

The family had a box camera in the 1930s. Later, Basu was gifted an Agfa camera which he used to carry during outings. Photos that decorate the family album include one of the bridge over the Yamuna at Mathura and another of the Laxman Jhoola at Rishikesh.

* * *

In 1943, Basu was one of two students from the government school who passed Class X in first division. With Jaideb no longer contributing to the family's finances, the need of the hour was a job. Both Basu and his father joined the Records Office at the cantonment. He was paid Rs 75 per month, Rs 25 more than his father. He also joined Kishori Raman Inter College[6] to pursue Intermediate Arts, which he completed in 1945.

Three years later, Basu, probably on the strength of his service at the Records Office during WW II, was offered a job as a draftsman with the Coastal Artillery in Colaba, Bombay.[7] He had enrolled for the Bachelor of Arts course at Agra University in 1946, but his efforts to graduate remained abortive due to work pressure coupled with a financial crunch. An offer that promised a better salary made Basu move to Bombay in 1948; after the First Battalion of the Somerset Light Infantry, the last of the British troops, left Indian shores.[8]

The ache of not being able to graduate would remain with him till his last days.

Bombay: Early Days

For years, the average North Indian male has deluded himself into believing that he is hero material. Basu was well-built, fair, with soft features and a sharp, near aquiline nose. At Bombay, Basu chanced upon an ad where a Madras-based producer was searching for a fresh face to play the lead in a film. Seemingly excited by the ad, Basu went to a studio for a photo session, only to beat a hasty retreat after being asked to pay an astronomical sum for designer photographs. His dreams of being the object of attraction on the screen took a nosedive; nevertheless, his predilection for cinema did not wane. The film was released in 1951 as *Bahar*,[9] where Vyjayanthimala made her debut. Karan Dewan, the male lead, was not a new face.

Before joining films, Dewan was a journalist for an Urdu periodical. Basu too ended up as one, drawing cartoons for a living. His work as a librarian gave him spare time, and he found part-time work as a political cartoonist with the weekly *March*, which was renamed *The Current* in 1949. His first published cartoon was on 15 August 1948, exactly a year after India had been declared independent. The cartoon featured a year-old ailing India surrounded by political bigwigs like Nehru, Azad, et al, in contemplation. The editor of *Current* was D.F. Karaka, who was especially happy with a cartoon Basu had drawn depicting a sadhu seated on a bed of thorns and reading *Current*.

A few months and around 20 cartoons later, Basu joined the offices of the Hindi division of *Blitz* near Fort, Bombay. His employment was contractual, and he would be paid Rs 10 for a cartoon. He would need to draw two cartoons per week, which were also published in the Urdu and English versions.

While cartoons were an extension of art, the satirical end products might have surprised even the pathologically reticent Basu. The act of drawing cartoons was fortuitous. Basu had put up in a small single-room set-up near Colaba, South Bombay. With not much to do before or after office hours, he had started investing in his hobby. A small drawing board, a bottle of Indian black ink, a few special sketch pens and pencils, and some paper was all he needed to pursue the act of drawing cartoons.

In 1949, Saroj Kumar's office closed down. He passed away at the end of 1950 after a short illness. Basu came down to Mathura for the last rites. With Jaideb settled separately in Ranchi, Basu was the head of the family on the rebound.

By this time he had met up with his school senior and friend Shankardas, who was known as Shailendra in film circles. Shailendra was yet to become an epochal figure. But he helped Basu visit a few film studios and personalities. Gyan Mukherjee became a friend. Another friend was his would-be brother-in-law Samar Chatterjee, a small-time actor. Basu, in an interview, recalled meeting singer-composer Hemanta Kumar Mukherjee, aka Hemant Kumar, who offered tea to him and Shailendra in glasses. Made of glass.

A few years before meeting the film folk, Basu had seen something which would change his vision of cinema.

Cinema Calling

The film society movement started in Europe in the 1920s; there are documented records of societies being formed in London, like the Film Society in 1925. However, the exact details of the first registered film society in India are vague. As per Vijaya Mulay, Ferenc Berko, a Hungarian photographer who was serving the Army in Bombay, started the Amateur Cine Society in 1937–38.[10] It was limited to technicians. Later, in 1942–43, it was registered as the Bombay Film Society (BFS). Screenings for members happened at the miniature theatre inside Eros Cinema, opposite Churchgate station. Post-independence, the Brits who were the main sponsors of this recreational cluster, left India.

> During my early days in Bombay, I had applied for membership at the BFS. I was told that there were no vacant seats. BFS was also a club for the elite, a lower-middle-class clerk like me was probably not welcome. I later joined a few film societies. Before that, I went around with Shailendra and met many film personnel.[11]

The monopolistic singularity of BFS in screening difficult-to-see films would soon cease to remain a monopoly. The contribution of the Calcutta Film Society was paramount in helping open up the market.

★ ★ ★

The Calcutta Film Society (CFS) was born in an attic in Ballygunge at the house of Chidananda Dasgupta in October 1947. Prasanta Chandra Mahalanobis, famed scientist and the founder of the Indian Statistical Institute, was the honorary president. Dasgupta and Satyajit Ray were the secretaries. For all practical purposes, the film society movement in Independent India gained momentum courtesy of the enthusiasm of the CFS. The first international film festival was planned by the government in 1952, and the CFS sent across a long list of foreign films of which many were procured by the Films Division for exhibition in the four metros.

The first phase of the festival was in Bombay, from 24 January to 1 February 1952. With a near-democratic framework of access to films of one's choice, it helped reduce the gap between the enthusiast and the cinephile.

It was at Bombay that Basu Chatterji saw *Bicycle Thieves.* It set him thinking. He is quoted as saying:

> Many people have asked me if *Bicycle Thieves* inspired me in thinking about cinema. The actors were non-professionals. The hero was probably a lathe operator at that time. My reaction to the film was very similar to other viewers. All felt that it was part of their lives. It could happen to anyone. I had a similar feeling during a few more films, one of which was Ray's *Pather Panchali* (1955). I was happy that Indians too could produce world-class cinema.[12]

Film festivals gradually became a norm in India. Jawaharlal Nehru understood 'art', and wanted Indian cinema to create a space for itself. Simultaneously, many more film societies were started in places like Patna (in 1951–52), New Delhi (1956), Madras (1957), Roorkee, and Bhopal (International Film Club in 1959), among others.

* * *

By 1953, Basu had moved from his Colaba shack to a 2BHK house in Daulat Nagar, Borivali East, a suburb that is now a part of Bombay. Savita's marriage to Bijoy Kumar Banerji happened in

1952 at Jaideb's place in Ranchi. In 1953, with Savita moving to Calcutta, the rest of the family shifted to Bombay.

From Borivali, Basu would board the local train to Churchgate from where he would go to his places of work. He made a few friends on the way, one among them being Dhruva Chatterjee, writer, and cousin of actor Soumitra Chatterjee. Sriman Barua, who had joined Reserve Bank of India, Bombay, in 1956, met Basu on a local train and moved into a nearby flat. Their emotional bonding extended beyond just being local train buddies. Chatterji Kaku (Uncle Chatterji) was the only uncle they knew, mentions Banya Barua, Sriman's daughter.[13]

On 20 June 1957, Basu was married to Keka Banerjee, a resident of Karol Bagh in New Delhi. Sonali, the couple's elder daughter, was born on 13 April 1958.

* * *

It is said that you can take a Bengali out of Bengal, but cannot take Bengal out of a Bengali. A growing suburb in the 1950s, Borivali had many Bengalis who had started the first Durga Puja in that area in 1953. It was the only Durga Puja in Bombay which was north of Bandra. Abani Dasgupta, percussionist and artist, was in charge of making the Durga idol. He was assisted by Basu. Bimal Roy, fresh from the critical success of *Do Bigha Zamin* (1953), was the honorary president in 1953.

The puja, an annual affair, was witness to nightlong musical soirees of Ustad Ali Akbar Khan, Allah Rakha, Manna Dey, Hemant Kumar, C.H. Atma and Salil Chowdhury's Bombay Youth Choir, among others. Abani Dasgupta, the pioneer of rhythm instruments like the dhol and the khol, would play the dhak, the sound of which is supposed to announce the arrival of the festival, which, for most, was more cultural than religious.

The cultural engagement helped Basu rub shoulders with the who's who of Bombay cinema. Unfortunately, Gyan Mukherjee passed away in 1956. Courtesy of Dhruva Chatterjee, and Basu's feverish moonlighting for cinema-related assignments, Basu would engage as a Public Relations Officer (PRO) with film-maker Hemen Gupta, albeit for a short duration. This activity was over and above his day jobs. Apart from *Blitz*, Basu had also started freelancing for *Free Press Journal*, and there was a time when he was asked to fill in the slot vacated by Bal Thackeray in 1960.[14]

Hemen Gupta, whose office was at Mahalakshmi, had just announced *Raaj Kamal*. Starring Pradeep Kumar and Madhubala, the *muhurat* was performed by Roberto Rossellini who was in India for his documentary *India: Matri Bhumi* (1959).[15] *Raaj Kamal,* despite the decorated start, had to be shelved, which led Basu to take up the role of a PRO with Raj Rishi Malhotra whose office was next door. Raj Rishi, as he was popularly known, had almost completed the shoot of *Ek Ke Baad Ek* (1960). Basu had designed two posters for the film, one measuring 30x40 cm and the other 20x30.[16] *Ek Ke Baad Ek,* a feature on family planning, was a disaster, and though Raj Rishi announced a few more films like *Armaan Bhara Dil*, *Saathi* and *Jahan Saathi Wahin Manzil* with Sharda (actor Vinod Mehra's elder sister), the leading lady of *Ek Ke Baad Ek,* none of them came to fruition.[17]

It was then that Shailendra introduced Basu to Basu Bhattacharya.

Assistantship

On 23 October 1960, Shailendra, in a letter to Patna-based poet and author Phanishwar Nath 'Renu', expressed the desire to produce a film on the story 'Maare Gaye Gulfam.'[18]

A few months later, in 1961, the *muhurat* was performed with the recording of two songs: 'Sajan Re Jhooth Mat Bolo' and 'Raat Dhalney Lagee'. The film was named *Teesri Kasam.*[19]

Disappointed that the films with which he was associated did not work, Basu had approached Shailendra for an opportunity. He was introduced to the director; his namesake with the surname

Bhattacharya. Basu Bhattacharya was a smart man who had a way with words. He was also among the assistants for Bimal Roy's *Parakh* (1960). His elopement and later marriage with Roy's daughter Rinki would be a matter of great concern for the conservative Roy family.

Nevertheless, the two Basus became good friends, and Chatterji became Bhattacharya's assistant for *Teesri Kasam*. Before joining as an assistant, Basu had to enrol as a member of the film directors' association, and it is there that he met fellow struggler Arun Kaul, who would remain a friend for life.

> Interestingly, Chatterji and Bhattacharya called each other Basu-da. Chatterji called Bhattacharya Basu-da as the latter was senior to him in the industry. In turn, Bhattacharya also added the honorific suffix as Chatterji was senior to him in age.

Bhattacharya also introduced Chatterji to a film society where he was a member. Named Anandam, it was started in 1959 under the aegis of Gopal Kumar Dootia, a critic and member of the Central Board of Film Certification, Bombay. Later, the society had, among others, film-maker Kumar Shahani and famed film journalist Uma da Cunha. Films for the public would be exhibited mostly at Tarabai Hall at Marine Lines.[20]

Shahani, who was associated with Anandam, mentions to the author:[21]

> For me, Anandam was important both because of nurturing it in its early days and because of my meetings with great film-makers, such as Ritwik Ghatak and Andrzej Wajda. We had our Anandam screenings at Ramnord Laboratories, established by Ram Chattopadhyay [in 1948], son of Harindranath Chattopadhyay, who had hoped to introduce Technicolour in India.

Basu Chatterji's association with Anandam was however limited to getting to see films that were beyond the access of the common man. 'I saw a lot of films during that period. And then became one of the founders of another film society called Film Forum.'[22]

★ ★ ★

A five-minute walk from Dadar East Railway Station (Central Line) towards Rooptara Studios lies the Hind Rajasthan Centre, also known as the Hind Rajasthan building. Situated on Dadasaheb Phalke Road, this building housed a film society named Film Forum in one of its numerous flats.[23]

Film Forum was started in 1964 [1965 according to another report] by K.A. Abbas. V.K. Cherian, in his book *India's Film Society Movement,* states,[24] 'He (Abbas) was also one of the key figures behind the film society Film Forum in Bombay, along with fellow journalist and scriptwriter V.P. Sathe, film-maker Basu Chatterji, Bikram Singh, a civil servant-turned film-maker, and Arun Kaul, who produced [*sic*] Mrinal Sen's *Bhuvan Shome.*'

Basu and Arun Kaul had to take up administrative positions this time—and not exactly honorary ones. They were designated as the secretaries of Film Forum. There was a small room where Basu would sit. It had a collection of film books, quite a few being his own, which served as the library. Membership was not a mandate for viewing films that were, like Anandam, screened at Tarabai Hall.

Film-maker Indraneel Kaul, son of Arun Kaul, in a chat with the author, points out something not widely discussed in connection with Film Forum.[25]

> There was a point in time when a lot of people were coming over into the world of parallel cinema. Film Forum was one of the many forays that had happened during the parallel cinema movement. It also intended to give literature its rightful place in Indian cinema. If you wanted to make a film based on an existing story, come, buy, pay the author and also give him due recognition, and then do whatever you want to. A lot of authors too were naturally coming over, as the process of

> copyrighting source material used for cinema was gaining in importance. Authors would solicit the help of Film Forum then to help them out in this area.

Film Forum also had its quarterly magazine. Named *Close-Up,* it was started in 1968. The second issue, dated October-December 1968, featured an interview with James Ivory and Ismail Merchant which was handled mostly by film critic Jag Mohan, a member of BFS who had joined Film Forum. Basu and Kaul supported him. The editorial board, apart from Abbas, V.P. Sathe, Basu, Jag Mohan and Kaul, comprised names like Mrinal Sen, Ram Maheshwari and Bikram Singh. Gopal Dutt was the official editor of the magazine. Present-day scribe and film-maker Khalid Mohamed would also have editorial duties thrust upon him in 1969.[26]

★ ★ ★

The mid-1960s found Basu slotted into the Bombay conundrum of multitasking. He was assisting Bhattacharya, managing Film Forum, organizing film shows, and also travelling to the offices of *Blitz* and *Free Press Journal* twice a week. Starting in the late 1950s, he was charging Rs 150 per cartoon, something which helped him chuck his job at Colaba. In 1966, a year after his younger daughter Rupali was born (on 2 July 1965), Basu bought his first major tangible asset—a flat in Adarsh Nagar, Bombay. It was still under construction, and the changeover happened in a few years.

Relieved from the pressures of a day job, Basu would use the time to hone his writing skills. His work in *Teesri Kasam* was typing out Nabendu Ghosh's screenplay. Ghosh, who knew precious little Hindi, would mostly use English as the medium of communication. Basu, in the meantime, had read the story well enough to write his version of the screenplay and compare it with the official one.

Outside work, Basu also wrote Hemen Gupta's obit for Film Forum in 1967, before the quarterly magazine was officially launched.[27]

★ ★ ★

In a span of a few years, Film Forum had created excellent connections with film institutes around the world. This included the British Film Institute, the cine academics of the USSR, France, East European countries like Poland and Czechoslovakia, and Asian countries like Ceylon and Japan.[28] Sound recordist Narinder Singh tells the author that they were treated to the best of Japanese films.[29] Film Forum also organised a retrospective of Indian cinema in Paris in collaboration with Cinematheque française in March 1967.[30] This was a publicised event, and the press conference in Bombay was one of the few occasions when Basu wore a suit. The photos were published in film magazines as well. Film Forum also honoured him with his first flight from Bombay to Calcutta.

Before Film Forum was established, the shutters of BFS were pulled down in 1962. The balance sheet showed an asset value of Rs 1500, which was transferred to Film Forum. A lot of members just came over, and one among them was fellow cartoonist Govind Saraiya, who was the secretary at BFS.[31]

After the completion of *Teesri Kasam*, Basu received a call from Saraiya to assist him for his first feature *Saraswatichandra* (1968).[32] Said Basu:

> 'Shailendra passed away after the release of *Teesri Kasam*. I always felt that the making of *Teesri Kasam* was partly responsible for his death. He had invested a lot of money, consequent to which he would worry about how to pay his creditors, and had started drinking heavily, something which proved fatal [. . .] Incidentally, during the last phase of both *Teesri Kasam* and *Saraswatichandra,* the relationship between the producer and the director became strained. The directors were not present during the editing phase, and I had to be there representing them. This helped me to a great extent in learning the art of editing. Today, I feel that the elbow grease which rubbed off on me during this stage of my life helped me a lot when I made my films.'[3]

The Variegated Sky

'When you stare into the abyss, the abyss stares back at you.'
—Friedrich Nietzsche

The Film Finance Corporation (FFC, later the National Film Development Corporation or NFDC)

It was a not-so-sultry April morning in 2015. Seated in a somewhat dusty but plush sofa was Basu Chatterji in his flat at the Ballygunge area in Calcutta. Usually under lock and key, the house was opened only on occasions when Basu or his family came down from Bombay. I had come down ten kilometres, with a short interview in mind. The session turned out to be seven hours long. And started with the making of *Sara Aakash*. Because my Sony recorder was malfunctioning, I rapidly took notes. The rapid part was redundant; Basu spoke in monosyllables and the answers took much less time than the framing and asking of questions. The smile never dropped from this one-time monolith's face. He was eighty-eight. For his age, his memory was reasonably good.

> It must have been around the late 1960s. I had completed assisting Govind Saraiya and had written a script based on the story of a Czech film I had seen. I took it to Himmat Singh at FFC. He advised me to submit a script based on an Indian story. My friend at Film Forum, Arun Kaul, gave me the book *Sara Aakash*. I read it in one go. It was not an easy book to follow—the manner in which it was written was

> complex—almost like the labyrinthine bylanes of Agra where the story was based. The story attracted me a great deal. It had a lot of emotional content. We purchased the story from Rajendra Yadav for Rs 21. I wrote down the script for the film in a week after which I took it to Bikram Singh who I knew through Film Forum. He liked it. Initial vetting done, my next port of call was B.K. Karanjia, who had replaced Himmat Singh at the FFC. He approved it. FFC granted me a loan of Rs 2.25 lakh (0.225 million) for the film.[34]
>
> ** In another interview, Basu mentioned an amount of Rs 1.60 lakh. This seems more plausible as the loan rolled out just a year ago for *Bhuvan Shome* (1969) was Rs 1.5 lakh.

Rachana Yadav, daughter of Rajendra Yadav, recalls a different line of approach about *Sara Aakash* though.

> Basu Chatterji had a sister who was married in Calcutta, Savita Banerjee. She was a good friend of my father and had taken the story of *Sara Aakash* to Basu Chatterji. It was through her that Basu Uncle got in touch with my father. My mother Mannu Bhandari was then teaching at Miranda House, and my parents were living in a place called Shakti Nagar near Delhi University. Basu Uncle wrote a letter first and followed it up with a visit to our place.[35]

Rupali Guha, Basu's younger daughter, mentions that both happened almost simultaneously.[36] And Kajol Majumdar, daughter of Savita Banerjee, goes back over fifty years in time:[37]

> My mother was married in 1952 after which she came to Calcutta. My parents used to stay in a house on Garcha Road, South Calcutta. From a very young age, my mother was the artistic kind. She loved painting, but her main interest was in literature, both Hindi and Bengali. She had the habit of writing, which she managed to sustain after marriage.

> Starting with short stories, she picked up poetry and started writing poems in the Haiku style, where you had three lines only. The dabbling in literature helped her connect with Rajendra Yadav and his wife Mannu Bhandari who were staying at CIT Road. Writer Kamleshwar also joined them when he came down to Calcutta. In all, the group grew in size and there were *baithaks* too at our place. Basu Chatterji, my mama (maternal uncle), would scout for good stories for cinema, and *Sara Aakash* was my mother's suggestion to him.

The search for a financer had been made easier following the changed directives of the FFC. The keywords were aspirant film-makers, Indian stories and low-budget films, preferably in black-and-white.

★ ★ ★

The Film Finance Corporation, or the FFC as it was widely known, was one of the three initiatives taken by the Government of India following the huge success of Ray's *Apu Trilogy* (1955-59) in the west. It was formed in 1960 and registered under the Companies Act, 1956. Shri Hariprasad was the General Manager of the Corporation. The activities of FFC, as defined then, were:

1. To finance the production of feature films
2. To finance the construction of cinema theatres
3. To grant permission for purchase of raw stock for production of films for which raw stock canalisation fee was charged
4. To import foreign films
5. To distribute and exhibit films imported by the FFC

Side by side, the Film Institute of India or the FII (later the Film and Television Institute of India [FTII] in 1971) was formed in 1960 and was made operational the following year with Gajanand

Jagirdar as the principal. Three years later, the National Film Archives (NFAI) was formed under the stewardship of P.K. Nair, India's best-known film archivist. The FFC was started almost simultaneously with the FII.

The financing procedure of the FFC, as elucidated by B.K. Adarsh in 1963 was:[38]

> The objectives of the Corporation's financing have set the pattern of selection of films for loans. Not all the money that is required for the production of a film is met by it. One-fourth of the total cost is to be met by the producer and the Board of Directors of the Corporation may, in its discretion, grant loans up to Rs 3.5 lakh for a single film [. . .] The Corporation also has the authority to scrutinise the script of the film. It thus makes sure that the proposed film conforms to its objectives. The Corporation has made a modest but a good start. The making of purposeful films is undoubtedly a slow process, but judging from the response from the film industry, it promises to be a sure success worth waiting for.

While the directive of the body was quite linear, with time, the FFC was being viewed as another film production company competing with commercial film producers. By 1968, the balance sheet was showing dismal deficits. Himmat Singh, the reigning chairman, resigned as he was contesting an election. B.K. Karanjia, who was one of the directors of FFC, became the chairman on the rebound.[39] Karanjia, with a background in running the country's best-known film magazine *Filmfare,* wasted no time in taking corrective action.

As the new set of rules was laid out, quite a few film-makers approached Karanjia. One among them was Mrinal Sen. His *Bhuvan Shome* (1969), co-produced by Arun Kaul, was released in his hometown of Calcutta on 16 October 1969. Sen, an admired film-maker in Bengal, managed to get a big theatre release. Elite, as the name suggests, was one of the elite halls in the city which pulled the commercial as well as the high-brow crowd. In sheer contrast to the lukewarm response reserved for cerebral films, *Bhuvan Shome*, despite its languid narrative, did quite well. Shot on location in Saurashtra, Gujarat, on a shoestring budget, it also brought to light some excellent technical faculties, including one who had graduated from FII on 5 August 1966.[40] This was Kewal Krishan Mahajan, the gold medallist in cinematography. It was KK's (as Mahajan became known) first feature film, as it was for a tall fellow, who till then had been rejected by All India Radio when he had auditioned for the job of an announcer. He did the voiceover in *Bhuvan Shome* for Rs 300.[41] Later, he signed on the dotted line for his first acting role on 16 February 1969[42] for Abbas, who was heading Film Forum. This was Amitabh Bachchan.

The critical response to Sen's first Hindi film was mixed. While most loved it, the house remained divided. Like Satyajit Ray, whose response was unclear; a blend of both good and bad.[43] But somewhere along with the praises and the occasional dissatisfactions, the term 'New Wave' cropped up. It would come to stay, at least for a few more years.

Basu, who was among the few reaching out to the FFC with Sen, was also acknowledged in the titles. By that time, he was in Agra with the cast and crew of *Sara Aakash*.

The Trip to Agra

The three men were on their way to Raja ki Mandi from the Agra Cantonment station. In the absence of a motored vehicle, the tonga was the preferred way of transport in a town where both the tonga and the cycle rickshaw ruled. It was the month of June, or July, in 1969. Two of the men came down from Bombay via Delhi: Basu Chatterji and K.K. Mahajan. The third joined them from Delhi—Rajendra Yadav. It was his ancestral home they were going to. The trip had the twofold purpose of understanding the milieu and scouting for some suitable outdoors. The journey was dotted with the shuffling of images of ungainly shops and tea stalls which were spectacularly devoid of women, though the occasional household help would make an appearance in sarees, the original colour of which was difficult to guess, let alone identify. While Agra as a tourist spot had grown in fame with every passing day, downtown Agra had lost most of its lustre post-Independence. The crowded roads bore a dry and forlorn look, bereft of either colour or the giggles of women with earthen pots one would observe near the countryside.[44]

In the preface to the book *Sara Aakash*, Rajendra Yadav mentions that by the time they were in Agra to scout for locations, Basu had already finished writing the script. Basu further mentioned that there were two areas where he was not comfortable: finding a suitable location, and trying to comprehend how a couple could have lived under the same roof without having spoken to each other for a year, as mentioned in the book.[45] Luckily, Pratibha and three of her four children had come down to Agra while Prakash was in the US teaching linguistics at Texas. They were living at Steele Kothi near St John's College where Prakash used to work before.[46] Meeting Pratibha Dixit was at the top of the agenda.

★ ★ ★

The process of translating the script into a screenplay had almost come full circle. Basu had initially approached Yadav, who refused on the grounds of unfamiliarity with the medium. He had suggested the name of his friend Kamleshwar who, by that time, had expressed an interest in cinema. Kamleshwar's treatment however did not have the right visual angle, and Basu decided to give it a try.[47]

The meeting with Pratibha happened at her place after two days.

The frosty relationship part was confirmed. The couple did not talk to each other for nine years. Prakash would go to college in the morning. After college, he would be engaged in giving tuitions, only to return late in the night by small-town standards. Pratibha would religiously perform the duties expected of a housewife.[48]

Viraj Dixit, the second son of Prakash and Pratibha Dixit, mentions, 'Since my father used to convey the details of his life to uncle Yadavji, the story of *Sara Aakash* is all about the story of my dad and mom living under the rule of Taauji (father's elder brother) and Taayaji (elder brother's wife) and how Taayaji behaved with my mom.'[49]

What was probably not discussed between Basu and Pratibha was that Prakash was not at all happy with his story being written by his friend and that too without his knowledge. He wanted to write it himself. Almost every evening, Prakash would come down to Yadav's ancestral house and discuss his woes. The practice ended with his stepping into adulthood and the consummation of marriage. The reason for not speaking to the wife was put down to inspirations from stories of Ram leaving Sita, Buddha leaving Yasodhara, Dushyant deserting Shankuntala . . .

⋆ ⋆ ⋆

M.L. Yadav was one of the many brothers in an Agra-based family. He had ten children—four sons and six daughters—of whom Rajendra Yadav was the eldest. Most of the Yadavs stayed in a house that might have dated back to Mughal times. It is said that the house had stairways leading to the Yamuna, which today is about 4 km away. Extending almost from the end of a lane to the main road, the house was built on a huge area and had five or six courtyards. Partitioned and extended over many years, demarcation of the construction vis-à-vis time was easy, with the Kakaiya bricks dating to the Mughal times unevenly protruding out of walls that desperately needed maintenance. A complete absence of planning dominated the structures, exemplified by areas where stairs would lead to locked doors whose keys had been lost decades ago. Shrouded in cobwebs, a few dead ends and rooms in the house had ghost stories associated with them as well. Moving around the house, Mahajan and Basu could probably make out that the walls were an anchor to old times, a smorgasbord of events that never got documented.

The building had five or six terraces, most of them separated by small brick walls. With no tall construction either within or around the same, it offered a 360-degree view of the town, and one could see important structures like St. John's College. For a house that had been compartmentalized and further divided to cater to human needs and egos, the terrace area was a huge unifier. In another life, the kids of the house had spent precious moments playing hide and seek, hopscotch, or *gilli-danda*, apart from feeding pigeons and flying kites.

* * *

Post the survey, the three sat down to enjoy the Agra special tea with a lot of cream. 'Fantastic,' KK beamed.

'Can we have this house for the shoot?' Basu was thinking aloud. The house strongly reminded him of his own in Mathura, and a few in Rajasthan, and he was told that the architects in the northern part of India had a style that was replicated in many places.

'This is a natural set. Building a set like this in Bombay could be . . .'

KK was cut short by Yadav—'We'll get this house.'[50]

The Cast and Crew

A young boy from Nahan in Himachal Pradesh, who called himself Rakesh Pandey, was fascinated by the theatre and left the small town for National School of Drama (NSD) in New Delhi after his Intermediate exams in 1963. At NSD, Rakesh met another young hopeful who called himself Subhash Ghai. Subhash was then in his final year at FII and advised Rakesh to move to Poona, considering that budding actors there were being trained specially for the cinema. Rakesh was getting a scholarship that covered his basic expenses, but on being told that FII had a scholarship programme too, he applied the next year. Along with Sadhu Meher, Jalal Agha, Rehana Sultan, et al, Rakesh was also selected for the two-year acting course. Ghai was there on the interview board.[50]

Life after passing out of the institute was not easy. Ritwik Ghatak was the vice-principal then, and his style was radically different from the requirements of the Bombay film industry. Most of the actors who graduated during that time had to struggle.

The struggle continued when Rakesh came to Bombay after his graduation. Visits to film houses yielded few results; promises by film-makers were increasingly obligatory. The first professional assignment came with a small role in an episode of the television series *Maya*, titled 'The Ransom of Raji' (1967), for which Rakesh travelled to Kashmir with his classmate Subroto Mohapatra. Veteran actor Manmohan Krishna, who played his father, recommended him to Satyen Bose who was making *Aansoo Ban Gaye Phool* (1969). In the meantime, Rakesh had started assisting Chandramohan Gupta in designing logos for films. One of his key assignments was to meet Shakti Samanta and take forward the design of the logo of *Aradhana* (1969) with the lotus on top.[51]

It was then that Basu Chatterji contacted him.

* * *

During the mid- and the late-1960s, Mrinal Sen used to visit FII as a guest lecturer. He had a great fondness for technicians who graduated from the institute. K.K. Mahajan and Narinder Singh were his first recruits from Poona. Singh had worked previously as an assistant in Ramanand Sagar's *Aankhen* (1968), and a Swedish TV series about women in India. Sen would use him first for *Icchapuran* (1970). KK's handheld camera-based photography of the railway line in *Bhuvan Shome* was most applauded. His name was on the publicity poster of the film when it was set for release in Calcutta—a rare achievement for a cinematographer, that too in his first film.

Basu believed in Sen's choices. KK and Singh were among the first he onboarded for *Sara Aakash*. For the lead role, he had another FII grad in mind—Subhash Ghai, who was also one of the eight winners of the Filmfare Madhuri talent contest in 1965. However, the image Basu had of Samar, the lead character of *Sara Aakash*, was of a young adult with sharp features and a lean body, and Ghai did not fit the description.

Says Rakesh in a discussion with the author:

> I had approached Mrinal-da at the FTII (sic) for a role in one of his films. Mrinal-da liked me but said— 'Rakesh, your features are very sharp. You are also very fair, almost like a prince. You see, I need less glamorous faces for my films.' When Basu-da was planning *Sara Aakash*, he needed a very slender college-going boy, one who also looked like a small towner. Mrinal-da recommended my name. Basu-da then called me during a film screening at his film club. This should be around the middle of 1969. Next, I was asked to come to his place at Bengal Chemicals in Worli to take part in an informal workshop. That is how my journey with Basu-da and the film started.[52]

Basu's search for the leading lady also led him to zero in on another FII student. Unfortunately, she, a Satyajit Ray protégé, was in her second and final year of college then and denied permission to act. Jaya Bhaduri. Another Bhaduri, Rita, daughter of actress Chandrima Bhaduri, was also considered, but she was probably too young for the role of Prabha. One conjectures that Yadav had shortened the name Pratibha to arrive at the name which was used in the book.

★ ★ ★

Himadri Dasgupta was a Bombay-based commercial artist. He knew Basu, and that he was making a film. Resource being a major constraint, Basu had spread the word around to look for fresh faces. Dasgupta knew Samir Chowdhury (universally known as Babu-da), younger brother of poet–composer Salil Chowdhury. He came down to Babu-da's place and discussed Basu's requirement of a young girl for his cinema. Madhuchhanda Chakrabarty, aka Madhu, Babu-da's youngest sister-in-law, had come from Calcutta to visit her eldest sister Manisha Chowdhury, who had played the youngest salesgirl in Satyajit Ray's *Mahanagar* (1963). Dasgupta liked Madhu, and after taking Babu-da's consent, put in a word to Basu.

Daughter of actress Madhuri Chakrabarty, Madhu had started acting quite early in life. Her role as one of the kids in the Bengali film *Dersho Khokaar Kaando* (1959) had elicited critical acclaim. She had subsequently worked in a few more films like *Madhyarater Tara* (1961) and *Dolna* (1965), but her crowning glory was the much-publicized dubbing session of *Deya Neya* (1963) where she had dubbed for Tanuja in her first Bengali film.

Madhu's dubbing story also includes the reaction of a bemused Uttam Kumar (the hero of *Deya Neya*) who, in a state of shock, said, 'Am I supposed to dub with this kid?' Madhu was then a class VIII student of South Point High School, Calcutta, and had come to the dubbing studio in her school dress.

It was probably Madhu's structural and facial similarity to Jaya Bhaduri which Basu found to his liking. She was asked to report to his Worli house for the workshop.[53]

There was one more new face needed for the film. Someone to play Munni, the hero's soft-spoken, caring and unfortunate sister who had been abandoned by her husband.

* * *

Nandita Thakur, the actress chosen for the aforementioned role, spoke to the author at length about the events which suddenly made her a cinema artiste:

> In the late 1960s, there was an exhibition of handicrafts at the Taj Art Gallery in Colaba, Bombay. Anjali Ghosh, my mother, was also one of the artists whose work was being displayed.

M.N. Gupta, the photographer who came to cover the programme, found my face interesting and sought permission to take my picture. Taken aback, I directed him to my parents who agreed. Gupta showed the pictures to the editor of the now-defunct magazine *Eve's Weekly*. The editor liked it and wanted to do a photo session, something which was arranged and completed in two to three days. And I was on the cover of *Eve's Weekly*.

The engagement with Basu-da started with a telephonic conversation. He had seen my photo on the cover of the magazine and got my number from their office. He was making a film for which he wanted me to play an important character. My first reaction to the call was a big no. But destiny had other plans for me. After about a fortnight, my husband (Santosh Thakur, brother-in-law of Shailendra) took me to Century Bazaar, Worli, for shopping. There, he met Basu Chatterji, his old friend, and introduced me to him. Basu-da recollected seeing my face on the magazine cover. Turning to my husband, he asked if I could work in his film. Because it was his friend's project, my husband said yes. And lo! I landed up doing *Sara Aakash*.

Being a complete newcomer in this field, I needed grooming. Initially, I was a little apprehensive. Gradually, I started enjoying myself. The cast used to meet at Basu-da's residence for rehearsals. I loved it. It was more like a family affair with Boudi (Mrs Keka Chatterji) and the kids. I enjoyed their company immensely.[54]

★ ★ ★

The three young characters in *Sara Aakash* were Samar, Prabha and Munni. A few pivotal roles remained to be cast: that of the father-in-law, mother-in-law and the sister-in-law, wife of the elder brother.

It was through the other Basu that Chatterji could avail the services of A.K. Hangal and Dina Pathak (nee Gandhi). Both these seasoned theatre actors were rookies in the world of cinema. Basu's spree as an assistant to Bhattacharya in *Teesri Kasam* helped in cementing a friendship with Hangal who had played a small role in it. In Dina, Basu had found the mother-in-law he had been looking for. Dina would get her sister Tarla Mehta, who, till then, had a rather uninteresting career graph in Hindi films. Basu had seen Tarla before in *Ek Ke Baad Ek* (1960) where she had played the pivotal role of Dev Anand's sister-in-law who dies during childbirth. She would play a sister-in-law once more.

A few peripheral roles were filled up with new actors like Jalal Agha and Aarti Bole, as the peppy pair of Diwakar and Kiran. Basu owed a favour to Shailendra, and his eldest son Shailey who was trying to make his mark as a lyricist was onboarded. The *Sara Aakash* script did not have any slot for a tailor-made song, and the budding lyricist was given the role of Amar, Samar's younger brother.

For the role of the elder brother, Basu requested co-film-maker Mani Kaul. Kaul was in the process of making *Uski Roti* (1970) with the financial aid of the FFC. Basu told the author, 'Mani and I were friends from the time we were strugglers. We had no money. The whisky we consumed was cheap. The glasses we used to drink were made of stainless steel. But there was a lot of heart. I paid him a pittance; Rs 300 is no remuneration for an artiste. But there I was, the producer, the director, the screenplay writer, the organizer, everything. One needs to go through the motions to appreciate the handicap.'[55]

The workshop at Worli was meant for formally introducing the cast and the crew via group exercises. 'I had very few dialogues and would spend most of the time gossiping with Keka boudi. I assume the process helped in gelling and creating a unified spirit, something we later understood, and I am still proud of,' says Madhu. 'Basu-da, however, hardly communicated. And he remained that way. Maybe he was shy. Or observing. Or both,' she adds.[56]

The Shoot

While recounting the memories of *Sara Aakash,* Rajendra Yadav had once remarked:

> There was a rumour in Delhi that Rajamandi (Raja ki Mandi) had suddenly become the centre of attraction of Agra. One day, I set out to verify it myself. Reaching Agra Cantonment, I took a rickshaw and asked the rickshaw puller to take me to the place where 'the shooting' was happening. En route, the driver blurted out what he thought were words of wisdom. 'We hear that the owner of the house where the film is being shot is making the film. Very soon the house will be sold. What kind of film is this? No hero, no heroine, no dance, no song . . . won't run a day you see . . .[57]

The negative feedback notwithstanding, the energy levels of the locals were at a premium high. For one, the weather was good—conducive to standing in the sun for hours without feeling the burning heat the place was infamous for. Secondly, apart from the Taj Mahal or Fatehpur Sikri, the town hardly had anything else to be excited about. Seeing a bioscope being filmed was one more.

★ ★ ★

It was on the fifth day (Panchami) of Navratri when Basu, along with most of the team, landed at Agra Cantonment junction. The squad included, apart from KK, Rakesh, Jalal, Dina Pathak, A.K. Hangal, Madhu, her mother, Nandita Thakur, her mother and her two-year-old daughter Panchali, Rajendra Yadav, Mannu Bhandari, and their eight-year-old daughter Rachana, a host of technicians including Prajnan Mitra, brother of Subrata Mitra (the ace cameraman) who came as the camera attendant. The Arriflex-2 model was a prized camera that Mitra would lend out to film-makers, and KK was someone he was fond of.[58]

Narinder Singh and Tarla Mehta came a day later.[59]

As an unwritten rule, the women travelled in first class. The men had second-class reserved tickets.

Basu was accompanied by his family. His sister Savita Banerjee too came with hers. Salil Chowdhury, the music director, had come to the shoot location for a short duration.[60] 'I had a choice between Salil Chowdhury and Hemant Kumar. Salil said, "Dada, humko dijiye [Dada, give me the film]." He did the whole background score for only Rs 10,000.'

The cast and crew were put up at a building masquerading as a guest house. Considering the size of the team, many of the male members had to sleep in the hall, which had been converted into a dormitory. The women had separate rooms. Nandita Thakur and her folks had put up with her uncle, Dr Manohar Roy, then the principal of Agra College. Nandita was also given a Hindustan Ambassador, as managing her toddler was important.[61]

Incidentally, vast portions of the film were to be shot at Agra College and its grounds. The Yadav and the Dixit families were influential; and they had managed the necessary clearances including police protection at the college premises.

★ ★ ★

In the 1960s, Agra was a peaceful and comforting town. While the migration from villages had happened post-Independence, agriculture still brought in most of the money. The leather and footwear industry had a good local presence. Iron foundries on the outskirts too provided employment. Tourism was a major money earner and promoted self-employment. The male-female ratio was high, and the unwritten code of conduct passed on from generations ensured that non-working women hardly went out of their houses alone. Women were rarely seen on their own at eateries, sweet shops or tea stalls.

Interestingly, though the demographic profile hinted at a deeply entrenched patriarchy, people were not prone to violence. Outsiders were readily accepted as one of Agra's own.

However, the first day of the shoot at Raja ki Mandi proved to be otherwise.

Madhu goes back in time recalling the same:[62]

> I was standing in front of a window for the shot. A crowd of a few hundred had assembled to see the shoot and were standing below. Could be mob mentality, but they were shouting at the top of their voices. Suddenly, a huge stone grazed my ear. I was shocked, as it could have hit my eye. I told Basu-da that it was extremely difficult to shoot like this. One, you cannot identify who hurled the stone. Next, you cannot ask them to go as this would create chaos. Basu-da found out a way. He said, 'We won't switch on the lights. Only when everything is ready, we'll say "Lights." And switch on the lights, open the camera shutters, and you know the action.'
>
> I was very scared during that scene. Thank goodness I did not have any lines in that shot. It was just some facial expressions, something which was captured very fast.
>
> I would have many more window shots.

In an article reminiscing about his days in Agra, KK too mentioned, '*Sara Aakash* had many windows. Many of them'.[63]

Narinder Singh also recalls the downsides of shooting in a place where the public did not know how to react to a shooting crew.[64]

> In a place like Agra, location shooting with sound was a major challenge. Being a small town, people had flocked to see the shoot. Even when the lead actors were new and not stars, the interest levels were very high. They were talking loudly, and it was difficult to silence them. In that situation, anyone would be nervous.

Inside the university, the police were called, so the crowd could not disrupt the shooting there. But while I was shooting inside the classroom, someone threw a firecracker which burst right in front of me. I wonder what kind of sinister pleasure one derived by the act.

The only way to counter such mischief was to keep one's cool. I did not react, and the shoot was completed without any more unsavoury incidents.

★ ★ ★

Most of the indoors were shot at the ancestral home. Rajendra Yadav's house, where he had shifted after marriage, was used as Jalal Agha's residence. Mornings for the crew began at either of the two houses. The cast and the crew would assemble and enjoy a typical Agra breakfast with *jalebi*, *kachori*, *moong ki daal ki pakodi*, *malai wala doodh*, etc.[65] They would generally move around the place in kurta-pyjama and chappals, to the amazement of the locals who found it difficult to equate them with the idea of the typical filmi folk who they thought moved around only in Impalas and other fast cars and dressed in Terylene shirts and dark suits.[66] At the least the ladies were supposed to dress up in Benarasis and Kanjivarams.

Basu-da would allow nothing of this, quips Nandita.[67]

> No artificial makeup, no costly sarees, nothing which could even remotely interfere with the fabric of the low-middle-class house the story was supposed to convey. Basu-da had given very strict instructions. No pressing of sarees either at the local laundry. We were clearly instructed to press the sarees under the mattress. No iron pressing. Apply kajal on your eyes via your fingers. Get dressed in costume after your morning bath. The sarees were given by the costume department. Blouses were stitched by tailors in Agra. Of the cheapest variety. The rate then was 25 paise or 50 paise per blouse.

All the malai-doodh and moong dal ki pakodi failed to control the butterflies in her stomach during the shoots though.

> During my first shoot, I was not told about the camera. I was mortally scared of the moving camera as I had never faced one in my life. Basu-da understood my limitations.
>
> He then had to coach me like a child. I had a college-going brother (Chandan Ghosh) who used to stay in a hostel. Usually, I would pack his bags during his trips back to college. Basu-da said, 'Imagine you are packing his bags. And reminding him of things to do. Don't be conscious of the camera. Speak whatever you would say to him when you are in the actual act of packing his bag.' So, I said, 'Write a letter to mom when you reach, etc.'
>
> And that is how my first shot was taken.
>
> Soon, he had set up an unwritten code that whenever there was a scene involving me, he would just signal to KK to start shooting without preamble.

There were technical challenges, too. Narinder Singh points out one which was Madhu's first spoken dialogue in the film.[68]

> Madhuchhanda did not have many lines in the film. Hence, to ensure whatever she said got due importance, we put in lots of effort. Like her first spoken line which I had to get recorded multiple times to get the exact emotion. Also, to get a very clean sound. The line was '*Daal toh maine chakh lee thee*'. This was a beautiful scene; the lady is innocent, she cannot fathom what is wrong. The pain comes out in the way she reacts to the rejection she faces from her husband. Hence, we wanted to make it perfect. I must have taken it 30 times till it came to what I was asking for. Basu left it to us, KK and me.

Technical hiccups were not only limited to indoor shoots. Many outdoor shoots had to be done with a hidden camera. Like the shot about the failed mission of a visit to the cinema (*Anmol Moti*, 1969).

This was during the initial phase of the shoot. Rakesh and Madhu were still unknown faces in Raja ki Mandi. They were asked to walk a certain distance apart from each other. Basu and KK were walking on the other side of the road; KK with the camera nicely camouflaged under a towel so that it was not visible to pedestrians who thought that the pair were a couple.[69]

A single take was required for a few other scenes too. Especially the one where Rakesh had to slap Madhu.

> I was asked to stand in the main courtyard where most of the shooting was done. Rakesh was extremely reluctant to do the shot, but Basu-da wanted it to be there. Rakesh was instructed to slap me suddenly; Basu-da wanted to capture the shock; the bewildered expression. He slapped me hard. Real hard. I staggered, lost my balance, and almost fell, managing to hold on to the broken brick wall separating the tap from the main courtyard. Rakesh immediately apologized, but I said it was fine as this is something he had to do as per the need of the film.
>
> Basu-da said nothing. He just said 'Cut!' and proceeded with the next shot of the day.[70]

⋆ ⋆ ⋆

True to his nature, Basu would speak little. There were times when even his 'Cut!' would be inaudible. Let alone talking, his reactions too were limited, leaving the cast bemused. Why does he not say anything, they would ask. KK, the go-to man during the shoot, would tell them not to worry, as the lack of a reaction meant that they could proceed with the next shot.

Basu did have to talk on occasions, though.

Tarla Mehta's Gujarati-accented Hindi was not exactly good news. Basu, who knew the local language very well, had to tutor her from time to time.[71] On the contrary, Dina Pathak, her sister, was equally at ease with expressions as she was with long lines in a mix of Hindi and Braj Bhasha. Tarla worked hard, and gradually perfected her diction to the extent that hers is considered among the best performances in the film. This is saying a lot, as the film had some excellent performances.

Except one. Basu's own.[72]

> There was one scene where the students are listening to an inspirational teacher. The actor hired for the shoot did not come. I had worked in some plays before but had never faced the camera. I tried to fill in the shoes of the missing actor myself. Oh, God! How I fumbled. I think for that short piece of twenty seconds (ten seconds in the final cut), we had more than ten retakes. This experience taught me something. Never underestimate the acting skills of professionals.

It would be interesting to note that the early days in Bombay found Basu sporting the Guru Dutt look. Fair, well-built, curly hair, soft face, and the mandatory moustache. While Basu would carry on the 'Hitchcockian trait' of appearing in cameos often, unlike Hitchcock, he never was dismissive of acting professionals.

However, he was dismissive of demands for good food. Lunch was prepared at the guest house with the mutton being procured from a shop outside. The menu would remain unaltered through the period of the shoot, which was three weeks. Especially the mutton preparation. The dish bhindi-mutton (a gravy of mutton and ladies' finger) might have been considered a delicacy in the northern part of the country—composer Madan Mohan was said to be an expert at cooking the aforementioned dish—but for the Bengalis there, this was a complete no-no. Says Madhu,

> Irrespective of the day, the side-dish was always Bhindi-Mutton. It used to come from a Muslim shop and was very well made, but the change of taste factor which we experienced vanished after two to three days. Bengalis would feel it difficult to believe that bhindi and mutton could co-exist in a single dish. I had a small tiff with Basu-da about our lunch.

> Basu-da himself was a foodie. But he too had to endure mutton and bhindi as he had to run the house on a very tight budget.

The after-shoot evenings were the most enjoyable times. The entire cast and the crew, barring Nandita who went back to her uncle's place, and Madhu, who would pay sporadic visits as her mother was also with her, would assemble in the hall. The shooting would be discussed threadbare. Basu had given them the liberty to speak their minds. Liquor flowed, though in moderation. Basu loved his whisky, and so did KK and Singh. Rakesh, a vegetarian and not fond of fermented malted barley, would pick up a bottle of beer.

Reminisces Narinder Singh:[73]

> Post shoot, we would assemble in a hall, sit on the ground, and celebrate. This became a daily ritual. Maybe we looked like a bunch of hooligans, all drunkards. But even senior pros like Hangal Sahab, Dina Gandhi, and her sister would take part in this fun-filled *adda*. We would have a drink and talk about the shoot. We became very good friends. The unit was so close, that nobody was told to do this, do that, etc. It all came so naturally.
>
> Interestingly, though it was the early part of our professional lives, we tried and did our work well. Maybe our collective intent was to do our best.
>
> The Yadav family too admired our hard work.

Rajendra Yadav had a few reservations though. The timeline of his story was the 1940s. Basu had made it 1969, contemporary; Yadav was not in agreement. However, many years later, in an essay recounting his thoughts about the film, he acknowledged his error of judgement.[74]

> The question was about the contemporariness of the story. Basu wanted to bring the story to the time when it was being shot. I believed that the original timeline should remain as it is. Later, I felt that making it a period piece might not work.

> The reality is that apart from New Delhi, Calcutta, Bombay, and a few big cities, time has not moved ahead even now. Barring names like Terylene, transistors and scooters, life is what it used to be before. Two or three megacities are expanding like banyan trees, and the fast-moving young Turks are trying to be part of the life there . . . the same young ones come to their hometowns during vacations, only to return by the time thoughts of change cloud their minds . . . till the time the key to marriage remains with parents, the intrinsic sorrow of *Sara Aakash* would continue to live on.

Yadav was also annoyed that only the first part of the story had been considered for the film. The novel had two parts, concluding with Munni's death. Basu had clarified that he was unaware of a second part. Assuming that this was rather an improbability, one feels that Basu perhaps wanted to end the story on a happy note. And that is what the last shot was all about.

Advertised as the shot which would terminate in a kiss, the schedule was at midnight on 7 November 1969. The location was the terrace of the ancestral house. KK would use a handheld photoflood for lighting the scene; in fact, budgetary constraints did not offer him the liberty to use fancy equipment.

This portion of the shoot took the longest time, after which it was pack-up.

The shoot was delayed. It started at 2.30 a.m. Autumn was making way for winter, and there was a cold breeze that night. The scene demanded Madhu to keep on crying. Rakesh, then very fresh, was perturbed seeing a girl cry so much and would miss his lines. Retakes after retakes followed. After some time, KK lost his cool and said, 'Pahari (the name by which Rakesh was known as he was from the hills), what are you made of? What's stopping you from reacting?' Rakesh said, 'All that crying is making me nervous and emotional. I am loving the scene too.' KK said, 'Don't be fascinated by her. Just react as you are supposed to, else Basu-da might push you off the terrace.' The exchange was however in the manner of banter, friendly, and was not to be taken seriously.[75]

In totality, there were seven to eight retakes. The kiss did not happen, but the embrace did, and it later became the still—taken by Vijay, A.K. Hangal's son—used to advertise the film. Madhu added,

> This was one of the very few shots where I had to check the script properly. Else, as I had very few lines, the script found a place at the bottom of my trunk, only to be referred to occasionally if I had a shoot.
>
> I did not use glycerine for this scene. I never used glycerine during a shoot. Recreating these emotions came to me naturally. I cried and cried so much that my face was swollen. By the time the shot was completed, it was early morning. Emotionally drained, I fell sick . . .[76]

★ ★ ★

For the Dixit and Yadav families, the shoot sparked off a lot of excitement. The consensus was that the cast and crew were very friendly, but at the same time, not very interactive. The entire film was shot at breakneck speed—three weeks. Normally, the shooting of one Hindi film song would approximately take the same time. During *Sara Aakash*, nobody had the time to socialize. Viraj Dixit remembers A.K. Hangal as one of the friendliest persons he had met. Rachana Yadav's memories are more of Jalal Agha, as he had a way with kids and used to play with her. Nandita Thakur was very talkative too, she recalls. Rakesh Pandey and Madhu were friendly but somewhat reserved in comparison.

Many from the family and friends' fraternity had blink-and-miss roles in the film. Prominent among them was Pratibha Dixit, the real 'Prabha', who viewers can find as the tall lady decked up in a dark silk saree and a large bindi just behind Madhu on her right (to the viewer's left) during the marriage scene.

Post-Production

On 9 November 1969, five months after the film had been conceived, the cans of *Sara Aakash* were on their way to Bombay. Basu and his extended family alighted in Delhi. They proceeded to the house of the Yadavs for the night.

It was the night of Diwali. There were firecrackers all around, as they were on their way to Shakti Nagar, remembers Kajol Majumdar. After a long time, the literati sat down to slacken their nerves by playing cards, which was something of a ritual in the northern part of the country on the eve of Diwali. Money would be lost and made. In business communities, the stakes could be in high volumes of cash.[77]

For Basu, the stakes were low. The money angle was nominal. He could not afford to lose money, having already spent almost all of what he had received from the FFC.

Back in Bombay, the sound recording took place at Bombay Labs. B.N. Sharma, the recordist at Bombay Labs, was indisposed, and the services of Minoo Katrak were sought. Basu-da could not afford Rajkamal Studio, mentions Madhu to the author.

The positive side was that the film did not have any songs, which helped control costs. The song sequence of *Bhool Jayen Saare Gham* from Mahesh Kaul's FII film *Rakhi Rakhi* (1969), starring students Radha Saluja and Suresh Chatwal, had been used as an insert. The composer of this song was Bhaskar Chandavarkar, who was then the resident music composer at the FII.

Basu needed some traditional songs though.

★ ★ ★

Salil Chowdhury, the composer known to cater to every kind of cinema, from the musical to the song-less, had a deep knowledge of almost all the facets of music. However, UP folk, especially folk of the Brij area, comprised a genre he knew little about. It is here that he came in touch with Rajendra Raghuvanshi. Raghuvanshi, a dramatist and musician, was the go-to man in Agra when it came to traditional music of that area. Salil sought his expertise. After sifting through an entire repertoire of folk songs of the Brij bhumi, a few were chosen and used as motifs in the film. The songs were recorded in the voice of local singers in Agra, adding authenticity.[78] Among the lot, the tune of 'Bane Teri Ankhiyan Soorme Dani' would later be used randomly by film-makers some fifty years later, sometimes with cockeyed lyrics in films starring Kangana Ranaut.

★ ★ ★

Dubbing sessions of *Sara Aakash* were nominal, barring for a few outdoor scenes where noise had crept in. This included the last scene which suggested a consummation of the marriage to follow. Madhu came down to the studio, saw the scene, choked while dubbing, and broke down . . . [79]

The editing of the film happened at Filmalaya Studio. Sasadhar Mukerji, one of the grand old men of Bombay cinema, having started his career in 1934 with Bombay Talkies, gave Basu the run of his dubbing facility and did not charge any fee. Mukerji was the guarantor for Basu in 1968 when he had taken his first script for approval to Himmat Singh. Though the script was rejected, the relationship between Mukerji and Basu stood its ground.

The relationship between the Mukerji and Chatterji families was also due to the 'Probashi Bengali factor', feels Rupali Guha.[80] Though they came from different backgrounds, Sasadhar Mukerji was the son of lawyer Haripada Mukerji of Jhansi, then part of the United Provinces (later Uttar Pradesh). The Mukerjis spoke Hindi at home. Or English. Basu could relate strongly to the culture, which was like an extension of his own.

Some running around by Basu, Arun Kaul, et al, and especially FFC's influence helped in ensuring a 31 December 1969 censor certificate for *Sara Aakash*. To expedite the process, the certificate was signed by K.D. Dixit who stood in for M.V. Desai, the chairperson who was not present then.[81]

The National Award

The date 31 December is of major significance for cinema in India. Unless cleared by the censor board by that date, a film is not considered by the Ministry of Information and Broadcasting for the National Awards for that year. *Sara Aakash* received its certificate on 31 December surely with the National Award in mind. As would N.C. Sippy and Hrishikesh Mukherjee hurry to get *Anand* certified on 31 December 1970 a year later. Apart from the prestige factor, National Awards added to the commercial clout of the film and also helped in getting it selected for exhibition in festivals in India and abroad.

Unfortunately, unlike *Bhuvan Shome*, *Sara Aakash*, in the absence of abstract elements and compounded by the failure to get a distributor for over a year, did not catch the eye of the literati then. Reviews were rare. Applause, if any, remained confined to the select few who managed the see the film with great difficulty in some small auditorium. Press conferences were limited, though Basu had arranged one in a well-known hotel then (as per Nandita Thakur, at the Taj Intercontinental, now the Taj Mahal Tower), after which one review by Mohan S. Bawa published in the *Sunday Standard* on 27 September 1970 said:[82]

> Basu Chatterji, one of the co-directors of the Film Forum, has just completed an offbeat, small-budget film, shot completely in Agra and edited and put together in Bombay. The film made with the finances of the Film Finance Corporation will be shown at the Locarno and Cork Film Festivals this year. Basu Chatterji has made a film that is surely Indian in inspiration and motivation . . .

One can only speculate how the technicians would have reacted had they seen the film then—especially the build-up to the main narrative. In the absence of any technical review in the public domain, the author talked to cinematographer-cum-author Yasir Abbasi on the opening scene of *Sara Aakash*.[83]

> For those times, this was a very different approach to filming a sequence. I was very, very surprised; this is something I did not expect. I can imagine how this would have shocked cinema buffs then. It's a completely different, experimental style. I saw it multiple times. The first time I saw it, it reminded me of the opening sequence in *Bhuvan Shome*. It is almost the same: in the former it is the train track, and here it is the lanes of the town. In *Bhuvan Shome*, music also plays a major part. Here, it is more visual. Music is secondary. One thing which hits you is that it's a documentary-style camerawork. The camera jerks, nothing is planned, you do not know what is coming next. The camera is handheld, focusing only on the walls, and sometimes on the streets. It shifts too, from the left window to the right, just exploring what is there on the way. There is pulsating energy in the sequence. This would remain even if the sequence were stripped of the music. Even today, this type of cinematography is not common at all.

The pulsating energy and the handheld camera which Abbasi talks about were probably a reflection of Basu's love for French cinema. Jean-Luc Godard's handheld camera in *Breathless* (1960) was an inspiration for film-makers in India then, but few could reproduce the candid dynamism as KK did in *Bhuvan Shome* or *Sara Aakash*. Fewer could think of an opening sequence like that, shot en route from the Agra Cantonment junction to the Yadavs' ancestral home. It was a sequence that Basu concluded with the marriage ceremony, the focal point of the film. It was his establishing shot: Agra, its raw exterior, the narrow roads, the relatively cleaner by-lanes, the old rickshaws pulled by older men, boys playing on the street, women hurrying, a Hindustan Ambassador halted in the middle of the road, cloth merchants selling their wares on the footpath near Raja ki Mandi station, and the wedding happening almost in tandem with a married woman next door dying by self-immolation.

The influence of European cinema was not only limited to handheld camera movement, but also a few flash-forwards that Basu employed—something not tried before in Hindi films. A few freeze shots of Samar were also used with dialogue in the background, a commentary on the state of his mind.

The marriage scene was shot by assistant Ramesh Gupta as Basu had to rush to Bombay for some important work at *Blitz*. Gupta, an alumnus of FII's batch of 1965, was a regular at Film Forum, and KK had also put in a word to Basu.

> I also suggested the running of Rakesh Pandey in slow motion. Basu used to proudly tell everyone that this is the work of Ramesh. He was very fair in that respect; never took credit for other people's work. It was my duty to suggest, and it was up to the director to fit the idea into his scheme of things. That he would accept and give credit where due was because he was very secure. Being a workaholic, he used to do everything himself, even the work that was supposed to be done by his assistants. This was possible as he was thorough and detailed, inasmuch as he had drawn sketches for the sequences in the film. Later, he made sketches only for complicated sequences, but the shot divisions and camera angles would be part of the screenplay.
>
> Another thing I must say, Basu never used very complicated camera angles. He followed the Satyajit Ray style to keep things simple. The camera should follow the character. Unlike Mrinal Sen, whose camera movements could be acrobatic and complex.[84]

In this context, it needs to be noted that Basu would cite the concept of the camera following the character in *The Cranes Are Flying* (1957) as an inspiration.

Despite the marginally unorthodox treatment, Basu's collage was much more than just a technical novelty. It was a story told with tenderness and insight into the human psyche. It was a story of patriarchy, of gender roles, social evils and mindsets that failed to evolve with time. It was a love story without the word 'love' being part of the script—except once where the sister-in-law teases Samar.

There were some endearing moments in the film. Like the pregnant sister-in-law tasting a pickle, the elderly father calling his adamant son a *suar* (pig), Prabha showing the photograph of her fiancé to a friend, Kiran cribbing about Diwakar's consumption of cigarettes, Samar using a hairpin as a bookmark, etc., the last two ideas probably inspired from Ray's *Apur Sansar* (1959). Basu also falls back on a short sequence from *Saraswatichandra* for the *suhaag raat*—the night the marriage is supposed to be consummated.

You have the voice of the local bangle-seller like a motif, the Vividh Bharti 'Vigyapan Karyakram' advertising *Nanha Farishta* (1969), Lata Mangeshkar's song 'Mitwa Re' from *Rahgir* (1969), and folk songs of Braj Bhoomi set up in contrast with the latest film hits like 'Phirki Wali' (*Raja Aur Rank*, 1968).

Basu's Agra came alive in all its earthliness, with unkempt walls and film posters juxtaposed with the vast expanse of the university grounds, Paliwal Park and the Shah Jahan Garden. Its cacophony comes through via the mismatch of scales between the natural sounds and traditional songs, the loneliness of the characters explored through patches of complete silence.

Why Agra, this could have been any other town in the northern part of the country. Agra is just a placeholder, and a notional one. Taj Mahal, the crown jewel of Agra, was used only in still shots and inserted during the title sequence, de-stressing its importance in the bigger picture.

Sara Aakash fetched KK his first National Award. He would go on to win three more, almost with boring regularity, till the award committees probably thought that other faces needed to be encouraged. Today, it does seem surprising that Basu did not win any National Award for *Sara Aakash*. According to him and many others who matter in the world of Indian cinema, *Sara Aakash* was his best work. It is not known what Basu's reaction was when the results were declared on 30 August 1970, but the reviews kept on coming after that.

Basu was subsequently at the University Centenary Auditorium, Madras (now Chennai) when the awards were presented on 21 November 1970. Among others, he met Utpal Dutt and S.D. Burman, luminaries with whom he would work later.

The Reception

It was probably around early 1960 when Bimal Roy—arguably Calcutta's best post-Independence export to the world of Bombay cinema in the last century—during a conference, blurted out, 'I am starved.'

It was a remark funny enough to raise eyebrows, especially given the fact that it came from Roy. His next remark however recounted a reality Bombay never wanted to face. 'I am starved for want of a theatre to release my film *Parakh* in Bombay.'[85]

Bimal Roy's *Parakh,* made on a shoestring budget with no stars to pull in crowds, was a film on the parallel stream. Distributors were unwilling to buy it. Cinema hall owners did not think exhibiting it would be profitable.

In April 2015, Basu Chatterji had a similar comment when discussing the release of *Sara Aakash*.[86]

> Film making, distribution, release, all are integrated. Often the making, censor date, etc. are paced to sync with the dates finalized with distributors and theatre owners. In this case, *Sara Aakash* had to wait as there were hardly any takers. Did the National Award for KK which happened late in 1970 help? Maybe, not sure. Rajshri picked up the film much later.

Four hundred and eighty-five days after the film received the film certification, *Sara Aakash* was released at Regal, Delhi. Despite positive critical reception, the film did not make headlines to match with *Bhuvan Shome,* or Hrishikesh Mukherjee's *Anand* (1970), which was released a few weeks earlier. However, the response by the average moviegoer baffled even the story writer, who said:

> Piqued by the leg-pulling of my friends in Delhi, I too had formed the opinion that there must have been something wrong with the film, else how was it being praised by all, irrespective of the demographical profile, from the tonga driver to the snob-intellectual? Even after playing my trump card to the theatre manager (Regal) that I was the writer of the story, he failed to help me out with tickets for any of the three shows on the seventh day. Mannu, Sanjukta, and I had to satisfy ourselves with *dosas* at the tea-house.[87]

The popular verdict was that *Sara Aakash* was a hit in Delhi. Rajshri usually played on a low scale, but an extra morning show had to be arranged for the film for the next hundred days. The miracle was the result of a TV viewing, during the time Doordarshan was limited to a 50-km radius in the national capital. It was shown on a Sunday afternoon as a special entry at the Delhi Television Centre. The response of that show prompted Rajshri to take the plunge.[88]

Rajshri played safe in Bombay, though. The morning show slot at Apsara on Grant Road was made available for the film, the poster of which, apart from the National Award mentions, also carried a blurb by *Variety*, New York—*One of the rare Indian films.*

Just below the title *Sara Aakash*, there was a line that had probably one of the first uses of the word 'art' to classify a Hindi film. 'An off-beat art film,' it said.[89]

Basu's Bombay

'More dreams are realized and extinguished in Bombay than any place in India.'

—Gregory David Roberts

Naseeruddin Shah, in his memoir, mentions an evening in Delhi in the early 1970s:[90]

> One evening in Delhi, with nothing better to do, I wandered into Regal Cinema and watched a movie called *Piya ka Ghar*, a family drama—a genre I abhorred, and the actors in it were hardly my favourites—but seeing it proved fateful. Playing all the important parts in the movie were, I realized, at least five graduates in acting from the Film and TV Institute of India (FTII), Pune.

According to Naseer, this film was one of the drivers which led him to try his luck with an acting course at the FTII. Had he been conversant with the story behind the film, he might have been a tad more respectful in his choice of words in his memoirs. A certain *Piya Ka Ghar* had a connect most unique with what would be Naseer's alma mater in the years to come.

In an interview with the author, film-maker Arunaraje Patil goes back over fifty years in time:[91]

> It was 1968. I was there as a student in the editing department. As part of the curriculum, Diploma films had to be made by

the students. Unfortunately, the films would have limitations as many actors would not get roles strong enough to display their talents. Thus, the institute decided on making a feature film during the summer vacation. The task of direction was given to the head of the acting department, Roshan Taneja, but it was all hush-hush.

Adds film-maker Vikas Desai, also an FTII grad:[92]

I was asked to be there as an assistant. Nobody except me from the student body was privy to the fact. I, fortunately, or unfortunately, told this to the student body. And then all of us went on strike.

Arunaraje continued:

While we had nothing against Mr Taneja, the fact that he and not the profs of the direction department was entrusted with the role, created a huge furore within the student fraternity. And we had our first strike. The I&B secretary at that time was probably Ashok Mitra. He flew down, met us, and asked, 'How are you guys going to do this?' We said, 'We'll show you.' We were a group of nine directors, twelve cameramen, nine recordists, and some twelve or thirteen editors. Vikash (Desai) and I were designated as the running in-charge. We said, 'We'll make a simple film. No offbeat stuff.' Chances of creating offbeat stuff were there with so many directors working together. The plan was that one would finish his part, and another would take over. Vikash and I were supposed to maintain continuity of style. We would interject and say, 'Come on, this is not avant-garde stuff, not a film by Truffaut or Goddard, etc. Keep it unassuming.' The first thing we needed was a story. Vikash suggested *Kuchambana*, written by the Marathi writer Va Pu Kale. This was about life in a city where three couples stay in a single room separated only by sarees hung from slings. Atam Prakash and Shobhna Shah played the young couple. Rehana Sultan played the sister-in-law.

> The gent opposite Rehana Sultan was played (probably) by Suresh Chatwal. A supervising person called Mr. Ghosh was there. Samiran Dutta was there as the second man. But we did all the groundwork. A.K. Bir would shoot surreptitiously at Chowpatty beach, students would stay in a huge dormitory at Vikash's bungalow . . . so many memories. This was probably the first instance of its kind in the world—the entire batch joining hands to make a feature film at the institute. It was an amazing experience.

Vikash adds:

> During a meeting, the production manager designated for the project, M.S. Sharma, suggested using the title *Piya Ka Ghar,* which was agreed upon by all. The name stuck.

The FTII film was later edited hurriedly and rather crudely, cutting down the footage to around forty-five minutes. It did not make it to the theatres. *Jai Jawan Jai Makaan*, made a year later, became the first official feature to be made by FTII. Atam Prakash later did mostly character roles, and we might recall the musician suffering from tuberculosis in *Anand* (1970). Shobhna could not make it big in Bombay and would get to do roles like Manmohan's second wife in *Amar Prem* (1971) or the murderess in *Do Gaz Zameen Ke Neeche* (1972). She did have a substantial role in Basu Chatterji's *Dillagi* (1978), and as one of Ashok Kumar's clients in *Chhoti Si Baat* where incidentally her character was named Shobhna.

Piya Ka Ghar was seen by some at FTII. This included Basu Chatterji who would, rather coincidentally, make a commercial film on the subject. He honoured the inspiration by not changing the name. Suresh Chatwal probably remains the only actor to have acted in both the *Piya Ka Ghar* films, essaying the same character.

★ ★ ★

Basu always returned a favour. Samar Chatterji, a small-time actor, was married to his wife's elder sister Ashima. He was a soft-natured human being who did not make it big in the industry. The roles he played were largely insignificant. The film he directed took almost a decade to complete. *Mr. Buddhu*, when completed in 1972 as *Pyaar Diwana,* was a film nobody remembered.

Samar had played a part in putting in a word for Basu in *Teesri Kasam*, mentions Rupali Guha.[93] Basu would return the favour, conflated with the sense of duty he felt he owed to his brother-in-law, by casting him in *Piya Ka Ghar.*

Quite a few films of the early and late 1950s were based in Bombay, the city of hope in a newly independent India. These films were often about youngsters migrating from far-off towns and villages to Bombay in search of work. In contrast, the films of the 1960s were an escape to places like Simla, Kashmir, Goa, Paris, Singapore and London where young men and women could devote their time to romance and music. Apart from food and shelter, they had access to bikes, jeeps, colourful sweaters, guitars and nightclubs.

Bombay was back in the centre of things in the 1970s, coinciding with the birth of the Angry Young Man. But Basu Chatterji's Bombay wasn't about the descent of the young man into crime and turning super-rich. It charted the journey of persistent people and families who took one step a day to improve upon yesterday's baseline.

Basu's Bombay story was made possible by the Rajshris. They had agreed on a commission-based profit-sharing system with Basu during the distribution of *Sara Aakash*. The Rajshris were happy with *Sara Aakash* and came to him with the offer of another film, the story for which was already selected by them. The proposal was to redo Raja Thakur's National Award-winning film *Mumbai Cha Jawai* (1970) [spelling as per the Censor Certificate dated 25 March 1970] in Hindi. This was another version of the original *Piya Ka Ghar.*

Basu found no reason to alter the name for his version. He also went back to FTII for selecting the leads and saw the film in the editing room. As told to the author:[94]

> I was a regular at the FTII [it was still FII then]. It was during talent scouting that I had liked Jaya Bhaduri and wrote to her father [Taroon Bhaduri] seeking his permission for her to act in my film *Sara Aakash*. While his reply was positive, Jagat Murari, the principal of FTII, did not approve of Jaya's acting as she was still a student. I was happy to have her as my heroine during *Piya Ka Ghar*. My first choice as the hero was a theatre actor, but the producer suggested Anil Dhawan, who was Jaya's classmate at Pune. I must tell you something, I never had any issues with my actors. All of them were good. It is the director's responsibility to get the best out of an actor.

Anil Dhawan, in an interview with the author, talks about his involvement with Basu:[95]

> A Kanpur boy who also studied in Lucknow for some time, I was the VP of the students' union and the captain of the cricket team at college in Kanpur, who, at the insistence of my sister, joined FTII and graduated in 1970 with Jaya Bhaduri, Danny and Rashmi who later became my wife. At the institute, we were taught about a very different kind of cinema. The kind of films happening in Bombay were a shocker, though I was lucky to work with some directors who were different. B.R. Ishara, Asit Sen and certainly Basu-da. We were introduced at the Rajshri office by Raj Barjatya and Basu-da chose me based on my work in *Chetna* (1970). Like me, Basu-da was also new, only one film old. His sense of writing a script was excellent. It was very tight and he would allow no change. Basu-da used to tell us in explicit detail, 'Do this, do that.' He would frown if you tried to do something other than that. Maybe it was because he was new

> and his career was yet to take off. Had he been established, he might have been more relaxed. The degree of his tension was reflected by how much of his handkerchief was in his mouth.

Madhuchhanda Chakrabarty was one of the first to report the handkerchief problem, which she had observed during the shooting of *Sara Aakash*.[96]

> Basu-da would start chewing a corner of the handkerchief. As the shoot progressed, more of the handkerchief would be in his mouth. If there were delays, we would tactically avoid him; we knew he was tense.

The habit of chewing the handkerchief was probably an extension of a childhood habit of scraping his tongue with his teeth.

Narinder Singh (who was not part of *Piya Ka Ghar* as the Rajshris had their own man, Dinshaw Billimoria, who had also worked with Bimal Roy) mentions how Basu used to crash the activities on the critical path.[97]

> Basu would methodically plan his shoots. He had a way of completing work on time as well. Suppose an artiste was not performing as per his requirement, Basu would say, 'Look left, look right, look up, look down,' and take shots. You ask someone to smile, he would normally put on a fake smile and it would be stupid. So, the intent was to get the correct expression and it was often achieved by means other than just acting out the scenes. Suppose somebody has to express that he doesn't like something, Basu would say look left and then look up. The combination could help create the expression Basu wanted. He was very much against wasting raw stock.

This was probably a reason why Basu would prefer trained professionals. They needed less handling. As long as they understood the character well, he was happy.

Anil Dhawan mentions an exception to the rule which delayed the shoot on a particular occasion.[98]

> There were times when the directions were not very clear. Jaya and I, both being new, were asked to board a local train from Churchgate and keep talking in a normal manner while KK and Basu would shoot from a car. Unfortunately, we had no idea where to get down and eventually landed at a station far away and took a taxi to the Rajshri office.
>
> But overall, he was extremely meticulous about how to complete the shoot on time. It was a learning experience for all of us who were new.

★ ★ ★

'Character is the very life of fiction,' advised John Gardner, the guru of the art of novel writing. And *Piya Ka Ghar* was a hamper of richly nuanced characters. Take the case of the smooth-talking Panditji-cum-marriage broker who, in the very first scene, 'sells' Bombay (as if it were the Eden) to Shyamlal, a gullible middle-aged villager. If the prospective groom for Shyamlal's daughter Malti was based in Bombay, what more could he ask for, asserts Panditji, in an obvious hurry to seal the alliance and pocket his brokerage. For the simpleton, Bombay signifies wealth and comfort. And that is a misplaced perception that the Panditji (Samar Chatterji) plays on. Panditji's sales pitch is that the boy's family has been living in Bombay for thirty years. 'Therefore, they have to be rich. If not, would they still be living in Bombay?'

'*Paanch manzile makaan me hai ladke ka ghar* (the groom's family lives in a five-storeyed building),' Panditji adds with a flourish. He craftily plays around with words, spicing them up with half-truths, likening the five-storey building called Bharat Mahal to a 'haveli inhabited by rajas and maharajas', but avoids specifics.

Shyamlal gulps down Panditji's sales talk, and happily agrees to the marriage of Ram Sharma (Anil Dhawan) and Malti.

In reality, 'Bharat Mahal' was a quintessential chawl in the Dadar suburb of Bombay—a community-dwelling of lower/middle-income families consisting of overcrowded and under-maintained houses adjacent to each other, with hardly any room for privacy. The common balcony for all houses on that floor was where the inhabitants would mill around. One needed to be careful to avoid water dripping from above and bumping into vegetable vendors while entering the building. The staircases were cramped by design and damp by default while the guardrails supporting the balconies looked dangerously brittle with age.

The creation of the chawl set was the brainchild of art director Bansi Chandragupta. Anil Dhawan says:[99]

> The chawl was in Dadar. First, all the outside shots were taken by Basu and his team. Then the chawl set was built at Rajkamal Studio. Bansi Chandragupta struck a deal with the inmates. 'Give me your furniture. I will replace these with new ones. I will take you to Dadar, you buy the stuff, I will get the same transported via tempo to the chawl.' This was a very intelligent move. There was absolutely no loss of continuity as the same furniture, upholstery, bed covers, cushions, etc., were used when a set identical to the house of Mr. Sharma at Bharat Mahal was constructed at the studio.

Inside Bharat Mahal, Basu introduced more of those delightful characters promised in the first scene. Ram Sharma was the chocolate-faced, evidently inexperienced young groom excited about getting married. Ram's parents were the pensioner Girdharilal Sharma (Agha) and Mrs Sharma (Sulochana Chatterjee)—both ever-smiling and warm to family and neighbours. Basu Chatterji's dialogues brought to the fore his skill of saying a lot with few words. For example, Mrs Sharma's lines, '*28–29 saal ho gaye is ghar mein. Ab yahi apna ghar hai. Gaon ko bhul hi gayi* (We have been living in this house for 28–29 years. This is our home. I have forgotten my village)' are a deep exposition—they tell us that, for the past three decades, the Sharmas' economic status hasn't improved enough for them to be able to move out of the chawl. It also tells us how young women from villages eventually adjust to city life. Can Malti? Chatterji lays down the premise around which the plot evolves.

Suresh Chatwal, who was in the film within a film in *Sara Aakash*, plays Ram's elder brother Shiri who runs a theatre group. The attractive Rajeeta Thakur, his wife, is also an actor in his theatre group. With a slender figure, washboard abs, her sari worn low at the midriff, her continual giggling, and her teasing of her brother-in-law Ram by refusing to show him Malti's photograph, Shoba's characterization is that of a fashionable Bombayite. In a connection most interesting, Rajeeta reprises her role of Durga in *Mumbai Cha Jawai*, where she was a debutant. Just that she was Shobha in *Piya Ka Ghar*.

The pair of Suresh Chatwal and Rajeeta Thakur playing the same roles in different versions could be a first.

Shiri and Ram's youngest brother Hari is a typical Bombay teenager who devours cricket, with the young local boy Sunil Gavaskar his favourite cricketer. Two other inhabitants of Bharat Mahal—the tailor Kulkarni (Keshto Mukherjee), a connoisseur of Hindustani classical music who often breaks into a song, and Kanhaiya (Mukri) who owns a taxi, are Girdharilal Sharma's longstanding card game companions and close friends. Another member of Shiri's drama troupe is Ram's friend and colleague at LIC, the jocular Arun (Paintal). Arun is a self-styled, self-appointed 'consultant' to Ram in matrimonial matters. In that claustrophobic house, card games, tea-breaks, bonhomie, laughter, leg-pulling, drama rehearsals and cricket commentary blaring over the big radio keep their faces glowing with happiness and contentment all day. They are cozy together. As Sharma discloses towards the end of the film, '*Hamare itne dukh hain ki agar hum unki chinta karne lage to hame sukh ki ek boond bhi haasil nahi ho sakti*

(If we permit our endless problems to overpower us, we can never find happiness).'

Into this milieu arrives Malti, who has spent a carefree childhood running in open fields and streams. She had an entire room converted into a playhouse for her dolls. Interestingly, the shock that the audience expects to see in Malti on being cheated into the reality that was Bharat Mahal doesn't come about. Instead, we see in her a sense of bewilderment, trying to find her way around the house amid the cackle of noisy neighbours.

Then comes the highlight of the film—the first night of the newlywed couple.

The 'bridal suite' is the kitchen—with a window that doesn't close. Ram is convinced that the room is dark because he has switched off the lights. But Malti feels bared because of the streetlights that bathe the kitchen in a bluish glow, and the music from a radio somewhere as well as the murmur of two neighbours chatting outside the window. Adding to the embarrassment, the sound of the fragile bridal cot creaking under Ram's weight permeates across the wooden partitions (purporting to be walls) for everyone in the house to hear. Ram is ready for lovemaking while Malti is stiff as a plank. What is implicit here is that Ram, a chawl-dweller in Bombay, is habituated to sleeping in semi-darkness and a pervasive aural disturbance. Whereas Malti, the rich village girl, needs inky darkness and total silence. The new bride discovers that in Bombay chawls, there is no privacy even for a conversation, let alone sex.

And then, unexpectedly, a loud alarm blares somewhere in the middle of the night and the whole chawl wakes up. That night, Malti learns an important lesson on survival in Bombay—running water is available in the mornings only for an hour a day. But when a fire breaks out somewhere (which is what the alarm was about), the municipal authorities release water for the fire engines—and the chawl dwellers get a bonus quota of running water.

> authentic. New shoes might have looked out of place as my character comes from a lower middle-class family. I also wore one of my trousers. We managed to save Rs 2–3, which we spent on having a dosa each while on our way back to the office.

Even back in 1972, efficiency in Bombay was as normal as rain. Shiri pooh-poohs Malti's 'perfectly matching' horoscope by saying, '*Do do rupaye me kundliyan banti hain Bambai mein* (Horoscopes can be doctored for as little as two rupees).'

Basu's Bombay in *Piya Ka Ghar* is expressed through images, underplayed exchanges, and sub-text rather than melodrama and high-pitched action. It is also a reflection of the urban 1970s where the radio was the lifeline. And ill-maintained record players which turned at a higher speed, resulting in the songs sounding hurried. One which we hear is 'Yeh Jo Mohabbat Hai' (*Kati Patang,* 1970), as the crane shot captures Malti, dressed as the bride, climbing up the stairs to her shanty on the third floor. The staircase scene, while being reminiscent of Aparna's entry into Apu's one-room terrace flat for the first time in Satyajit Ray's *Apur Sansar*, also touched upon the song Ray had mentioned in his 1970 story *Sonar Kella*. Coincidence? Most likely.

And throughout the screenplay, Hindi film songs, snippets and references to Hindi films run like a motif. Bombay without the Hindi film industry is incomplete. Basu chose his background songs and radio programmes with care, including his favourite—AIR Vividh Bharti's staple programme *Vigyapan Karyakram*, which in the film starts with an ad of Nirodh, the condom popularized by the Congress government during the family planning movement titled *Hum Do Hamare Do* (We two, our two). Later in the evening, we hear the famous *Saz Aur Aawaz* programme where a song and its instrumental version would be played in the reverse order as Dipak Kapadia's slide guitar belts out the tune of 'Mujhse Bhala Yeh Kaajal Tera' (*The Train*, 1970), probably underlining that songs from Rajesh Khanna's films were the most popular ones then.

The Dharmendra-Asha Parekh-Vinod Khanna dacoit saga *Mera Gaon Mera Desh* (1971), which was running to full houses around that time, also has its quota of songs. 'Sona Lei Ja Re' plays on the radio, while 'Maar Diya Jaye' is heard at a loud volume by some late at night—definitely by blokes with little consideration for others. A sober song, and an older one like 'Ae Malik Tere Bande Hum' (*Do Aankhen Bara Haath*, 1957) is heard in the morning, though it could well have been Basu's tribute to V. Shantaram whose studio was the stage for his set of Bharat Mahal. And the re-recording also happened there with Mangesh Desai behind the mixing machine. Hindi cinema and songs being an understood and accepted way of life is also expressed with Shobha often humming a few, from 'Dilbar Jani' (*Haathi Mere Saathi*, 1971) to 'Yeh Dil Diwana Hai' (*Ishq Par Zor Nahin*, 1970). Ads of *Khamoshi* and *Abhinetri*, both releases of 1970, are major displays at Churchgate Station.

In a comic sidelight, Ram attempts to borrow a page from Dharmendra's art of serenading the woman in *Jeevan Mrityu* (1970)—but his efforts fail and he stops taking advice from Arun thereafter. A five-second shot of Dharam is seen, shooting for the fictional film *Aan Milo Balma*, probably a backhanded compliment to the Rajesh Khanna-Asha Parekh-Vinod Khanna starrer *Aan Milo Sajna* (1970). An ad of the now-discontinued carbonated soft drink Gold Spot shot by Shyam Benegal—who was yet to shoot a feature—with Rekha, then only a film or two old, as the model, is hanging at the reception of a hotel.

Looking back, *Piya Ka Ghar* stands out as a reflection of urban India of the early 1970s. A time when nostalgia for the past was on the decline. With a rising influx of people into the cities, the foundations of an agrarian society were under the radar. Politicians had no qualms in switching allegiance for personal gain. Friends and extended family on long train journeys would halt en route and drop in unannounced, assured that they would be offered a place to stay, albeit reluctantly. Films became faster; even the retired male with a rudimentary knowledge of English would want to see Westerns. Though 'Beatlemania' was largely unknown outside of the ultra-rich, and fewer knew of a certain Cary Grant, Gregory Peck with his wooden act was the larger-than-life hero, who became popular with *MacKenna's Gold* (1969) which had a record run (then thirty-two weeks in the city). Working wives hummed the latest songs, an indication of how film music permeated their subconscious.

Basu's 1970s had come to stay. His choice of songs used in the background, has remained in public memory even now, fifty years later. Like Laxmikant-Pyarelal's choice of instrument in the song 'Yeh Jeevan Hai'—the acoustic guitar. According to Nirmal Mukherjee, a rhythm guru who was a sitting member of Rajesh Roshan's team, Pyarelal had used four guitars with chord inversions in this F major song.[103] Kishore Kumar, in his first song for a Basu film, sang it in a whispering cadence.

This extraordinary song, among the finest of music directors Laxmikant Pyarelal, was shot with a special three-wheel tripod trolley that was brought from Calcutta, recalls Anil Dhawan.[104] This helped KK in manoeuvring the camera through the barely walkable spaces inside the chawl set. I will sing this song, said Basu to the producers when confronted with the question of lip-synching. He had it all planned out, scripted to appear as a leitmotif in the film. In the end, it was a KK meeting KK song; Kishore Kumar's voice is given a visual dimension by K.K. Mahajan.

★ ★ ★

Piya Ka Ghar, with its simple, caring lot, would go on to become Basu Chatterji's signature style. Perhaps like the Bengali films of the 1950s, he felt that it was the characters on the fringe who would add a world of value to the story. In inept hands, *Piya Ka Ghar* could have devolved into a mushy tearjerker. Basu infused the narrative with an intrinsic comic charm, friendly banter and funny moments. For example, the scene where Sunder, a co-passenger, gets engrossed in a game of cards and misses his stop, thereby having to pay a hefty fine. Basu's technical expertise like the jump cut from the train to the tonga, the excellent set design, and realistic night photography—something neglected in Hindi films till it went digital—were traits that would come to define his work.

Glitches like Gauri Shankar (Raja Paranjpe) not shown younger during Malti's childhood can be ascribed to oversight and takes nothing away from the overall product. Basu however could have exercised caution in the areas of costume and continuity. Rajeeta Thakur changing her saree four times in almost back-to-back sequences was not the best example to set. These lapses in continuity would become an accepted part of his otherwise very entertaining films.

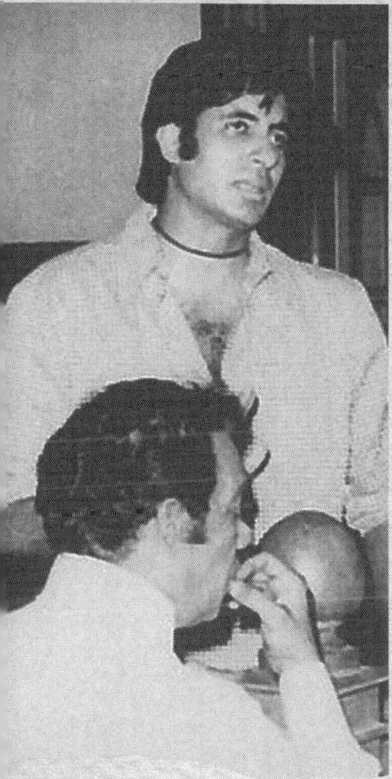

BOOK 2

The Common Man

'Thomas Hardy said happiness is just an interlude in the general drama of pain. I am concerned only with these interludes'

—Basu Chatterji

The Birth: The Idea

In Hindi cinema, everyone knows what happens when the leading lady falls in love with the hero. She marries, and lives happily ever after, provided the film is not a tragedy or an art film that nobody understands. The presence of a third angle, if any, is that of somebody with negative traits. Most probably a villain who gets beaten up in the end and often locked up behind bars. Or killed. Also, leading ladies of Hindi cinema do not fall in love with more than one man. A visionary like Mehboob Khan in *Andaz* (1949) hinted at this unexplored angle. Hrishikesh Mukherjee in *Anuradha* (1960), or Raj Kapoor in *Sangam* (1964) tried to circumvent the rule, but these were again films with a sombre undertone. Bhattacharya, the other Basu, had dealt with a similar storyline in *Anubhav* (1971) only to lose the plot with a climax very chauvinistic.

In his films, Basu Chatterji allowed for the possibility of a woman falling in love more than once. The story, devoid of melodrama, would be humorous, entertaining the public even while doing away with the overt sentimentalism, inane action-packed fights and the mandatory six-song routine that were a staple template followed by most of the movies of that time (and now).

These light entertainers, with a deeper subtext, were recognized as a new genre and christened as 'middle-of-the-road cinema'. Films with characters we encountered in our day-to-day lives, finding a bit of ourselves in them, who would encounter situations that reflected our own experiences. Falling in and out of love was one.

* * *

Post *Sara Aakash*, Basu's trips to Delhi were marked by a mandatory visit to the Yadav residence in Shakti Nagar. He used to love the place and would not mind staying over. It was during one such Delhi trip that he discussed the cinematic possibilities of *Yehi Sach Hai* (1966) with Mannu Bhandari.[105]

Mentions Mannu Bhandari in her autobiography:[106]

> In 1970 (actually, 1969), Basu Chatterji created a space very different for himself in the world of art films after adapting Rajendra Yadav's *Sara Aakash*. In stark contrast to the established world of art films which distanced the viewers, Basu not only brought back the viewers but also made them empathize with the characters in the film. The success of the film was a source of joy for Rajendra, and Basu-da floated the idea of making a film on my story *Yehi Sach Hai*. Needless to say, I was delighted; but was concerned how a story that had been written in the form of a diary articulating the innermost contradictions of a girl could be adapted for the cinema. When I put forward my reservations to Basu-da, he suggested I leave the task to him and give him the go-ahead. The ardour of seeing my story in the form of cinema overpowered my apprehensions.

Yehi Sach Hai was based on the confessions of a male friend to Mannu Bhandari; a friend who was caught between two women in his life. Mannu Bhandari had done a gender role reversal.

The transformation of this simple story told on screen in a simpler manner happened in a rather complex process. Starting in early 1972, it was rejected by two producers till a young engineer thought otherwise.

★ ★ ★

Suresh Jindal was an electronics engineer from the University of California, Los Angeles, and had spent a few years in the US working in the aerospace industry, before settling in Delhi. In May 1972, he had just read the review of *Piya Ka Ghar* in the *Times of India.* Vijay Rahi, who Suresh had never met, but whose sister was a friend of Suresh's elder brother Ramesh, had dropped in. Rahi had come with the intent of pursuing him to become a film distributor for some films he had in mind, mentions Suresh to the author in an interview.[107] 'I pointed to the film name on the paper and said that I was willing to produce a film if the director of *Piya Ka Ghar* was willing.'

Rahi knew Basu, and arranged a meeting between him and Suresh at his flat, where Basu shared the cinematic treatments of three films he had in mind. During their next meeting, Suresh had zeroed in on the story by Mannu Bhandari. Basu was circumspect; he mentioned that two producers who had given him the signing amount for the film never followed up on the project.

On being asked why he chose Mannu Bhandari's story, Suresh had an interesting answer.[108] 'Sir, our society is so conservative that for a girl who is already engaged, to even mention another man's name makes her a "fast girl" and a vamp of low character. The story has a liberating aspect that our country needs now.'

According to Suresh Jindal, the signing amount was paid in the form of traveller's cheques the same day. Basu had already formed a team and wanted to continue with the same, and in a couple of days, the crew comprising KK and Narinder Singh had been paid their signing amounts.

Basu had mentioned to the author that Jindal had initially agreed to go ahead with two out of the three alternatives he had shared with him.

Yehi Sach Hai is the story of Deepa, a Kanpur-based girl who is in a dilemma, not knowing who to choose: Sanjay, her boyfriend, or her teenage love Nishith, whom she bumps into after three years (changed to five years in the film) during a trip to Calcutta. The name Nishith suggests a Bengali origin, though we cannot be sure as the characters do not have any surnames. Probably to strip off cultural and caste backgrounds and make the characters appeal to as large a section of the north Indian audience, Basu renamed Nishith as Naveen. The other three names, including Ira, Deepa's friend, remained unaltered in the script, though Deepa had a surname, Kapoor.

Basu named the film *Rajanigandha* (or *Rajnigandha*, depending on the pronunciation and the spelling you choose to use). The major task at hand was finding Deepa, Ira, and Naveen. And Sanjay, who would be the prototype for the 1970s common man.

Sulagna Biswas puts it aptly and succinctly in her article:[109]

> One of the most flawed boyfriends Bollywood has ever seen, Sanjay's talkative, obsessed about his job and promotion, always late, forgetful about movie tickets and compliments . . .

Finding Amol Palekar

A story before Suresh Jindal decided to produce *Rajnigandha* . . .

Like most small-towners, Basu was an early riser. Post *Piya Ka Ghar*, he would be at work by 7 a.m. By 8.30 a.m., the ceiling fans would be switched off in the rooms where the others would be sleeping. It was their wake-up call.

Those who woke up early would find Basu in his chair, sometimes on the floor, writing his screenplays. Except for the days when he had a morning shoot. This was the time when Basu cut down his professional assignments for *Blitz*.

The script of *Rajnigandha* happened during the early morning sessions when *Piya Ka Ghar* was in the making.

★ ★ ★

The first actor Basu had in mind for the role of Sanjay was Amitabh Bachchan. He was yet to become the Alpha Male then.

History could have been very different had Basu stuck to his original choice.

Shashi Kapoor was offered the role of Naveen. Suave, slick, with leadership qualities that extended beyond the college campus to wield influence in college selection panels, he was, as defined by Sulagna Biswas,[110] the original LinkedIn Man.

Sharmila Tagore was Basu's first choice as Deepa. Independent, but not a renegade. Observant, sentimental, committed, steadfast and yet ambivalent.

The plan fell through. Shashi Kapoor was fine with playing Naveen, subject to the condition that the film was sold to distributors at the existing rate for a Shashi Kapoor film, something Basu was not comfortable with. Sharmila was out of the contention too, but the reason is not known. Maybe Basu wanted fresher faces. Meanwhile, Basu flew to Calcutta and offered Aparna Sen the role of Deepa. Aparna, who probably had not seen *Sara Aakash*, felt that the story of Deepa was ordinary. Her refusal prompted Basu to pitch it to Mallika Sarabhai. She was referred by Yogesh. Both Yogesh and Mallika were working in *Sonal* (1973) then. Basu met Mallika in Ahmedabad and the dates for a few shoots were fixed. However, Mallika was planning to do her MBA and later walked out of the film.

In the meantime, *Piya Ka Ghar* was released in Calcutta. News of its critical acclaim reached the cognoscenti. Aparna Sen, being one of them, had a change of mind and wrote to Basu expressing a desire to play Deepa. A few days after Basu acknowledged the mail, Aparna came down to Bombay to complete her part of the shoot of Tapan Sinha's *Sagina* (1974). Basu met her, and when the discussion boiled down to money, Sen said she was fine receiving in kind as a small film-maker like Basu would find it difficult to compensate her at the market rate.

The contract with Suresh Jindal had been finalised by then. Said Basu:[111]

> I discussed the possibility of giving Aparna Sen a Fiat car. It would have cost us around Rs 32,000. But things began to get topsy-turvy when she refused to work with the Naveen I had in mind—Samit Bhanja, who I had seen in *Guddi* (1971) and liked. While the producer and I were fine with the monetary arrangements, we started to become sceptical of starry tantrums. This is when we consciously took the decision of taking all new faces.

The search for rookies thus commenced. Basu, for a short time, had also mulled trying out Rakesh Pandey, but he was preoccupied, as told to the author.[112]

> Basu-da wanted me to do *Rajnigandha*. At the time, I was doing a film with Mohan Segal called *Intezar* (1973). The set was at Rooptara Studios. Basu-da came down to the set, and said, 'I am doing a film called *Rajnigandha*. It is about a girl and two boys. It will take 20 days to shoot.' I said, okay, when do you want to start? He said next week. I said, 'Basu-da, I am doing this film, and it will take at least 15–20 days here on this set. I can manage three to four days at the most if you shoot in Bombay.' He said, 'No no, the producer might run away.'

* * *

In addition to his National Award-winning screenplay for Shyam Benegal's *Bhumika* (1977), theatre veteran Satyadev Dubey—who people would recall as the weekly waged stevedore who confronts the goons only to be run over by a truck in *Deewar* (1975)—made one extremely significant contribution to Hindi cinema: Amol

Palekar. Dubey had directed the Hindi play *Aadhe Adhure,* starring Amol, who was acting in Marathi plays at the time.

Basu loved his acting, and Amol was Basu's original choice for *Piya Ka Ghar* (1972), but producer Tarachand Barjatya's son Raj Kumar Barjatya, who was there at the theatre with Basu, opined that Amol was too simple-looking for a hero.

Suresh Jindal, however, had no issues in accepting Amol, a postgraduate of JJ School of Arts, Bombay, as the Sanjay of his film. Basu was happy with the onboarding, about which he told the author:

> Amol was then working with Bank of India. He was a part-time actor. I was fond of Marathi theatre and had seen Amol in a few plays. He used to come to film shows arranged by Film Forum as well. Raja Thakur, the maker of *Mumbai Cha Jawai* (1970) had also put in a word. Amol had played a small role in his film *Bajiravacha Beta* (1971). After he was rejected by Raj, I proposed his name to Suresh Jindal.[113]

Amol had talked about his first business meeting with Basu with author Balaji Vittal:[114]

> There used to be a café named Samovar inside the Jahangir Art Gallery. I met Basu-da and producer Suresh Jindal there. Mr Jindal did not talk during this meeting. But the interesting part was that Basu-da did not talk much either. He narrated the story of the film like this. '*Amol, kya hai, ek ladka hai, mano tum. Aur ek ladki hai. Nayi ladki hai, Vidya Sinha hai uska naam. Usse miloge tum. Toh, ye dono hai . . . aur . . . yaar ye tum padh lo na* [Amol, there's a boy. You. And a girl, a new actress called Vidya Sinha. You will meet her . . . you two . . . oh, why don't you read it for yourself].' Basu-da handed me Mannu Bhandari's story.* Following my acceptance to do his film, he gave me

* Mannu Bhandari's story is twenty pages long, and not two pages as reported in many features.

> the script as well. After reading that, I kept wondering how someone who was so ill at ease narrating a story could write a screenplay in so much detail. Even the dialogues were there. He was extremely eloquent in the cinematic language. Once you understood that, communication becomes easy.

The choice of Naveen came through an old connection. Preeta Mathur Thakur, wife of the late Dinesh Thakur, tells the story in an interview with the author.[115]

> Mohan Rakesh's *Aadhe Adhure*, one of the most powerful plays in Hindi of all time, was one of the first ones to be staged by Delhi-based Om Shivpuri's Dishantar. Basu Bhattacharya loved the play and wanted to make a film on the same. It was during this phase that Dinesh Thakur, who had portrayed Om's son Ashok, was introduced to Basu Bhattacharya. *Aadhe Adhure*, the film, did not happen, but Dinesh Ji was offered the role of the third angle in the marital triangle *Anubhav* (1971). So different was Dinesh from the chocolate-faced film stars that Tanuja's initial reaction to him was, '*Yeh kala kauwa kaun hai* [Who is this black crow]?' They became good friends.
>
> Dinesh also became close to N.C. Sippy. It was through the circle of mutual friends that Basu Chatterji cast him in *Rajnigandha*. Interestingly, Amol too had played Ashok in Satyadev Dubey's production of the same play.
>
> As Dinesh, a post-grad in Hindi literature, had a strong background in Hindi theatre, he was also given the additional task of working on the diction of the cast, apart from helping Basu with the dialogues.

The two theatre artistes were given the job of mentoring Vidya Sinha as well. Said Basu:

> Vidya Sinha, who played Deepa, had acted in a film [author's note—*Raja Kaka*, 1973], but I selected her just by seeing

> her photograph as a model in a magazine. Another girl who I had in mind but was left out in the final process was Heena Kausar. Vidya looked younger than she was, one of the reasons I selected her.[116]

A workshop, in Basu Chatterji style, was arranged to familiarize the main artistes. The bubbly Rajeeta Thakur was the only repeat actor from Basu's previous film *Piya Ka Ghar.*

The Making

The first shot of the film had Deepa appearing for an interview. To quote Vidya Sinha from an interview with Roshmila Bhattacharya,[117] 'The first scene required me to be in a tizzy over an interview and since I was really nervous, I got away with my first shot.' What she did not mention, or perhaps did not know, was that other people involved in the shot were probably much more nervous. Basu did not have actors chalked out for that scene and was relying on amateurs. One who refused was Praba Mahajan, KK's wife, who had played the lead in Kumar Shahani's *Maya Darpan* (1972).[118] A day before the shoot, there was nobody to play the woman on the interview board. Basu made an SOS call to his friends, and one of the people he called was Nandita Thakur's mother. As Nandita Thakur mentioned to the author:[119]

> My mother Anjali Ghosh was a beautiful woman in her youth. She was a beauty contest winner once, at the Lady Jane Dundas Hostel of Scottish Church College, Calcutta. One day, she received a request from Basu-da to play a small part in a film he was making. '*Boudi, ekta choto role aache, kindly kore din* [Sister-in-law, there's a small role where I need you. Kindly do not say no].' My mother, with no prior acting experience, was driven down to the school where Basu-da was shooting and spoke three lines—in her heavily Bengali-accented Hindi—as per the script. Certainly, her nervousness was far less than mine when I did my first shot for *Sara Aakash.*

The other two interview board members were also, to quote Basu, his '*yaar dosts*'. On the right of the screen, you would see a face near-forgotten today, Gopal Kumar Dootia, incidentally the founder of the film society Anandam and one of the most well-known faces in the Bombay film circle then. The gent on the left of the screen was Raj Prakash Gupta, one of the producers of Basu's *Manzil*.

Convent Girls' High School at Prabhadevi, Bombay, was the site of the interview sequence. Both Sonali and Rupali were students there. It was a connection that would take them back in time when they were in skirts and their hair in plaits.[120]

Location shooting was something Basu always preferred. Apart from flexibility with time and space, it also came cheap.

While the budget was not a major concern for *Rajnigandha*, Basu, always with an eye for economy when it came to film production, had some of the crew, including himself, do cameos. One would recall him decked up in the choicest of winter clothing including a striped muffler watching *Kahin Din Kahin Raat* (1968) at Rivoli in Connaught Place, New Delhi. One might miss Suresh Jindal, though, who with his long hair and drooping moustache looked very different then. He was accompanied by his niece.[121] An unlit cigarette dangling from his fingers was not the best example to be set in a cinema hall, but that was something Basu wanted to show—a total disregard for statutes by the people in India. This sequence at the cinema theatre is very important, in the sense that it captures the producer, the director, and the lead actors in a single frame. Both Suresh Jindal and Basu were there during one more sequence each as well. Suresh, in the background at the open-air coffee house in Delhi, and Basu, wearing a dark grey sweater with his back turned to the camera at a bus stop. Around thirty minutes into the film, viewers would also notice a disgruntled Narinder Singh standing in a queue in front of a phone booth. Those were the days when the telephone was a luxury. Rajiv Suri, the executive producer, and also one of the producers of *Manzil*, played a steward at Flora, Worli. Basu and his family were regulars there.[122]

* * *

The first phase of the shooting happened in Bombay. Delhi-based Dinesh Thakur came down and roamed around the streets with Vidya in tow. The shoot was completed in approximately two and a half weeks. Mannu Bhandari's story touched upon landmarks in Calcutta like the Coffee House, Dharamtala, Dhakuria Lake, and Sky Room, the best restaurant in the city, which had to pull down its shutters in 1993 due to persistent labour trouble. In Basu's story, Bombay replaced Calcutta. He and KK would walk the city with Dinesh, Vidya and sometimes Rajeeta, capturing landmarks the viewers would know courtesy of their exposure to the cinema from Bombay. For the academic Deepa, these were just names till then. Her eyes explored the contours of the city just as Basu's, when he, as a young hopeful from Mathura, had come down to work, expecting, among other things, to do his graduation and follow it up with a jab at the civil services exam. It was probably his failure to graduate on account of economic compulsions that he wished to see his characters well-educated. Especially his heroines. Deepa is seen pursuing her PhD, something not very common for the heroine in Hindi cinema then.

Multiple scenes of the couple eating around the city were also captured. Was this because Basu was a foodie himself? Basu put on his angular smile, something which was more of a boyish grin when confronted with this question at his Ballygunge residence.[123]

A few shots were taken at Basu's Worli flat as well, one among them being the scene where Deepa is seen attempting suicide by hanging from a fan.[124]

The crew moved to Delhi for the next phase of the shoot. Vijay Rahi magnanimously lent his flat at the posh A-Block, Defence Colony. Most shots of Vidya standing on the balcony and staring at the road, engrossed in thought and waiting for Sanjay or the postman, were taken there. KK also took some panoramic views of the city, including familiar landmarks. While Delhi boy Dinesh played the urbane, slick and dependable Bombay adman, Amol, a resident of Bombay, travelled to Delhi for his part of the film. The locale shots were more of old Delhi, tipping its hat to tradition in contrast to the razzmatazz that was Bombay, laconically and amusingly typified by the party which had, among its cast, Mrs Chitra Palekar, wife of Amol, in a blink-and-miss role. The party was a microcosm of the advertising world. People forgetting dates and commitments and taking pride in the esoteric, like the cinema of Michelangelo Antonioni in a know-it-all manner, only to go into hibernation when asked simple questions like, What was the story? The party scene was arranged with associates of KK and friends of Suresh Jindal from Alliance Francaise. A few there were also assisting Basu.[125]

For a story based on a dilemma, *Rajnigandha* had its music crafted to underline the confusion. Salil Chowdhury, fresh off the success of *Anand* (1970) and *Mere Apne* (1971), returned to Basu's team. He was an automatic choice, said Basu to the author.[126] Suresh Jindal too mentions that music sittings at Salil Chowdhury's Peddar Road flat, named Himgiri, happened during the time he and Basu were scouting for actors. Yogesh, who the author met multiple times, laid out the complete story of how the songs of *Rajnigandha* were made.[127]

> I was a big fan of Basu Chatterji and had seen *Sara Aakash* thrice. The flash-forward methods he employed in the film appealed to me very much. Incidentally, he too had liked my work and had approached Salil-da with a caveat—I want the same guy who wrote the lyrics for *Anand* (1970). I had no other work then, and *Rajnigandha* happened to me.
>
> For the title song, Basu-da sketched the outline of the situation of a man arriving to meet the woman with a bouquet of rajnigandha flowers. I was working with Salil-da for a film named *Mere Bhaiya* (1972) where he had composed a background score using a lot of wind instruments, including

the saxophone and the flute. I was fond of the tune and asked Salil-da if he could reuse it for the title song, which he ultimately did. I wrote to the meter given to me by him. After the recording was done, Lata Mangeshkar told me, '*Bahut accha likha hai* [It has been written beautifully].' It was a memorable day for me.

Now, there were some discussions between Salil-da and Basu-da. When I asked them, Salil-da said, 'Basu-da is saying that the song has come out lengthier by a few seconds.' Perplexed, I enquired how it was possible. And even if it was so, all that needed to be done was to edit the extra seconds. It was then that we were told that the song sequence had already been shot! The song was in the background and hence there was no lip-sync. I had written the second *antara* as

'Apna unka kya doon parichay
Pichle janmon ke naate hain
Har baar badalkar ye kaya
Hum dono milte aate hain,
Dharti ke is aangan me,
Rajnigandha phool tumhare . . .'

Then I saw part of the film and the song sequence at the studio, and my general feeling was that the lyrics did not tie in well with the situation. I went to the Irani restaurant across the street, sat down at a table, and did a rewrite of the second antara. It had a more contemporary feel. To Basu-da, it would have made no difference, but I would have rued the fact that my song failed in its attempt to capture the essence of the film.

'Rajanigandha Phool Tumhare' brought Salil back to the Binaca list after *Anand*. The song, with the leading notes of Sunil Kaushik's twelve-string guitar, is partly reminiscent of the prelude of Simon & Garfunkel's *Sound(s) of Silence* (1964), and remains a favourite with many even forty-five years later, and not just on account of nostalgia.

If Lata's impeccable rendition of this intricate melody is most loved, 'Kai Baar Yun Bhi Dekha Hai' surely is the cherry on the cake. Discerning, sharp, with a reverb creating a halo of sorts.

To top it all, the dazzling songs were situational, certainly not decorative adjuncts in a story where silence was used to communicate more than the words spoken.

In a discussion with the author, Preeta Mathur dissects the song situation for 'Kai Baar . . .' as heard from Dinesh Thakur:[128]

> You see, the unusual part of the song was that it was not ready when the picturization was to take place. It was not yet fixed or decided. Basu-da gave them the background. Both the actors were told, 'These are the emotions. You have to portray them.' Just that, nothing else.
>
> But if you see the song on screen, it so beautifully matches the visuals and the expressions of the characters. This is the brilliance of a director and an editor. How they mix the song with the visuals to fit in with the emotions. That was amazing. Basu-da had given them these instructions. There is this dichotomy in her mind. Should she go with him? Should she not? She is confused. And he isn't saying anything. Probably he is afraid of rejection, or he does not want to pre-empt. And she is thinking, 'Why doesn't he say something? Why doesn't he help me decide?' The taxi ride, you see—he is very careful, very concerned, very courteous but not saying anything more. He is just not taking it to the next level despite doing all that is needed in a manner most decorous . . .

This marked a rare occasion in Mukesh's career when he was not singing for the male protagonist. Rather, his song represented the crux of the story, and he pulled it through with his deep bass and controlled passion. This thought-provoking song on 2x4 with syncopated beats, a touch of Bossa Nova and arranged with lots of brass and wind obligatos, came to Mukesh on the rebound; engaging Lata as envisaged originally would have cost the producer Rs 3000. Mukesh charged only Rs 1000, a token amount, mentioned Basu to the author. The change of playback singer was the reason for the delay in the recording.[129]

Said Yogesh about his writing for the already composed song by Salil Chowdhury:[130]

> Salil-da, who was a great poet himself, would never permit me to be inspired by him as far as writing lyrics was concerned. He would shoo me away if I followed his style of writing. 'Kai Baar Yun Bhi Dekha Hai' was written to the tune of a Bengali song Salil-da already composed. But I had to use my imagination to fit the situation.

Salil Chowdhury was another reason why the song was married so nicely to the visuals. His expertise in handling background scores came into use; one would notice the rhythm picking up only when the taxi starts moving. The background music was used to signify the moods of the characters too, and one might go back and check Chowdhury augmenting Deepa's tension by adding a C sharp note in the progression 'F-G-F-C(low) / F-G-F-C(high)', in the scene when she has been kept waiting by Sanjay for over an hour. The composition also helped separate the characters of the two cities. Delhi saw a dominant use of Indian instruments, both string and wind, while Bombay's was more rhythm-based. George Fernandez's muted trumpet was one of the attractions in 'Zindagi Kaisi Hai Paheli' (*Anand*, 1970). The instrument found prominent use in *Rajnigandha* too, especially in the sequences involving Bombay. And in 'Kai Baar.'

. . . *And the Aftermath*

Over two months and Rs 7 lakh[131] later, *Rajnigandha* was complete. Being a rookie producer working with almost all debutants, Famous Cine Laboratories and Studios had given Jindal a 50 per cent credit on the processing costs.[132] While this would have acted as a buffer, the market reaction to the sales pitch was dismal. Distributors rejected the film simply after hearing its name. '*Kiski gandha*? *Kaun si gandha*?' They would ask, and surmise—'*Class ki boo aati hai* (reeks of class).'[133]

Jindal went to quite a few of them, including the financiers of *Anubhav* (1971), a Sindhi family. '*Tukka lag gaya, lag gaya* (we just got lucky),' they said about the success of the film, not interested in taking any more chances. Among other distributors who backed out was Shakti Raj (a distribution company floated by Shakti Samanta and Rajesh Khanna). They had held on to the agreement for three months, and then dropped it, Jindal said to the author.[134]

It was the Rajshris once again. They picked up the film almost two years after it was canned. It is not known what the selling rate per territory was, but assuming a mark-up of 25 per cent to cover interests and producer's profit, Rs 1.50 lakh per territory—a total of six territories—should have been a decent bargain.

Jindal sold it for £16,000 in the UK, which, in 1974, translated to approximately Rs 3 lakh.[135]

The censor certificate carried the spelling *Rajanigandha*, the way a Bengali would pronounce it. The title read *Rajnigandha*. The spelling on the censor certificate was courtesy of the clerk. To change the same would have taken another three months. Jindal decided to let it go to avoid any further delay in the film's release.

Rajnigandha was released on 20 September 1974, 10 days after it received the film certificate.

* * *

Jindal goes back in time in a discussion with the author:[136]

> The premiere of the film happened at the Akashwani theatre, a government-owned theatre hall near Mantralaya in Bombay. The hall had never been used for a commercial film release

before. Rajshris being the innovative kind, arranged two shows at the auditorium. A release of two shows per day was something unheard of in the industry. But I was a newcomer, and I relied on them. I remember going to the first show with my production manager Rajiv Suri who was also the producer of *Manzil*. We went to the auditorium, first floor, and waited. Patiently. We thought that nobody had heard about the hall then.

In show business, a lot depends on how you promote your product. Not being given three shows itself was like a defeat. However, the Barjatyas had a lot of confidence. Gradually, the tickets started selling. When the last ticket was sold, we were so happy — we shook hands, laughed, and almost cried with happiness. '*Yeh toh sara show bik gaya, mazaa aa gaya* (all the tickets have been sold, feels great)!'

Then the show started. The audience was laughing at every punch line. And this is something which gave us confidence. Word spread. Then the film was exhibited at two other theatres in Bombay. One at Dadar (Plaza), and one in Worli. The film had silver jubilee runs at all three halls. Something unprecedented. It went on to do a silver jubilee in all the major cities, including Madras, which was a graveyard for Hindi cinema then. It was a small hall which could accommodate around 300 people. But it ran for twenty-five weeks, and that is something which made us very happy.

You make a film where you have put in all your savings and money, and then it finds no takers . . . it was so frustrating. And then suddenly, this. The feeling of the extraordinary success was difficult to define.

The fourth estate woke up to the news. What was this film, where a woman dilly-dallies between two men and finally settles for one where the other is not a villain? Rather the one she chooses is anything but hero material. In a format where the heroine would inevitably fall for men with multiple virtues, this was anticlimactic.

Rajnigandha went to become one of the most applauded films of the 1970s. A bunch of fresh faces, their simple, uninhibited deportment, despite being caught in a mesh with life-changing implications, was something the average Hindi film viewer had not seen before. The complete absence of patriarchy in a society that was still evolving was also viewed as a major shift from films where women had to play roles subservient to their male counterparts. A man accepting an intellectually and academically superior wife was an idea abominable even in the topmost echelons of society, forget the middle class where alliances were arranged to ensure financial security for the girl. Chatterji's Deepa was evolved, futuristic without being selfish, someone who saw beyond the masculine types society eulogized.

A little-discussed and apparently overlooked aspect of *Rajnigandha* is the use of colour to demarcate the relationships. Deepa's scenes with Sanjay are radiant, while the indoor sequences with Naveen seem to carry an unsaturated tonality. This may have been partly inspired by KK's experimentation in *Maya Darpan* (1972).

It was the understated technique and the crisp, visual storytelling that gave the film its freshness. Even the best of film-makers in Hindi cinema then would not look beyond a tried and tested formula. Basu's common man was born when Rajesh Khanna was gradually losing his box-office clout to Amitabh Bachchan. A new star on the horizon was Rishi Kapoor, whose debut in *Bobby* (1973) was what dreams are made of. For a film to be successful then, you either needed a very strong romantic angle, a milieu where music made more sense than the spoken word, or someone convincing enough to take the bull by its horns. Basu circumvented the paradigm, and rather successfully too. He, with his ear to the ground, identified with the ordinariness of people and circumstances and told their story in a manner not tried before. It was devoid of gimmicks, but had a lot of heart. And with an undercurrent of humour all along. Characters in *Rajnigandha* did not oscillate between extremes.

They would not break into a song at the slightest provocation. There was little or no indication about the artistic abilities of any of them. Their romantic faculties too were limited, and their anger subsided once they were out of college. And most importantly, they spoke in a language the average educated man on the street used.

People who had become progressively tired of the excesses in the name of entertainment loved this film. Basu also had a name for his audience. He called them the balcony class.

Basu became big after September 1974.

Suddenly, Amol Palekar and Vidya Sinha were big too. Sans the romantic demeanour of a Rajesh Khanna or the impressive voice, physique and screen presence of Amitabh Bachchan, Amol was a face the common man started identifying with. Especially in the metros. Vidya Sinha could no longer walk down the streets casually to have her regular quota of *pani puris*. But somewhere, the man who would corner the deepest compassion was Dinesh Thakur. As Roshmila Bhattacharya tells the author, Dinesh used to constantly receive marriage proposals after *Rajnigandha*. Women found within him a hero almost in the format of Mills & Boon—who ultimately and unfortunately does not get the girl.[137]

Agrees Preeta, his widow:[138]

> Basu-da was the one who gave Dinesh ji this great break. He became a tragic romantic hero in the eyes of the people. One who did not get the girl. Other women had such a soft corner for him. So, the whole image that Basu-da created was of a sincere, dedicated man who does everything for the girl but loses her to someone who was the antithesis of all that he stood for. A great fan following was ensured after this. He went on to do many roles in films and theatre after that, but nothing like *Rajnigandha*.
>
> It also created adversaries. Here was this guy who was not so well-known, and suddenly he has this sacrificing lover image which gives him a huge fan following with women writing letters proposing marriage.

Rajnigandha, however, was not without its flaws. Continuity for one. During both the train journeys, the saree Deepa wears while boarding changes when she disembarks. Anachronism for another. The poster of *Seeta Aur Geeta* (1972) can be seen inside the theatre where the film on exhibition is *Kahin Din Kahin Raat* (1968). It is not a re-run, the story has moved back in time to the late 1960s when both Sanjay and Deepa are final-year undergrad students. One who has seen *Kahin Din Kahin Raat* knows that the song 'Qamar Patli Nazar Bijli' happens within the first thirty minutes of the film and not after the interval as shown in *Rajnigandha*.

Despite the bloopers, *Rajnigandha* was a game changer. It shattered a few archetypes. A hero needn't be handsome, dapper or rich to win the heart of the heroine. The heroine could be in love with two men simultaneously without her conscience pricking her like a cactus. Images could also speak for most of the time without the story seemingly flying off like a tangent over the heads of the audience. For a near-songless film, the background music needn't be loud to create drama. The act of joking about marriage was not the privilege of men alone. Women too could be cocky and confess, if partly in jest—*shaadi hui hai, pyar thodi hua hai* . . . (I'm only married to him, I'm not in *love* with him).

Coming of Age

Films we loved in our childhood often do not age well. Action films typically seem outdated with changes in technology. Stunt films, which kids devour, are generally dodged later. The historical or mythological tale tends to drag. A glycerine fest which could be a big hit during its time normally does not retain its charm in the years to come. Arthouse films, with complicated camera angles and storylines nobody understands, are often labelled as classics, with most, including the reviewer, not having seen them.

Love stories with sad endings have a greater shelf life as they generate a sense of nostalgia. Films with hummable songs also make the heart grow fonder. Comedies age well as they are fast-paced. The operative word for a film which retains recall even some fifty years later is 'well-made'. And it is often a merger of heart and technology, like the films of Sir Charles Chaplin.

Nearer home, parallel cinema, which to the masses is projected as a simplified version of arthouse cinema, could be construed as slow and antiquated by viewers used to fast cuts and digital prints. Well-made parallel cinema ages well though. While there is little nostalgia for Mrinal Sen's National Award winner *Mrigaya* (1976), Shyam Benegal's *Ankur* (1974) still attracts viewers. As do most middle-of-the-road films, a watered-down version of parallel cinema. A good story told simply always has takers.

Like *Rajnigandha*. During the 1970s and the early 1980s, Rajshri's distribution network was formidable. In small towns, they pitched the film for noon shows. In metros and large towns, they would conveniently use it as a filler between two big banner films. During the era of television, VHS, and later VCD/DVDs, it became a post-lunch favourite with housewives. Today, it has had multiple runs in middle-class households where Hindi is understood.

However, people who saw the film later had a few complaints as well. Nothing much happens. And there is no climax.

Probably this is what Mannu Bhandari also foresaw. The diary format was difficult to streamline in the form of a script, though Basu had to a great extent managed the downsides by dramatizing a few key moments. The sudden introduction of Naveen at VT was one. In the story, it is Ira who receives Deepa at the Howrah station, and it is only a chance meeting with Nishith which happens at the coffee house. On screen, this could have appeared contrived. And without the surprise element which the unexpected sight of Naveen had created.

Fate was kind to the film. Suresh Jindal, in his obituary of Basu Chatterji, describes it in his no-holds-barred manner:[139]

> *Rajnigandha*, like everywhere else, was running to packed houses at Metro Cinema in Calcutta. I was sitting at my

> nephew's office in Calcutta when he got a phone call that left him speechless. I asked him what happened.
>
> 'Chachaji, it was the Rajshri office (distributors of the film) saying that *Rajnigandha* has got the Filmfare Award for Best Film . . .'
>
> 'It CAN NOT BE. The whole industry knows that for Filmfare Awards all winners buy copies of the magazine and nominate themselves, since it's voted by the readers. We have not FILLED A SINGLE FORM . . . so how can it be? Send someone immediately to buy today's *Times of India*. I CAN'T believe it. You HAVEN'T been filling any forms behind my back, HAVE YOU??'

Rajnigandha won two, and not just the best film award. It was the first film in the history of Filmfare to win for best film as well as the 'Critics Award' for best film. This was Basu's second Filmfare award, having won for the screenplay of *Sara Aakash*. But his best award in his opinion came from a dedicated set of fans he had created.

> I got many letters after *Rajnigandha*. One letter was from a woman from Pakistan. She wrote in Hindi mixed with Urdu, 'How truly you have described. We all had a lover in our college days but we never married him. We married someone else.'
>
> You see, this was common in almost 90 per cent of the Hindu middle-class families as well.[140]

Basu was also swarmed with offers within weeks of the film's release. One was from the house of B.R. Chopra.

The Romance

Suffering from unpronounceable 'diseases' such as 'Improper conditioning and defective verbal communication', 'unstable self-evasiveness' and 'unstable paranoidical frustration' was Arun Pradeep, Basu's common man in *Chhoti Si Baat.* The name was a hat-tip to Basu's friend and partner at Film Forum, Arun Pradeep Kaul.

Unlike Sanjay, Arun is neither talkative nor focused on office politics. His needs have evolved. He has already received a promotion in his organization. Unfortunately, he is gauche, keeps running his fingers over his thin moustache, proffers a limp handshake, tugs at the top buttons of his shirt, and has a defensive body language. Though hard-working enough to get promoted to Grade II Supervisor recently, he cannot assert himself over anyone at the workplace, be it the betel-chewing peon Pandu (Noni Ganguly), or his junior Raman who, busy listening to the cricket commentary over the radio of India's run chase in the cricket match against MCC, shoos him away. The common man's confidence takes a beating.

In his classic book titled *Story*, author and writing coach Robert McKee advises scriptwriters on the character design of the protagonist. 'Deep within the protagonist, the audience recognizes a certain shared humanity.' He adds, 'The unconscious logic of the audience runs like this: "This character is like me. Therefore, I want him to have whatever it is he wants because if I were he in those circumstances, I'd want the same thing for myself."[141] What Arun wants is Prabha Narayan, a dainty working girl who he sees every morning at the bus stop on his way to work. Prabha's office is somewhere in the vicinity of Arun's in the Nariman Point area. In Arun, the audience can see themselves, thus infusing credibility into the character. Arun's agony may well be that of thousands of others seated in the auditorium and thus, they all wish that he wins over Prabha.

And here comes one more hat-tip. Prabha was probably a name Basu fancied from the time of *Sara Aakash* where the leading lady had the name. Shobha's sister in *Piya Ka Ghar* is also named Prabha. Colonel Julius Nagendranath Wilfred Singh, the titular character in *CSB,* also mentions losing a Prabha sometime in his life.

And the inside story was that Basu used this name also because his cinematographer K.K. Mahajan married Prabha (spelt Praba), the lead actress in Kumar Shahani's *Maya Darpan* (1972) [christened Aditi in the film].

But all is not well. Prabha likes Arun for sure but is tickled at his timidity. She isn't coquettish but has fun teasing him, waiting amusedly for the poor guy to make his first move. Let alone make the first move, Arun is too flustered to even respond promptly to Prabha's standard pre-mobile-phone-era conversation starter, 'Excuse me, time *kya hua* (what's the time)?' at the bus stop one morning.

Though reticent and anything but forthright, Basu's common man on a love mission is observant. He pays great attention to details, keeping a mental note of the colour of sarees and the handbag, the way the lady sits, and the literature—Denise Robins' romantic novels—she reads during her daily commute to the office. He is also desperate enough to stalk her morning and evening, to and from office, lying in wait for her outside her office, standing close to her in the crowded bus or right behind her in the lift lobby, and sometimes right till the gate of her house—though his intentions are extremely honourable. His obsession level is high; he even knows which floor the girl lives on. As warned by her colleague and confidante Deepa (Nandita Thakur), and by a neighbour, this twerp could be more dangerous than what met the eye. Which, fortunately, he is not. And the girl understands that.

Basu's common woman was uncommon for her time. Prabha is compassionate, observant, not the kind to play the victim card, owning up responsibilities at the office. And with a mischievous sense of humour.

Arun has competition though: Prabha's colleague Nagesh (Asrani), the smarter and the more resourceful of the two. He assumes that Prabha is dedicated to him by default; apart from sharing rides to the office on his scooter, she is his table tennis partner as well. Male privilege? Perhaps. The effect it has on

Arun, who has little understanding of women, is rather strong. With nervous frowns replacing the smiles, his resultant impetuous responses include daydreaming in the manner of Walter Mitty. How Arun gets rid of his pathological shyness, combating emotional extremes—euphoria and despair—through professional guidance, and finally wins the girl is the story.

Throw the kitchen sink at the opponent. All is fair in love and war.

The art of winning in love through rules not entirely fair ended up as a raucous comedy. It made Basu big, he became the go-to director for producers wanting to make a critically and commercially successful film on a tight budget. Incidentally, Basu had not changed his leads from *Rajnigandha*.

> For *Chhoti Si Baat*, I needed a hero who would look gullible enough, and Amol was fine. I wanted to take a new heroine as Vidya had become very busy. B.R. Chopra suggested we stick to the *Rajnigandha* cast. They are a hit pair. And they are fresh. And Vidya was signed.[142]

★ ★ ★

At another level, *Chhoti Si Baat* is also about the Bombay of the salaried middle-class working in mid-sized family-owned organizations within the city. It eschews the picture-postcard imagery of the skyscrapers, the Marine Drive, or the other extreme, like the slums of Dharavi. It is arguably one of the few Bombay-based stories that do not have a single shot of the Arabian Sea. Instead, we see queues at bus stops and lifts, packed buses, crowded lifts, even senior executives of the company travelling to work by buses and trains, people scurrying amidst honking traffic, always appearing to be in a tearing hurry to reach their offices, rushed lunch hours, frequent glances at their wristwatches . . . Basu's is the clockwork Bombay of the everyday officegoer because the film was about people in that category. Even the houses shown in the background are representative of this 'median'—neither poverty nor opulence.

Basu appears too as one of the passengers on a bus from Bandra to South Bombay—in a blink-and-miss role. The bus route depicted in the film was number 86 (Bandra—Backbay Bus Depot). Part of it was also shot at the Shivaji Park area.[143]

Bombay's heritage leisure spots that the characters visit help give that sheen to their personas. One of Arun's bosses romances at the Pamposh restaurant in Bandra. Arun suggests that he and Prabha go for tea at Gaylord Restaurant and a movie at Eros. The luncheon meeting between Prabha, Arun, and Nagesh (in which Nagesh overwhelms Arun with his pompousness) takes place at the famed Samovar Restaurant inside Jehangir Art Gallery. Later in the film, they lunch at Flora, the city's oldest Chinese restaurant.

The offices are also an extension of the lives of people in the metropolis. Test cricket is a way of life, and employees, including executives, switch on the transistor radio to listen to the running commentary. After-office hours recreation is a given, and we see both Arun and Nagesh fighting it out for supremacy in table tennis and chess. The shots of the office were at *Indian Express*, mentions Nandita Thakur to the author.[144]

Cricket and Bombay have often been a part of Basu's cinema. However, he could have exercised more caution during the re-recordings. In *Chhoti Si Baat*, the commentary heard on the radio was of the third Test between India and England, played at Chepauk in January 1973, not the one at Bombay. In *Piya Ka Ghar*, the Irani Trophy match of 1971 is heard on the radio when Hari shouts—Gavaskar scores a century; something which happened at Georgetown, Guyana, 13,920 km away, and seven months before. There was no live commentary in India for that series. Had it happened, it would have been at night.

The names Prabha Narayan and Arun Pradeep do not indicate a Maratha nativity, suggesting that their careers may have brought them to Bombay; this is reinforced by the fact that Arun, who is the only child of his deceased parents, shares a room with Mohan (Devendra Khandelwal), while the story remains silent about Prabha's family background. Nagesh Shastri appears to be domiciled in Bombay because of his claims to have coached Sunil Gavaskar, meaning he must have resided in Bombay for at least five to six years. These are upwardly mobile, cultured young people who have found a foothold in midsized corporates. And Arun's financial status (perhaps due to his frugal lifestyle) appears stable enough to be able to pay the bill for three at Samovar Restaurant, purchase a motorbike paying Rs 3000 on the spot as well as remit the 'tuition' fees of Rs 1000 upfront to Colonel Julius Nagendranath Wilfred Singh of Khandala.

Said Basu Chatterji in a chat with the author:[145]

> There was a British film called *School for Scoundrels* (1960). The basic plot of *Chhoti Si Baat* was derived from that. The role of Julius Singh was modelled on the character called Dr S. Potter. This was also my first work with Ashok Kumar. We became good friends. Ashok Kumar was very impressed with Amol Palekar, especially at the complete absence of mannerism, something accompanying theatre artistes.
>
> There was also this cameo by Amitabh Bachchan, used to show that Singh is an important man who is consulted by even the best-known actor of the country. Amitabh was shooting at the same studio, and I had requested him for that twenty-second act, something which he did gratis. [Contrary to what has been publicized, Amitabh was shooting for *Faraar* (1975) and not *Zameer* (1975) when this cameo happened.]

Amol Palekar, in a discussion with scribe and author Balaji Vittal, goes into part-flashback, part-academic mode:[146]

> I still remember this press conference we attended in Madras when *Chhoti Si Baat* was released with big fanfare. One of the senior journalists asked Basu-da, 'This film has been copied

from *School for Scoundrels.*' And Basu-da, in his inimitable style replied, 'Not one, but I have copied *Chhoti Si Baat* from two films. The other one is *The Secret Life of Walter Mitty.*'

Chhoti Si Baat was such a lovely adaptation. He had taken the basic idea but it was not a shot-by-shot copy. He cast the characters into the mould of a common man. Kurosawa made *The Hidden Fortress* an absolute classic. But he took two major liberties—

1) He took a Shakespeare classic and removed all the dialogues of Shakespeare
2) He incorporated whatever was not there in the Shakespeare script. Is Lady Macbeth pregnant? So, her wanting her son to get the throne becomes a logical motive. Sir Lawrence Olivier sought permission from Kurosawa for the theatre version of *Macbeth* which Kurosawa was doing. Look at the mutual respect while taking all the ideas.

Ajay Prabhakar, who assisted KK in the film, adds:[147]

B.R. Chopra had a story department. They wanted Amol to dress up well, and said he be given a Fiat. Dada flatly refused and said, no, no Fiat. Only a motorcycle. There were more differences, but Basu-da did not relent and changed nothing.

Basu was right. With a salary of Rs 800–1000 per month, it is very unlikely that Arun could afford a car. A bike, and a second-hand one at that, was definitely a better idea, than the cars that both male leads had in the original version. As for his resolve of not changing anything in the film, he could have been a little careful while editing the scene where Arun arrives at the Colonel's bungalow. Arun, in chappals, is suddenly seen wearing shoes while climbing the circular staircase, only to change to chappals once he is on the balcony.

Said Basu Chatterji,[148]

> When the film was completed, B.R. Chopra and his wife saw it in their private theatre. And he called me and said, 'Basu, what have you done? We will get beaten up. This won't run for even a day. I'm sending you a copy of *School for Scoundrels*. Just copy it.' And I was left thinking whether he was serious about asking me to re-shoot the whole film? Fortunately, around that time, Chopra went away to Dehradun (or somewhere) for 15–20 days on personal work. He had a business manager called C.V.K. Sastry who was not privy to this exchange between me and Chopra. I took the money from Sastry and completed the post-production work. Some people like Jeetendra saw it and liked it very much. The film was released and became a superhit. And Chopra sent me a telegram saying, 'Happy proved wrong.'

Adds Ajay Prabhakar,[149]

> When the film was released, the logo of B.R. Films was not there. After the film started doing very well, that was inserted at the beginning of the film.

The *chhoti si baat* between Basu and Chopra was resolved. Basu went to the extent of refusing to extend the film beyond his script. Selling the film to the theatre owners was a challenge as the length of the film was two hours, as compared to the average length of two hours and thirty minutes with an allowance of twenty minutes on either side [*Zameer*, a B.R. Chopra production, received the censor board certificate the same year, and advertised on a hoarding in *Chhoti Si Baat* was two hours and twenty-four minutes long (the digital version is curtailed and cut to two hours and ten minutes)], but the Rajshris, who were the distributors in the eastern part of the country, clubbed it with a documentary on the composer Madan Mohan made by the Films Division.

★ ★ ★

One might take notice that while Basu's common man Amol Palekar became one of the most sought-after actors thereafter, Vidya Sinha failed to hold on to the position accorded to her by *Rajnigandha* and *Chhoti Si Baat* by venturing into films of the commercial variety. The aesthetics of the 1970s mainstream cinema did not quite suit someone whose predicament had already been penned in the last antara of 'Kai Baar Yun Bhi Dekha Hai':

'Jaanoon Na, Jaanoon Na/ Uljhan Ye Jaanoon Na / Suljhaaun Kaise Kuchh Samajh Na Pauun.'

The Musical Romance

Neither Chopra nor Basu had envisioned the unprecedented commercial success of *Chhoti Si Baat*. Love stories sans mushiness were not the rule in Bombay then. A comic love story was a genre specific to Bengal. Bengali humour, which was more situational than slapstick, was probably genetic and manifested itself in the screenplay and dialogues of *Chhoti Si Baat*. The middle-class filmgoer, especially the urban lot, loved the film. The consensus was *Chhoti Si Baat* is a story well-told. The characters, not limited to the leads, are nicely sketched. Apart from Ashok Kumar, Amol Palekar, and Vidya Sinha, artistes like Chandrashekhar Dubey (Gurnaam), Amol Sen (Pinto), Rajendra Nath (Mauni Baba), Devendra (Mohan), Nandita Thakur (Deepa), Rajan Haskar (Nausherji Batliwala), and Noni Ganguly (Pandu Dhole), among others, add value to the script. Says Nandita Thakur:[150]

> Basu-da wanted the characters to look natural. I was to play a Christian girl and had to cut my hair as Basu-da wanted me to have a bob cut to fit the role as the office secretary. I did not have very long hair at that time, but Basu-da wanted it to be shorter.

Actors Dharmendra and Hema Malini were roped into the film almost at the last minute, as Basu had to step out of his comfort zone and shoot a typical song sequence. The shoot was completed in half a shift during the phase the crew was winding up at Khandala. The song, titled 'Janeman, Janeman', became an instant hit. Said Basu:[151]

> I came to know of Yesudas through Basu Bhattacharya, for whom he had sung a song. I was doing *Chitchor* at that time and had suggested his name to the producer. Around the same time, he also sang for my *Chhoti Si Baat* as Salil Chowdhury knew him too and was also very fond of his singing. As I was not in favour of the song and dance as used in Hindi cinema, I made the hero go to a cinema hall [Sterling Theatre in Bombay] and watch a film where the song was sung by the hero and the heroine of the film being exhibited.

'Janeman, Janeman', the Yesudas–Asha Bhosle duet, was extended to the lead pair as well. Shot around September/October 1975, this completed the shooting, and the post-production had to be hurried to ready the film for a censor stamp that happened on 31 December. Released on 9 January 1976, *Chhoti Si Baat* did not win any National Awards but won Basu a Filmfare award for the screenplay. Like *Rajnigandha*, *Chhoti Si Baat* too had two songs that were used in the background, both of which, 'Na Jane Kyun' (sung by Lata Mangeshkar) and 'Yeh Din Kya Aaye' (sung by Mukesh), with jazz-style phrasing and chords, became iconic. Mukesh did not take any money for his song, said Basu, 'He was delighted as he had won the National Award for best singer for "Kai Baar" (*Rajnigandha*) and sang this song out of sheer gratitude.'[152]

But it was Yesudas, not Mukesh, who would be the lead singer in Basu's next film.

* * *

The Hindi film song has mostly been undermined by film critics, and often by film-makers who have aimed for constructs beyond the run-of-the-mill. In the 1970s, the main three purported to have promoted middle-of-the-road cinema were Hrishikesh Mukherjee, Basu Chatterji, and Gulzar. Apart from Gulzar, both Hrishikesh and Basu have, from time to time, expressed apathy towards the use of the traditional film song. Paradoxically, both were knowledgeable about the grammar of music. Hrishikesh was a trained sitarist, having played for AIR, Calcutta. Basu was self-taught. He spoke about his dabbling with music thus:

> I used to sing. My elder brother (Jaideb) too used to sing. He had a Dwarkin-make harmonium, a very famous brand in those days. I had bought a small sitar [actually a slide guitar and not a sitar, and the interviewer was mistaken] for Rs 3 from a Christian boy in Mathura who sold it off for money. I could play the harmonium and the sitar then.[153]

Later, in the 1970s, Basu had started studying notations in Hindustani classical music. In his impeccably artistic handwriting, he had also documented the corresponding notes in Western music.

Basu, in a discussion with Gulzar on the use of music in cinema, had accepted Gulzar's point of view. He also mentioned the same, albeit two and a half decades later.

> Gulzar and I have had a debate on the use of music in cinema. While I initially felt people in my world don't really break into songs at regular intervals, Gulzar had a different explanation. He told me that by the same logic, music should be done away with since a hundred violins also don't start playing in real life.[154]

Following the success of *Rajnigandha*, the Rajshris, who had been unswervingly distributing Basu's films, approached him for their second production with Basu. Though it is not known who gave Basu the idea to film *Chitta Chakor*, a short story by Subodh Ghosh.

Not among Ghosh's best, this was one story that Basu moulded, in more than one way, to give it a feel of practicability. And to add value to the screenplay, he turned his weakness—a dislike for songs as they are placed in Hindi cinema—into a strength by making the hero a singer. And one well-versed in Hindustani classical music.

Basu named the film *Chitchor*. Started almost in parallel with *Chhoti Si Baat*, the writing and the polishing of the screenplay took six months.[155] A screenplay that had four beautiful songs on a track intrinsic to the film.

With a picturesque village adding width to the story, the Rajshris decided to shoot the film in CinemaScope.

And Basu added a name to his portfolio. A name he would keep on repeating whenever the opportunity permitted him to do so. Madhupur, then a sleepy hamlet in south Bihar (now Jharkhand). Meera, a character in Ghosh's *Chitta Chakor*, lived there.

★ ★ ★

Basu fell in love with the name 'Madhupur'. Like most of his characters, it had no regional bias. There could be a Madhupur in Bihar, in Bengal, in Odisha, in Madhya Pradesh, in Rajasthan, for that matter, any state in India. Basu's Madhupur was in Maharashtra: Panchgani. He changed a few names in the story and moved the location to the fictional village of Madhupur, a place that enchanted the viewer with its wide expanse of silver oaks, coconut trees and native flora, as it did through its water bodies. The houses chosen for the shoot included a bungalow which has developed into a tourist attraction over the years.

Incidentally, till quite some time, the viewer not privy to Basu's secret—which he divulged later to the press—thought that *Chitchor* was shot in the sleepy hamlet of Madhupur.

★ ★ ★

The selection of Amol Palekar was by default. The Barjatyas, who were sceptical of Amol when proposed for the role of the lead in *Piya Ka Ghar*, wanted him in *Chitchor*. Basu did not want to repeat Vidya, and a few auditions were arranged by P.K. Gupta[155], the production manager of Rajshri. Among the girls shortlisted was the rookie Bindiya Goswami. Unknown to her, Bindiya was asked to pose in front of a special type of camera.[156] As recounted by Ajay Prabhakar:[158]

> We did not have a lens for shooting in CinemaScope. We used an attachment behind the zoom which was mounted on the camera (probably Arriflex). The Rajshri people had imported the zoom attachment for converting the format to CinemaScope.

As per Basu, Bindiya, who was very young then, had some puppy fat and was not considered fit for the role.[158] By the time Rameshwari, an FTII grad of 1975, was brought for the audition, Zarina Wahab, two years her senior at their alma mater, had already been finalized. In his book *The Legends of Bollywood*, publicist Raaj Grover writes in detail about Zarina, a shy, reclusive small-towner who spoke no English[160] till she joined FTII, and her screen test.[161]

> Photographer Dheeraj Chawda was a favourite of film magazines and film stars. I was quite friendly with him. I met him one day and asked him to shoot some nice pictures of Zarina. But he took me aside and said in a hushed tone, 'You are wasting your and my time.' However, on my insistence, when he looked at her through the lens of his camera, he was stunned. He said, 'Wow! What a photogenic face!' I simply smiled, and Dheeraj took so many photographs that Zarina was tired at the end of the session. It wasn't for nothing. The next issue of *Filmfare* devoted two pages to just Zarina's photographs . . .

> My relationship with the founders of Rajshri Productions was such that I didn't need to take an appointment to visit them. I got to know they were planning a film with Basu Chatterjee [*sic*] as the director and Amol Palekar as the hero, and that they were looking for someone to play the lead actress's role. Without wasting any time, I took the photographs of Zarina taken by Dheeraj and showed them to Basu Chatterjee and Kamal Barjatya. They liked them but felt they didn't relate to the simple village girl they had in mind. They had to take a call on the heroine for the film in two days. So the same afternoon, I met another photographer friend Girish Shukla and fixed a shoot for Zarina to capture the village girl look. I called up Krishna, the costume designer at Ajanta Arts, and asked him to bring the ghaghra choli that Waheeda Rehman had worn in *Reshma Aur Shera*. When Zarina wore the same outfit and posed for pictures, she looked every bit a village girl. Girish Shukla captured about ten to twelve images of Zarina, which I then gave to Basu Chatterjee. He was very happy to see them and immediately finalized her as the lead heroine.

In an interview with the author, Zarina goes back in time, with a version slightly different from that of Grover:[162]

> After graduating from FTII in 1973, where my classmates included Shabana Azmi, the late Preeti Gangoly, Kanwaljit Singh, the late Rita Bhaduri, Neelam Mehra, Adil Aman and Shailendra Singh, among others, Dev Anand Sahab offered me *Ishk Ishk Ishk* (1974). We went to Nepal for the shoot, to Kathmandu and other places. The offer for *Chitchor* happened a year later perhaps. One of my 'Muhbole Bhai' [someone I call a brother] was Raaj Grover. He took me to Rajshri Productions to meet Tarachand Barjatya, who assured me that he would get back in case of an opportunity. After a month, I received a call from them for a screen test. There were two

more girls there for the screen test as well. It happened on the terrace of the office of Rajshri Productions. Within a week they called me and said—'You are selected.'

The screen test was taken by one of the photographers of Rajshri, I do not exactly remember who. I can never forget this day when the three of us were subjected to a screen test almost together. I was not very sure about the outcome but was happy that I got it. Before going there, I was advised to wear a short saree, if you recall, something like what I had worn in *Chitchor.*

The same getup I continued in the film.

The *Sara Aakash* pair of A.K. Hangal and Dina Pathak was back playing the elderly couple. Pathak played the heroine's mother, beavering away to keep the prospective groom(s) happy, manipulative at the same time when confronted with an unpleasant truth. Hangal, as Headmaster Pitambar Chowdhary, was given a fitting wig; his effortless manoeuvring of expressions based on the situations in the film was an act that remains with you forever. The naturally giggling Zarina, who was an excellent fit for the role of Geeta, recalls them as institutions. 'So much to learn. I was learning from them all the time. I consider myself blessed to have worked with such senior and brilliant artistes.'[163]

There were two more FTII products in the film. Zarina's classmate Kamal Bir Kaur, rechristened Ritu Kamal, played Meera, her elder sister. She would continue to play bits-and-pieces roles in Basu's films. And Vijayendra Ghatge, a grad of 1974, made his debut. Entrusted with the task of mentoring him, Amol was his roommate at Panchgani.

But the main star of *Chitchor* was Master Raju. Till then, both Amol and Zarina were only a film (Hindi film) old. Raju was a child star and one who was in high demand. He and Master Alankar were among the best-known faces in the 1970s. Debuting as a four-year-old in *Amar Prem* (1971), his replication of the siren played during the blackout sessions of the India-Pakistan war of 1971 in the song 'Sa Re Ke Sa Re' (*Parichay,* 1972) had made him a household name.[164] Having travelled to Panchgani during *Parichay*, he would be travelling for a longer duration this time.

'He was very good even when young,' says Arup Gangoly, who was an assistant to Basu Chatterji from *Safed Jhoot* (1977).[165]

The schedule, initially planned for forty days, was cut short by almost half, Zarina confirms:[166]

> We finished the filming in 27 days. Out of which, 23 days happened at Panchgani. Two hotels had been booked. The unit was in one, and the staff in another. I was accompanied by my mother or at times by one of my sisters. Early morning, we used to go to the place designated for the shoot, which would happen from 9 a.m. to 6 p.m. It was less of a shoot and more of a picnic. Never felt we were shooting. No night shoot happened except one. The positives of the outdoor shoot was a complete absence of distraction, hence things were very much under control.
>
> The rest four days, Basu-da had put up a set at Rajkamal Studios for the song 'Tu Jo Mere Sur Mein'.
>
> Working with Basu-da was complete fun. I had worked with Dev Saab (Anand) who was very energetic, disciplined, always walking at jet speed with all of us falling behind. Basu-da was a natural. No tension, no histrionics. 'Be natural. Don't try to act. Feel and use your intuition.' Being natural he meant no makeup too. 'You are playing a village girl, I don't want any artificial gloss,' he would say. I used to surreptitiously apply lipstick, after which he would raise his glasses on his forehead, observe me and say—'Why did you apply lipstick? Wipe it off.' He used to hate makeup. Rest assured, 99 per cent of my shots were without makeup. For the remaining 1 per cent, I would manage to apply lipstick or kajal. That's how we did the film. He was a very spontaneous director, would pick up

> cues from the discussions we had. 'What did you say? Come again, what did you say? Let's use this in the shot. Repeat the discussion.' This happened on a few occasions, including the one where Master Raju was telling the joke about how a hearing-impaired would ask for water and a blind man for a pair of scissors. We used it and I was told that people loved it. It was all so spontaneous.

The picnic aura was also due to the bonding which happened there. Most had come down with their families. Basu had his trademark cameo, standing at a railway platform. This happened at the request of Zarina. Till then, all the films where he had done a cameo were successful, a fact which was at the back of her mind. Basu's daughter Rupali played Geeta's (Zarina) niece, her third act in her father's film and a speaking one at that, the previous two being in *Us Paar* and *Chhoti Si Baat* where she had no lines.

While the general feeling was that of a picnic, the planning which happened behind the scenes was pretty rigorous, especially to overcome the technical challenges. For one, the camera had an additional contraption enabling the shoot in CinemaScope. Also, avoiding multiple shadows, which were bound to happen, as there were many reflectors to maintain uniform light.

Cinematographer Nadeem Khan, in the article 'The Boss and I', talks about K.K. Mahajan, and how he mitigated the challenge.[166]

> My earliest recollection of his work was *Chit Chor* [*sic*] which I saw when I was still in FTII (I think sometime in 1972) [his memory has failed him, it has to be in 1976 or later] . . . Cleanly photographed, one particular shot intrigued me no end. A long tracking shot in a verandah of a bungalow in Mahabaleshwar, two people walking and the camera tracking with them, no big deal so far . . . but what struck me was in spite of the characters being very close to the wall there was only a soft single shadow throughout! Remember folks, HMIs did not exist then, and one had to use multiple reflectors to fill the entire area, leading to multiple shadows!

> *Aur yahan toh ek hi shadow tha* (And here it was only one shadow)! The shot stuck in my mind, and so when I got a chance to ask the great man—'Sir, *aapne kaise kiya* (Sir, how did you do this)?' He smiled and said 'guess'. I couldn't. He said, 'Simple (that was his greatness . . . simplicity to achieve astounding visuals) six double bed sheets stitched together stretched out on two trees . . . constant fill throughout.' Wow! When I became a cameraman this piece of equipment was my mandatory companion!'

This contraption made by the production team was used for bounced lighting for the outdoors, says Ajay Prabhakar, who was KK's assistant in the film.[168]

* * *

The romance with the mistaken identity and waking up to reality thereafter was the story of the film. Basu did not unscroll a panorama of emotions, preferring to keep the narrative simple. Multiple layers were woven through the characters surrounding the lead players: the incredible generosity of the mother taking an abrupt nosedive, the sudden indifference of the otherwise mild and accommodating headmaster, the nine-year-old playmate growing up one afternoon in winter . . .

The contrast between the boyish insouciance of Deepa's father and the pragmatism of her mother is also one of the high points of the film, and it is often through images that the same is established. Especially her dominance.

The film is not without a few logical flaws though. The date of the marriage, as planned by Geeta's parents, is on the fifteenth day of 'Maagh', which roughly translates to late January. While discussing this, they mention that it is a month and a half away, which means the discussion takes place in December. Vinod (Palekar), a few days later in the story, tells Geeta that he is planning to take a long leave for marriage around Dussehra, a festival that usually takes place during October. Also, Geeta has appeared for her matriculation, an examination which would be held during summertime. Strangely, the results have not been published even after six months.

Having said that, *Chitchor*, with its fluid and articulate camera movement, neatly written screenplay and exemplary music, was arguably Basu's best-told story. It proffered a heartfelt glimpse into a semi-rural, semi-urban India, and the disarming and difficult-to-disentangle simplicity of its people and customs. It also broke the paradigm that the foreign-returned city-slick is a rogue. The characters, including that of the postman (Chandrashekar Dubey) and the school clerk (Shail Chaturvedi), were nicely outlined with empathy and understanding and devoid of sentimentalism.

★ ★ ★

Zarina was there during the first show, which took place on 11 June 1976, at one of the three theatres—Ambar, Oscar and Minor (she could not remember which one)—at Andheri, Bombay. She says:[169]

> Me, Basu-da, we all were there. The reaction of the people was extremely agreeable. I did not dress up for the occasion, this was no premiere show, just a normal show. I was not wearing any makeup. Nobody there recognized me; I could enjoy the film without being distracted. Nobody knew me either, I was not famous. There was no publicity. No mention of artistes going to the show. I was like a part of the audience.
>
> Never expected *Chitchor* to be this big a hit. I intended to work in good films, and the concern was not how it would do. It was a jubilee hit, probably a Golden Jubilee, I'm not sure . . . I was ecstatic. I started getting multiple assignments and I, who had struggled for quite some time, bought my first flat.

Chitchor, apart from becoming a sentimental favourite in due course, was the third back-to-back Basu Chatterji–Amol Palekar film to celebrate a silver jubilee. The unique success helped Basu earn the sobriquet of 'the director with the Midas touch'.

The consensus was—here is someone who completes films in a record time with little-known actors and limited resources, mostly shooting outdoors, and makes films which are not only commercial successes, but are also extremely healthy entertainers. The films are devoid of sex, violence, crude hyperbole and mandatory songs.

Talking of songs, *Chitchor* had four, all of which were chartbusters. The rookie rule applicable to the stars could have been extended to the music department as well. Basu was working with songwriter-composer Ravindra Jain, someone who was generally associated as the house composer of the Barjatyas. Jain used to sing at temples in Aligarh and later in Calcutta where he had turned composer. He went to Bombay in 1972 at the invite of Nari N. Sippy. Pandit Subir Chakrabarty, who had spent quite some time with Jain in Calcutta says:[170]

> He was a unique talent. What you call an inborn talent. He did not methodically learn classical music but had a tremendous sense of the same. He was not the greatest singer around, but he could see music. Literally. He was in some ways like Rahul Dev Burman, a raw, freak talent. He could compose classical-based songs without having a clue about the raag. To top it, he could compose a song in a raag and move to a completely different raag within the same framework, something which would leave us flustered and ecstatic at the same time. The kind of notes—high notes—he sporadically touched while singing were not only difficult, but were also almost impossible for singers apart from the Lata Mangeshkars and the Asha Bhosles. The same can be said about his phrasing too.

It was classical music that Basu wanted for the film. And Jain produced his best-known score of all time. Basu mentioned:[171]

> We had recorded 'Gori Tera Gaon Bada Pyara' with Yesudas. This was around the time I had also recorded 'Janeman Janeman' for *Chhoti Si Baat*. After hearing Yesudas, the

producer said, 'Why don't you take him for all the songs?' So Yesudas became the voice of Vinod in the film.

'Jab Deep Jale Aana', the first duet of the film, was based on a tune Jain had composed for Usha Ganguly's play *Mitti Ki Gadi* (a Hindi play based on the famous *Mṛcchakatika*) in 1970 at Calcutta. It became the melodic high point of the film, especially for the use of the catchphrase of Raag Yaman— Ni Re Ga Ma Ga Re Sa Ni. It was selected as the best classical Hindi film song of 1976—Swami Haridas Award—by the Sur Singar Samsad, an institution dedicated to the cause of Hindustani classical music in Hindi cinema. The song also fetched composer-lyricist Jain the Dr V.D. Arora award for Best Lyrics as well. Yesudas and Hemlata were adjudged the best singer duo and presented the Tansen Award. Yesudas also received the National Award for 'Gori Tera Gaon Bada Pyara' while Hemlata won the Filmfare award for 'Tu Jo Mere Sur Mein'. In no time, Yesudas became a rage and was roped in by Richardson-Vicks as their brand ambassador for the Vicks cough tablet. Another interesting point is that two songs from two of Basu's films won National Awards with only a year separating them.

> In hindsight, Basu might have wondered why he had let go of the song 'Teri Galiyon Mein Hum Aaye' (*Minoo,* 1977) which had been composed for *Chhoti Si Baat* by Salil Chowdhury. Only the tune was retained as part of the background score. While on music, one might spot a distinct similarity between the motif of Kabir Khan's *83* (2021) with the first line of the recurring background score of *Chhoti Si Baat.*

Chitchor, for a short period, brought back light classical music in Hindi films. Though the icing on the cake was the breezing chord-based melody, 'Aaj Se Pehle, Aaj Se Zyada', the two versions epitomizing joy and sorry respectively.

Talking of music and sorrow, bits of both were part of his only failure till then. *Us Paar.*

⋆ ⋆ ⋆

The three, almost back-to-back films of Basu where Amol was the hero are today acknowledged as the common man films in Hindi cinema. Basu's common man was an extension of the small-towner in a big city or an alien environment. Visually you can be sure that the common man in Basu's films is not a Bengali from Calcutta. Or a South Indian from Madras or Hyderabad, at a time when Bangalore was just a sleepy little town loved for its weather. A double name, like Arun Pradeep in *Chhoti Si Baat,* reconfirms that Basu did not drift from the concept of the North Indian Hindu as a hero either, it is just that he embodied no superpower—neither verbal nor muscular. The Mumbaikar in his film did not speak like a typical *Mumbai ka chhokra* either. He might have been planted in the city by a job. He could be a second-generation Mumbaikar as well. Devoid of the Marathi accent, though his common man remains a doyen of Marathi theatre and cinema, Amol Palekar. In defining relationships in the three films, the interactions were more leavened by humour than by assumed seriousness, which often is tagged to love. His ability to tweak a common line of thought by astutely separating the layers resulted in very different subtexts in each of his films. Understated elegance in *Rajnigandha*, hobbled by insecurity in *Chhoti Si Baat* and the fear of lamentable consequences if married to the poor overseer in *Chitchor.*

The Misses

'Failure is the condiment that gives success its flavour.'
—Truman Capote

Romancing the Circus

More than two and a half years before Basu's common man got the endorsement of the critic and the crowd, he was searching for a subject for a film. *Rajnigandha* was not planned yet. *Piya Ka Ghar* was in the making.

Said Basu:[172]

> Suresh Jindal, who had seen *Sara Aakash* in Los Angeles, wanted to make a film for me. I had a script ready. Jindal had also selected S.D. Burman as the composer. In the interim, he also agreed to produce *Rajnigandha* (1974) but walked out of the first film he had agreed to produce. Who knows, maybe he was hard-pressed for money. I decided to turn a producer myself. Today I realize that was not a good thing to do.

Things were delayed. Getting the buy-in of distributors and financiers took time. *Piya Ka Ghar* would be released in May 1972, the success of which triggered one more film in October 1972: *Manzil,* the shooting of which had to be stalled after a few reels. *Rajnigandha* was nearing completion by then. And Basu was jobless. He had stopped contributing to *Blitz*. He did not have expendable money. Ramesh Gupta, who joined as Chief Assistant, his second stint with Basu, also put in his money. As he mentions:[173]

> It was part-financed by me. You see, it was supposed to be made by Suresh Jindal who was not interested. Basu was very bullish about the film. He had put in some money as well. At that time, I was planning to buy a flat in DN Nagar in Andheri West. A flat there was priced at Rs 5000 then. Now it is in crores. Anyway, I had some Rs 8000–9000 which I had kept separately for a flat. Suddenly, in an emotional moment, I decided to invest the money in the film. I got the money back, but that was in a piecemeal manner, in instalments of Rs 500–600. I could not buy the flat then. I bought it in 1982 for Rs 92,000.

The script Basu had chosen took him back a few years.

★ ★ ★

1968. The occasional film show organized by Film Forum was like a sanctuary from the overdramatization that was 'commercial cinema', the landscape of which had practically changed with colour. Except for the select few, the gullible millions in India had lapped up the cultural chicanery which came in the form of a three-hour-long package.

One of the members of Film Forum was Ronodeb Mukerji, the eldest son of S. Mukerji. *Tu Hi Meri Zindagi* was an ambitious film that he had made during that time under his father's banner. While this unfortunately remains the only film he completed in his lifetime, he forged a camaraderie with many of the associates, including Basu. The drinking sessions helped strengthen the bond between the two, despite the age difference of a decade. Rono had his four-wheeler, and Basu would accompany him to S. Mukerji's Filmalaya Studios where he saw many film people for the first time. This included Ashok Kumar, who would be one of his main anchors in later years.

Basu did not waste much time articulating to Mukerji that he wanted to make a film. Mukerji was okay with the request and suggested Basu finalize a story. 'You people see so many films; why don't you choose one from those?'[174]

* * *

In 1968, Basu, using the services of a certain Mr Novachek (another interview mentions it as Novacrin) of the Czechoslovak Consulate in Bombay, had organized a Czech film festival. From the lot exhibited, *Romance pro křídlovku* (1966), aka *Romance for Bugle*, a teenage love story, had caught his attention. Said Basu, in a chat with the author:

> I was very moved by the film. I floated the idea to Mr Mukerji, who suggested some changes after hearing the story. The story was about a group of gypsies. He wanted to have them replaced by dacoits. In the end, I stuck to my script. The FFC mandated a guarantor and a co-guarantor for the loan to be approved. Mr Mukerji was a guarantor and asked one of his distributors for a collateral guarantee. I approached Himmat Singh with the letters and my script.[175]

The guarantees did not help. The script was rejected by Himmat Singh.

Later, when Himmat Singh had been replaced by B.K. Karanjia, the script was again rejected with B.K. suggesting—'Why don't you write something about near home?[176]' And that is how *Sara Aakash* was made.

The script of the Indianized version of *Romance for Bugle* was lying with Basu. Refusing to split hairs on the selection of the cast and crew, Basu wasted little time. It was the old team, almost, with Moushumi Chatterjee (who was working in *Manzil*), Jalal Agha,

Raja Paranjpe and A.K. Hangal in the pivotal roles. Rishi Kapoor, still awaiting the release of *Bobby* (1973), was one of the actors Basu wanted as the lead, a role eventually played by Vinod Mehra.[177] Maybe this happened at Moushumi's suggestion; Vinod was the hero in her first Hindi release, *Anuraag* (1972). 'I signed *Kacche Dhaage* (1973) first, but *Anuraag* was released earlier,' mentions Moushumi to the author.[178]

Vinod had a soft face, probably a key reason for him getting on board as the jilted lover.

Cineye Films' second venture had a formal name. *Us Paar.*

The outdoor happened at Srirangapatna near Mysore. Some scenes were also shot at the Shivasamudram falls.[179] For Basu's children, it was their winter holiday, and a trip to Mysore and Bangalore served as a great motivator. They travelled to Mysore via rail and road. And from there to Bangalore where Mrs. Chatterji suffered a slipped disc, forcing the family to take a flight back to Bombay. It was the family's first flight together,[180] in the winter of 1973 when the equations in Hindi cinema were in the process of changing forever. *Zanjeer* (1973), *Abhimaan* (1973) and *Namak Haraam* (1973) had been released. Henceforth, getting dates from Amitabh Bachchan would be a challenge.

⋆ ⋆ ⋆

Otakar Vávra's *Romance for Bugle* was a black and white film. Like the European films of that time, the plot was simple, the dialogues sparse, the camera angles complex and the characters real. The leads (Jaromír Hanzlík and Zuzana Cigánová) were teenagers. Even Miriam Kantorková, who played the seductress Tonka, looked innocent in a scene most sensuous, a bath in the stream where she was in the nude. The backlighting was diffused, fashioning a feel of illusion. Terina (Cigánová), the central character and the love interest of the soft-natured hero (Hanzlík) and the gruff gypsy Viktor (Štefan Kvietik) had died some thirty years ago.

Us Paar was made in colour. Premiering on 6 June 1974, 755 days after Basu's last release *Piya Ka Ghar*, it had the naïveté of the original but suffered major logical flaws. Anachronism for one. In the mid-1940s, the tariff for three shots at the balloons in a village fair could not have been 25 paise. This amount was high enough to fetch you more than two litres of milk. While taking the story thirty years back in time, Basu had forgotten to consider factors like inflation. And dress designs.

The investment of time and detail, the key to *Sara Aakash* and *Piya Ka Ghar*, was found wanting too. Unlike European films where the story played a role often subservient to the eloquent visuals, commercial Hindi films demanded a strong storyline and a series of connected incidents. While *Us Paar* retained the languid pace of the original, the length of the film was one and a half times that of the former, a couple of passages surely expendable. The use of bright and saturated colours also failed to underline the tragic tone of the story. Also, in no position to circumvent a few rules of commercial cinema in India, Basu had to unnecessarily stretch the film to fit into the framework of show timings.

Basu, however, was honest with the intent; there was no visible pointer in artfully manipulating the tragic story by introducing characters common to Hindi cinema, like the crafty villain, the scheming mother-in-law, the dishonest village priest, etc. In the absence of the well-known tropes, the viewer was bored with the staid narrative. In the final count, Basu failed to translate the agonizing heartbreak of the lead pair into the viewer's own. *Us Paar* failed to cross the Rubicon and was a commercial disaster.

As seconded by Ramesh Gupta:[181]

> When I read the script of *Us Paar*, I told Basu, that this is not going to work. In a film, the process of falling in love is interesting. But when you start a film with a boy and a girl already in love and planning to elope, the interesting part is already lost. But he said, 'No no, I've seen a Czech film where it worked well.' He did not accept my take on the subject.

> Like I told you, an assistant can give a suggestion, but it is up to the director to accept or reject the same.

Basu spoke about the predicament.[182]

> I was not as experienced at that time as I am today. I should have forgone the film. I would not have put money from my resources, which I did. I used to put '*hundis*' of Rs 5000 and make the film. I was a good paymaster. *Us Paar* did not do well financially.
>
> The film was also much longer than it should have been. Even after the film was completed, we found out that the edited length was coming to a few minutes less than what was mandated by the hall owners. I had to hurriedly get a song composed, recorded and shot. That added little value to the film, but I had no choice.

The song in question was 'Aye Mere Man Main Hun Magan'. While force-fitting the nicely sung Mohammad Rafi song into the film, and using a few more songs, Basu might have taken solace in the fact that the music remained the reason the film continues to engage the viewers. Yogesh, who Basu would later name as his favourite lyricist, went back in time in a discussion with the author about his work in the film. And his first with the grand old man of Hindi film music in the 1970s: Sachin Dev Burman.

⋆ ⋆ ⋆

To quote Yogesh:[183]

> I had no work those days and went to Basu-da who asked me to pick between two music directors—S.D. Burman and Laxmikant–Pyarelal. [Author's note: One assumes this happened pre-*Rajnigandha* and the choice was probably between *Us Paar* and *Piya Ka Ghar*.] I had stuck a friendship

> with Manna Dey after my first film *Sakhi Robin* (1962). I was also working on a film by Prabhat Mukherjee called *Sonal* (1973) for which Manna-da [Manna Dey] was the music director. When I solicited his advice, he bluntly told me to go for S.D. Burman.
>
> I had seen Burman Dada before but never dared to talk to him. Anyway, I took a risk and went to meet him at the Jet on Linking Road, where he used to stay on the first floor. I introduced myself after giving Salil-da (Salil Chowdhury) and Hrishi-da's (Hrishikesh Mukherjee) references. Burman Dada wasted little time. He had heard about me working with Basu-da, and played a tune on his harmonium, and asked me to write lyrics for the same. He wanted me to write lyrics like Gulzar, for a folk-based tune and gave me the example of 'Mora Gora Ang Lai Le'. Prabhat Mukherjee had gifted me a small Dictaphone—a voice recorder which Dada named *Khilona*—in which I recorded the tune. I went back a few days later with a set of lyrics, and Burman Dada said okay to the first one. The song was 'Tumne Piya Diya Sab Kuch Mujhko'. That's how I began my journey with Dada.

'Tumne Piya' was an atypical SD composition. Contrary to his free-flowing style, it was heavy, but at the same time spontaneous. The song had the touch of a couple of morning raags (Todi, Lalit, Bhairavi) in the *mukhra* while the antara would dovetail into folk, caringly heartfelt. Folk was the mainstay of the other Lata Mangeshkar solo, the playful and rhythmic 'Yeh Jab Se Hui Jiya Ki Chori', where the voice of Moushumi Chatterjee was mixed to go along with the visuals. The use of a solitary, conclusive, and deceptively sad 'Oo', almost terminating the song, was an SD specialty. He loved using elusive phrases, with the listeners salivating for more. Basu also recalled the song with excitement as SD would enjoy singing '*Hui*' in a loud tone, almost like an exclamation.

Unfortunately, Lata's brilliant solos were perceived as too sophisticated then. Thankfully, their recall now is arguably more than what it was in the last millennium. Like all premium old wines, they have matured with time, with the right quantum of the surprise element one would love to hear even during multiple hearings. Adding value to the timeless melodies, among others, is the unusual lyrical candour, the delightful obligatos—sometimes on the flute, sometimes on the strings, Moushumi's spirited lip-synch and near-virginal beauty.

The playful 'Pyaara Hindola Mera' marked Moushumi's entry into the film. As it was Asha Bhosle's in a Basu Chatterji film. Moushumi goes back in time:[184]

> *Us Paar* was my first shoot in the Bangalore-Mysore area. It was around the time of *Zehreela Insaan* (1974) as well, which was also shot in the south at Chitradurga. During the shoot of 'Tumne Piya', I was almost seven or eight months pregnant; and you would observe that throughout the song I was sitting. The transition from afternoon to sunset was done under natural lights by KK.

The bard in SD stepped in to take centre stage with 'Piya Maine Kya Kiya'. Though written with SD in mind, it was sung by Manna Dey who negotiated a plethora of long notes, often complex, and an amazingly soulful *taan*, as one finds Kamli (Moushumi) being forced to leave the village, signifying curtains for the love saga. It was Manna Dey's swansong for SD, and probably one of his most memorable ones.

And the film was SD's only one for Basu, which he mentioned to the author:[185]

> Sachin-da was a pain in the neck but in a lovely way. Every other day he would say, '*Basu, ekta notun sur eshche. Shune jao* (Basu, I have just thought of a new tune. Come, listen to it),' while I would be running around for money.

> He was one music director who worked harder than the producers. He would be in a state of frenzy while working, obsessed, and extremely passionate. Every situation posed a challenge for him, and he worked on it until he was satisfied, only to come up with more alternatives the next day. The man was immensely talented, as talented as Salil Chowdhury, who was my favourite composer. He scored brilliant music for *Us Paar*. I would have loved to do more work with him, but unfortunately, the opportunity never arose.
>
> During the making of *Us Paar*, he was very upset when I'd included some pre-recorded music as the background score for the climax of the film. He heard it but didn't object. I had bought the canned music from a small-time composer at a paltry sum of Rs 15,000. If I had recorded the background score with him, it would have cost me Rs 40,000. He probably understood the pain of a first-time producer who was working on a shoestring budget.

The failure of *Us Paar* pained Basu; it was a project after his heart. Did he take solace in the fact that the film was discussed over the years for its music? Probably. It took him back in time, recounting the gay abandon with which Lata Mangeshkar had sung two of the most evolved scores of Sachin Dev Burman.

Hui. Basu sang it in tune at the ripe young age of 88.[186]

⋆ ⋆ ⋆

Despite the failure, Basu did not let go of his self-deprecating sense of humour. In an interview with N. Bharathi in a film magazine in 1977, Basu, discussing that there would be confusion galore due to the existence of two Basus, Chatterji and Bhattacharya, mentioned:[187]

> At the moment, because I'm supposed to be the successful one, I find people telling me that I make good films like *Anubhav*. Then they turn around and say, what kind of rubbish

does Basu Bhattacharya make? Films like *Tumhara Kalloo* and *Us Paar*!

The White Lie

In the Bombay film industry, the late Basu Bhattacharya remains an enigma. On the one hand, his touches of altruism have been acknowledged by people who were close to him; and, on the other, his penny-pinching impudence is part of folklore. While a few might vouch for his generosity, professionalism was something his name never got tagged to. But most would agree that he had a fine sense of humour, which could be self-deprecating as well. Like the incident Sai Paranjpye mentions in her biography:[188]

> And then I met Basu Bhattacharya. He was the chief guest at the launch of Bollywood film historian Firoze Rangoonwala's latest book. He spoke very well, making fun of everybody, especially of himself. 'It is said that the success of a film depends on its stars. I beg to differ. I made *Aavishkar* with the topmost stars of the time—Rajesh Khanna and Sharmila Tagore. It flopped. Obviously, my "flop value" outstripped their "star value".'

Basu considered the other Basu (Bhattacharya) his guru. This is surprising as Bhattacharya barely managed to complete a handful of films. One among his many incomplete films was *Ashamapta Kavita* (Unfinished Poem), which was being produced by Shyamal Mitra. A song based on Shyamal's own 'Gaane Bhuban Bhoriye Debo' (*Deya Neya,* 1963) had also been recorded by Yesudas. The cast included Devendra and Sharmila Tagore, who was then pregnant.[189] Like the 'Unfinished Poem', the film too remained unfinished.

But in the process, Shyamal met Basu Chatterji.

★ ★ ★

Ashim Kumar Bhattacharya[190] was one of those rare Bengalis who made a name for himself in Bhojpuri cinema. His roots in Varanasi were the reason behind his expertise in Hindi; in fact, his attempts at playing the hero in Bengali films like *Harano Prem* (1966) and *Ram Dhakka* (1966) [one of those films which had Manna Dey composing the music] were met with abject failure. While he carried on playing the occasional sidekick in Hindi films, Bhojpuri cinema gave him fame.

The Bhattacharyas stayed at Santacruz. Like most Bengalis, they used to congregate at the North Bombay Sarbojonin Durga Puja held by the S. Mukerji family in the Podar School compound. Basu Chatterji too had become a regular after his friendship with the Mukerjis. Manik Dutta, the small-time actor, was a member too. He was a common friend who introduced Ashim Kumar to Basu. A small role for Ashim Kumar in *Chhoti Si Baat* followed, and he set upon a higher goal—film production.

Rajeev and Rana Bhattacharya, sons of Ashim Kumar, say:[191]

> Father wanted to make a film on a medium budget. Shyamal Mitra had the rights to a story by Samaresh Basu, *Chhutir Phande*, which had been made into a Bengali film. Basu Chatterji purchased the rights from him, and subsequently, he was also asked to take over the music direction. This was during the phase after *Rajnigandha*. My father was already acting in *Chhoti Si Baat* and this probably helped in the decision-making process. The film was named *Safed Jhooth* and was financed by Raj Rajpal, a businessman.

The budget for *Safed Jhoot* was around Rs 40–50 lakh. A four-week-long outdoor schedule was planned in Mysore. Some patch-up shoots had to be done at Khandala, and at INS Hamla, at Malad West, Mavre, Bombay. The indoor shots were in locations like offices, etc. Studio shoots were minimal.

It appears that Mysore, with its distinct organized small-town charm, was one with which Basu had fallen in love. The production team had managed to book the Circuit House, and it was used as the bungalow in the film. The lake, Kaveri River, etc., were all in and around Mysore. The cast and crew stayed at Metropole Hotel, presently known as Royal Orchid Metropole Hotel. The team had a few new assistants which included Arup Gangoly, Ashok Kumar's son. 'I mostly had to manage the continuity and the costumes,' he told the author.[192]

Ashok Kumar had a pivotal role in the film. Around that time, he commanded a high fee almost in six figures for each day of the shoot. However, considering the budgetary constraints, he lowered his price considerably. The film group was like family for him too as apart from his son, his son-in-law Deven Verma also played a key character.

* * *

Samaresh Basu's *Chhutir Phande* had not one, but two reproductions in Bengali. The first was in the form of a play written by Gautam Roy in 1972. The second was the eponymous Bengali film which received film certification in 1975. Directed by Salil Sen who had his roots in theatre, the dialogues, mostly of the tongue-in-cheek variety, were the strength behind the success of the otherwise bland film. The actors—Soumitra Chatterjee, Aparna Sen, and Utpal Dutt, among others—were industry veterans known for their dramatic and oratory skills, while Robi Ghosh was a name you immediately associated with comedy. They carried out their roleplay in a manner astute enough to cover up the snags in the slack screenplay, which were many.

On the flip side, while Basu's screenplay was tighter, it lacked the momentum to create a strong impact. The general feeling was that it would all be well in the end, never mind how. This 'how', which was something viewers eagerly looked forward to in a Basu Chatterji film, was found to be missing. The story of a man being forced to stay away from his wife on his honeymoon should have been treated like a tightrope walk, even in a comedy. In this case, the humour came at sporadic intervals, without much action in between. In effect, the narrative failed to snowball into something cohesive. Barring Ashok Kumar, who put in an act strong enough to match Utpal Dutt's in the Bengali version, the characterizations left much to be desired for. Vinod Mehra was too soft-faced for comedy. Mithu Mukherjee in her second Hindi film displayed the oomph and the coquettish manner she was known for rather well, but her role stymied her abilities to go beyond the timid curvy young thing.

Some diversion came in the form of an interesting, eponymous cameo by Amol Palekar. Shyamal Mitra's music was pleasing to the ear; a few of the songs being remakes of his tunes in Bengali. 'Sara Belaye Aaji Ke Dake' was recreated as 'Neele Ambar Ke Tale'; 'Aha Mori Mori' (*Bon Palashir Padabali*, 1972) became 'Tere Mere Liye'; and 'Chori Chori Jaiyo Radhe' was almost a literal adaptation of 'Dheere Dheere Chole Radha' from the film *Phulu Thakurma* (1974). Only 'Matwale Pal Ye', shot in natural evening light by KK, was later made into a basic Bengali song 'Bhalo Laglo Ei Subhokhon' for Arundhati Holme Chowdhury.

★ ★ ★

Basu's memories of *Safed Jhooth* were not something he cherished or endorsed. Rana Bhattacharya attributes it to several factors:[193]

> The overall time to finish the film was more than one and a half years. This was primarily due to two reasons. Basu Chatterji became very busy. He was directing many films at the same time, including Rajesh Khanna's production *Chakravyuha*. All these added to the delay. The delay led the distributors to reduce the selling rate. This happened everywhere, except Maharashtra, where Shakti Raj stuck to their word and did not reduce the price.

> Amber, Oscar, Minor were three halls in Andheri West. Now there is Shoppers Stop. Pramod Chakrabarty's *Dream Girl* was released in Amber on 19 August 1977. On the same day, *Safed Jhoot* was released at Oscar. It had a decent run, but the film only broke even due to the compromise on the selling rates per territory as mentioned.

The conscientious believer in the adage 'cinema for art's sake' did not respond to the film kindly. Basu was branded by *Filmfare* as someone who had shattered the promise of *Sara Aakash* with films like *Safed Jhooth* and *Chhoti Si Baat*.[194]

While a plethora of negatives clouds the appreciation of the film, it had a few Basu touches though. Not someone to advocate the use of song and dance without a purpose, Basu made Anita (Mithu Mukherjee) a singer and Ashok Kumar, for all his vitriolic behaviour, a connoisseur of Hindustani classical music. The company where Mr Gulati (Ashok Kumar) is an executive is real: Weston TV, which was a leading CRT TV manufacturer. A blink-and-miss moment is when Vinod Mehra mentions his suit was tailor-made from Kachins, a garment shop that would cater to the requirement of the Bombay film world in the 1970s. Basu himself had a cameo as the proprietor of one of the Kachins outlets in *Mazaaq* (1975)—his longest one, around forty-three seconds, with multiple lines of dialogue. In a film neither produced nor directed by him.

It probably gave him the confidence to try out a longish cameo in *Safed Jhooth* as a customer who is refused a room at the Circuit House. Between the two cameos, Basu had greyed. A mop of unruly white hair would now greet the viewers during his cameos, the number of which would come down with time.

The Urban Love Story

Rain, Bombay, and Basu were synonymous. Basu loved the rain, and did not think twice before filming it when the opportunity arose. His conviction was well-reasoned. If we can film during the rain, let's do it. KK's expertise on the handheld Arriflex also gave him the freedom to explore the city without being noticed.

The title shoots for *Priyatama* (1977) were about rain, using it as a metaphor to flesh out the character of Dolly, the leading lady. The physical feel of droplets lightens her eyes as she gently collects a few and rubs her hands against her face. And takes a life-changing decision. She wants to marry. Well, that's how the film started.

Arup Gangoly, who was an assistant in the film, reminisces:[195]

> A major part of the title song of *Priyatama* was shot on the road and during the rain. This is at one end of Bandra Carter Road. There used to be no buildings then. There was nobody on the street then. Hence it was easy to shoot. Now it is very crowded, shooting such scenes is next to impossible.
>
> Other shots like children walking with umbrellas on the streets were all stage-managed. We got the children, the umbrellas, etc. They were all junior artistes. Among them, one man who was confident enough to talk would be in touch with us and strike a deal with the director. How many men and women he wanted, and what clothes they would need to wear. Rates would differ based on that. The ad hoc rate in those days, per head for each shift, was Rs 300 for women, Rs 500 for men and Rs 1000 for foreigners. A higher fee for a foreigner with dancing skills.
>
> In 'Cham Cham Barse Ghata', the title song, the junior artistes were made to walk as per the script. It was all pre-planned. The song, the stanzas, the shot divisions, what to shoot, and where. Basu-da was a master when it came to scheduling the shoots.

Basu Chatterji, in a discussion with the author, also mentions the song:[196]

> The *Umbrellas of Cherbourg* (1964) was an inspirational film for our generation. The dance of umbrellas in the *Priyatama* song was my tribute to the film.

So was the use of solid colours in the film. Neetu Singh getting into the taxi with a stole and coming out without it was surely not. This went unnoticed during the final cut.[197]

Despite the minor gaffe, 'Cham Cham Barse Ghata' was Basu's most stylized song shoot till then. The lashing of the sea on the Worli Sea Face was a tribute to his fascination for Bombay. Overlaying (dissolve) of two different shots was used for part of the song, which in turn had Rajesh Roshan, the music director, using double-track voice recording. One track had the main melody, and the other the harmony, both sung by Asha Bhosle. Something R.D. Burman had started in Hindi cinema with 'Kya Janu Sajan' (*Baharon Ke Sapne*, 1967).

★ ★ ★

Sabita Bose, wife of writer-cum-director Chittaranjan Bose, aka Ranjan Bose, talks to the author about how *Priyatama* was made:[198]

> T.C. Dewan was a film producer who had done *Resham ki Dori* (1974) where my husband wrote the screenplay. The film did reasonably well, and he wanted to do his next film with Ranjan. He reached out to Basu Chatterji, with the caveat that the film will have Ranjan writing the screenplay. Basu was initially against the idea; he always wrote his screenplays. This is when Basu and Ranjan were formally introduced.
>
> For finalizing the screenplay, Basu and Ranjan would go over to a hotel named Plaza in Andheri. This helped them work on the story uninterruptedly for a few days, after which both families would go to the hotel to welcome them back home. These sessions also would happen at El Taj in Khandala.

Priyatama was a very different film as compared to the previous comedies of Basu Chatterji. It was about the upper middle class, a societal stratum he had avoided exploring till then. The story of Vicky, a TV producer (one of Jeetendra's best performances) in a clingy relationship with the naïve but unreasonably demanding daughter of a millionaire was not the idea of a romance Basu seemed comfortable with. While he did not fall into the familiar trap of melodrama, family pressure, economic discrepancies, gender-based role-play, etc, *Priyatama* did not have the compactness of his earlier comedies. The reasons for the differences between the couple leading to a legal battle were flimsy. The sudden reconciliation, something which happens in a matter of minutes, also defied logic, as there is nothing to suggest the build-up of repentance within. In totality, the film lacked the emotional bonding to make the viewer feel for the characters. The humour element was more actor-oriented than situational. Basu had chosen a stellar cast though, including I.S. Johar and Asrani, who played important cameos that helped sustain interest in the film.

Strategically, the film had a well-timed release, just three days after it got its certification on 20 September 1977. Money spent was recovered fast. It was a success and completed a silver jubilee which was celebrated by T.C. Dewan, but unlike with *Chhoti Si Baat* and *Chitchor*, the recall would wane over time, though a few moments stood out which continue to attract viewers.

One was Basu's cameo. It came almost halfway into the film when Jeetendra, in a hurry to reach home, collides with Basu playing a pedestrian who is reading a newspaper as he walks, the act staged almost out of the climax in Satyajit Ray's short story *Patolbabu Film Star.*[199]

Basu's romance with the radio continues in this film too. You get to hear a song by Lata Mangeshkar as part of the programme *Bhule Bisre Geet.* The characters are also established through metaphors, for example, Renu (Asha Sachdev) hums 'Piya Tose Naina Laage

Re' as she dresses up; the poster of *Love Story* on the adjacent wall is in sync with her character as the girl crazy for marriage.

Says Sachdev in an interview with the author:[200]

> I was not there in the film initially. Then somebody put in a word. Basu-da called me for a trial shoot, and he was very happy with the results. I got onboarded instantly. My role was of a simple girl, and I had my hair cut accordingly. The actress who I replaced was Rita Haskar.

Rita Haskar also played an important role in the film as Anna, Ravi's secretary. She, Sachdev, and Rakesh Roshan were the livewires in a script that became more dependent on the performers than on the visual narrative. This is unfortunate, as the film started with the promise of being a canvas of colours, the depiction of rains being very graphic.

Rakesh Roshan talks about his role in the film:[201]

> I was signed as the lead for this film by Basu-da. This was my second signed film for him, after *Khatta Meetha* (1978). After some days, Basu-da came to me and said, 'Producer T.C. Dewan is insisting on having a well-known star in the lead. However, there is another very good role in the film, and you know about it. Would you play that role?' I said, 'Basu-da, it doesn't matter; if a producer insists on having a star as the lead, I am fine with playing second fiddle.' We had a clear understanding on this, absolutely no acrimony. Jeetendra, when we met, told me, 'Guddu (Roshan's nickname), I can drop out of the film. But then the producer will take some other star.' I assured him that there was no question of him dropping out, and we were doing the film as friends.
>
> The great thing about Basu-da's films was that we never felt that we were going for a shoot. It was all so fun. He was strict with what needed to be done, but never imposed it upon us and gave us the freedom to interpret the characters

> based on our experience. He would only call out if there was melodrama or overacting. *Priyatama* was like working with extended family; both Jeetendra and Neetu were good friends. So, there was no tension, which is perhaps reflected in our faces in the film.

Blogger-cum-critic Sukanya Verma puts the characters of Renu and Vicky in perspective.[202] 'If Sachdev, who won a Best Supporting Actress Filmfare trophy for her Big Ethel in Ali MacGraw glasses chasing [Rakesh] Roshan's perennially disgruntled Jughead is refreshingly droll in its contrast, Roshan raises laughs with his 'not amused' interjections. He's happiest strumming the guitar [author's note: played in the film by Arvind Haldipur on his Japanese 'Kay'-make twelve-string guitar[203]] to younger brother Rajesh Roshan's lilting tunes, the winsome 'Koi Roko Na Deewane Ko'.

Rakesh Roshan goes back in time:[204]

> The composer was my younger brother Rajesh. Maybe because he was doing it for his elder brother, he put in more effort. It was a lilting melody, and both Basu-da and I selected the song almost instantly when it was composed.

It is the long notes of this F-sharp minor-based composition in Kishore Kumar's high-pitched yet phenomenally deep and oh-so-resonating voice that has remained the final takeaway from the film. One is curious—was it written by Yogesh for the sequence as depicted in the film? In an interview with Balaji Vittal, Yogesh clarifies how the lyrics were finalized.[205]

> Basu-da was a very finicky director at times. While writing 'Koi Roko Na Deewane Ko', I had to write about twenty-five different options for the mukhra. After I took it to him, he said, 'Have you written all the mukhras and the antaras?' I said, 'No, these are alternatives for the mukhra.' 'So many of them? Let me read these through,' and he read through

> and shortlisted five, advising me to sit with Raju Roshan and complete the composition. The antaras came during the final sitting.

Rajesh Roshan, though, has a contrarian view.[206]

> Basu-da gave me a free hand, and never, never, interfered in my work. The most he would say is, 'Raju, I don't like this word in my song.' And I would readily have it changed to his taste.

With lyrics like *'Yeh bheega bheega mausam / Yeh bheegi bheegi raahen / Chale do hamrahi / Bahon mein dale baahen'*, it was most probably meant for depicting the rains in Bombay. Unfortunately, Basu had already earmarked another song for the opening sequence.

And the Ones Which Rocked

'A happy family is but an earlier heaven.'
—George Bernard Shaw

Certainly Not Sour

Rita Mehta, daughter of the late Russi Karanjia and erstwhile editor of *Cine Blitz,* recalls an interesting anecdote in a discussion with the author:[207]

> You know, my father was a very straight-cut man with a sense of humour. He once was admonished by the Lok Sabha for calling Acharya Kriplani 'Cripple-loony'.[208] The police took him away and came to arrest the deputy editor as well, as the intent was to cripple the working of the tabloid. Now, the person sitting in the deputy editor's chair was not the deputy editor, but his brother Savak, who looked very similar, though they were not twins. Poor fellow, he got arrested without a clue as to why. His brother in the meantime kept on working, and *Blitz* was published as usual.

Basu too recalls the deputy editor:[209]

> The deputy editor at *Blitz* was a nice gentleman who was fond of me and gave me the freedom to work twice a week. I used to submit my artwork and an invoice which he used to approve. The practice went on for many years till I left the organization during *Piya Ka Ghar.*

The deputy editor was called Homi Mistry.

Homi Mistry had played multiple roles in *Blitz,* graduating from the position of an accountant to suddenly being in the limelight for his coverage of the Nanavati murder case in the late 1950s. He also represented the organization for the fixation of wages and rates of journalists.[210] Also vested with signing authority, he would approve the invoices which Basu and other freelancers would submit.

Mistry's detailed coverage of the Nanavati case had probably inspired Basu. The make of the gun in Amol Palekar's dream in *Chhoti Si Baat* was Smith and Wesson, the model used by Nanavati to kill Prem Ahuja. He had fired three shots too.

Either way, Basu wanted to acknowledge Homi Mistry in some manner. The opportunity came in *Khatta Meetha* (1978), another film of Basu which opened with a song. This was also the film where the titles were in English. Till then, Basu had been using mainly Hindi, at times partly supplemented by English.

★ ★ ★

Contrary to belief, *Khatta Meetha* was not directly inspired by the Henry Fonda and Lucille Ball starrer *Yours, Mine and Ours* (1968). Basu had seen *Bizim Aile* [*Our Family*] (1975), a Turkish film, at Tehran or Tashkent in the mid-1970s. He had the habit of frequenting film festivals abroad even when his films were not nominated or sent for exhibition in the non-competitive section. The idea for indigenising this real-life story was taken ahead by Gul Anand, a charming man with a deep interest in good cinema, who bought the rights to the story. Once he had started writing the screenplay, the first thing Basu did was to name the lead character Homi Mistry.

Rita Mehta mentions another interesting anecdote about Homi:[211]

> He was a very kind-hearted man. Soft-spoken, and formally dressed for office. Both he and his brother Savak worked with

> the *Blitz*. A cute story I remember is Homi being in love with a girl to the horror of his mother who was against the alliance. Can you believe this? Working, well-paid, famous, everything, but his mother still would not let him marry the girl he loved. As much as Homi was a devoted lover, he was also a good son and waited till his mother passed away to marry the girl.

Basu would use part of the story as a match for a character he named Dara. It was enacted on the screen by Deven Verma. His mother, played by Piloo Wadia, was a Parsi who served as a consultant for the film as it needed approval from the community before the release. She helped Basu understand customs specific to the Parsi community, though he had some idea about the same, having worked in a Parsi office for two decades.

Dara and his mother were not original characters either. Dara was based on Sener in *Bizim Aile,* a role played by the famous Turkish actor Sener Sen. Basu and Gul Anand had bought the filming rights; changes to the story were not permissible in the contract.[212] It was almost a literal adaptation, though the dialogues were original. Some stray characters and events, like cameos by Keshto Mukherjee, Amitabh Bachchan, and a Parsi marriage, were essentially Basu's own. As were the songs.

* * *

The challenge in *Khatta Meetha* was selecting the ensemble cast. Ashok Kumar, who was a default member of Basu's team by then, was the first actor to be onboarded. David and Ruby Myers, aka Sulochana, were roped in for the cameo of the friendly neighbourhood couple. Interestingly, both were Jews.

Rakesh Roshan and Bindiya Goswami followed.

In an interview with Priyanka Bhatt, Rakesh says:[213]

> Basu-da was a family friend of ours. My mother, as you know, was a Bengali. Being Bengalis, the families knew each other,

> before Basu-da was a director and I an actor. I started my career as an assistant to H.S. Rawail and worked with him for two-and-a-half years but got into an acting role soon with *Ghar Ghar Ki Kahani* (1970). When Basu-da started making films, I went to him and requested if he could consider me for a suitable role sometime. He gave me a good opportunity in *Khatta Meetha*. And then in a few more.

Bindiya's first professional connect with Basu also happened around the same time, as she recalls:[214]

> My first professional meeting with Basu-da happened at the BR Films office. By that time, I had signed *Mukti* by Raj Tilak, Chopra's son-in-law. The production house was the same, and we were there at their office in Khar. I was young then and was accompanied by my mom. Raj Tilak introduced us to Basu-da. I remember talking to him, and during the discussion which happened then, I smiled. Incidentally, I had two devil teeth you know, that looked like fangs. The discussion then turned to my teeth, with people trying to find out solutions varying from straightening them out, getting them filed or capped, but finally, everyone decided to keep them as they were.
>
> Sometime before, for another film, I do not remember in detail, he was testing a camera and doing a few screen tests in the process. I think it was not specific to a film. That was done at the Rajshri office, which was situated near Siddhi Vinayak temple. I think the screen test is still with them. This was for a camera, a new camera, not a film or an ad.
>
> [Author's note: This served as the screen test for *Chitchor* (1976).]

A major challenge was to get an actress to fit in the role of Melek, as portrayed by Adile Nasit in the original. The ask was for a middle-aged lady, short, sweet and plump, the variety Bombay films did not offer apart from the likes of Manorama. Basu had seen some theatre of Pearl Padamsee. She was also a friend of Bharati Gangoly, Ashok Kumar's daughter, who was part of her theatre group. She fit the role from the physical angle. Her acting abilities were never in doubt.

Basu Chatterji took on Pearl Padamsee with the assumption that she was a Parsi, mentions Arup Kumar Gangoly, who was an assistant in *Khatta Meetha*:[215]

> Basu Chatterji was okay with Pearl even after he was told that she was not a Parsi as he was aware of her acting skills. Pearl, a doyen of English theatre, was from South Bombay, an area where people did not know good Hindi. Understandably, she had major issues in memorizing the dialogues. We knew each other for years, and she would often solicit my help to get the pronunciation right. Even then, she would, at times, struggle, and had to work hard to get the phrasing correct.
>
> I was very closely associated with her. I lived in South Bombay then and would travel to the north of the city for some of the shooting or dubbing. I used to take my car, so Basu said, 'Why don't you bring her along?'

Dinesh Shankar Shailendra, who was also an assistant in the film, mentions that the Sippys—who were the co-producers along with Gul Anand—and Basu had jointly decided to have Pearl as part of the cast. Pearl did have issues memorizing Hindi dialogues and often wrote them down in English and pinned the sheet on Rakesh Roshan's shirt.[216]

'But Pearl was an astonishing actress. She did carry a bit of theatre with her though, and Basu-da would ask her to tone it down as on the screen everything would be magnified manifold,' mentions Rakesh Roshan. Her final output was no less than brilliant.[217]

Agrees Bindiya. 'Pearl! She was like an institution. As she came from theatre, we were like, "She does not need to be told anything!" We kids were in awe of her.'[218]

The entire cast and crew would travel for the shoot which happened in Panchgani and Mahabaleshwar. Some of the shooting was in Bombay as well, mostly before the trip. Recounts Bindiya:[219]

> The shooting of *Khatta Meetha* started in Bombay. My first shot was in front of this bungalow named Aradhana, which is right opposite Amitabh Bachchan's bungalow Jalsa. The scene had Rakesh Roshan dropping me home. I play a Parsi girl; the experiment we had done was wearing a short wig. I think that's the picture that is out everywhere. It is in black-and-white. If you Google it, it comes up. I thought it was very cute, very Parsi-looking. We shot two scenes that day—me walking home, and another with my screen father Pradeep Kumar. Then we reshot the whole thing as Basu-da decided to go with my natural hair. My hair was up to my hips, pretty long. He said, you have got natural looks, so there's no need for a wig. Jalsa was then N.C. Sippy's house, and incidentally named Bindiya.

The Bombay shoot also included a few days inside the machine shop of the Godrej Plant at Pirojshanagar, Vikroli. A report from the Godrej Archives mentions the following:[220]

> Mr B.S. Wadiwala, who then worked at the opposite plant i.e. the Typewriter Plant, says, 'I had witnessed the shooting which lasted for a couple of days and took place on the road from our old VIP Canteen to Plant IX. Yesteryear actors Ashok Kumar, Deven Verma and David alight from the bus along with other workers and proceed to their workplace through the first bay entry.'
>
> Inside Plant IX, most of the scenes were shot at the machine shop milling section. Ashok Kumar who personifies the character of Homi Mistry in the movie is seen as the supervisor of the section, a role played in real life by Mr A.R. Kulkarni (later Safety Head). Mr Robert Lasrado, part

> of the Design Department in the same plant, recognized his colleague Mr Bhosle in one of the clips and recollected the day vividly: 'It was a typical shooting scene with spotlights, reflectors, and curtains to cut distraction.' Mr M.K. Bam, who worked night shifts at the Electronic Data Processing Plant nearby, recollects the early morning chaos and confusion as the production unit prepared for the day's filming. It was not the customary siren but the arrival of crew members, buses and shooting equipment that signalled the end of the night shift. In the evenings when it was time to report for his shift again, Mr Bam remembers catching up on the day's events with off-duty day-shift employees. Unlike the pompous and unapproachable cine-stars of today, the cast of *Khatta Meetha* effortlessly mingled with employees and non-crew members. Mr Lasrado particularly remembers superstar Ashok Kumar as 'humble and approachable'. Funnyman David, true to his name, was always 'jolly and easygoing'.

The scenes involving Rakesh Roshan and Bindiya Goswami walking around were shot at the BPCL Refinery at Chembur masquerading as a college campus. Basu-da had hired something over there, and decided to shoot the scene outside. He had also hired some junior actors and made them walk. The BPCL management was fine to rent out the premises as long as they were paid, mentions Arup Gangoly.[221]

★ ★ ★

Memories are short; the cast was not very sure of the length of the shoot at Panchgani. Some claimed it happened for three weeks, some six. Basu had shared a bound script with all, including all the assistants. He also expected his actors to know their parts well. Two bungalows had been hired—one served as Ashok Kumar's, and the other was for Pearl.

Newly-weds Basu and Keka Chatterji (courtesy of Rupali Guha)

Basu-da with wife, Keka Chatterji, and daughter, Sonali, at Hemen Gupta's son's wedding in 1978, at Holiday Inn hotel (courtesy of Jayanta Gupta)

During the making of *Rajnigandha*: Basu-da with Mannu Bhandari, Vidya Sinha, Amol Palekar, Dinesh Thakur and Suresh Jindal (courtesy of Rachana Yadav)

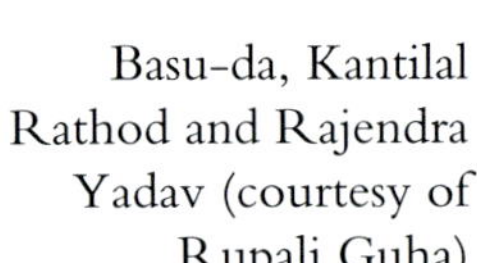

Basu-da, Kantilal Rathod and Rajendra Yadav (courtesy of Rupali Guha)

Basu-da with Amol Palekar and Kamleshwar (courtesy of Rupali Guha)

Shailendra (courtesy of Amla Mazumdar)

Basu Bhattacharya (artwork by Indro Ganguli)

Govind Saraiya (artwork by Indro Ganguli)

Editor G.G. Mayekar (artwork by Indro Ganguli)

Mrinal Sen, Salil Chowdhury and Basu-da (courtesy of Rupali Guha)

Basu-da, Rajkumar Barjatya, Tarachand Barjatya, Dr Ashok Bhattacharya (son-in-law), Sonali (daughter), Mrs Rajkumar Barjatya and Keka Chatterji (courtesy of Rupali Guha)

The Chatterji couple in Moscow, July 1977, with Harish and Tarla Mehta (courtesy of Rupali Guha)

Basu-da and Dharmendra at the Cairo Film Festival (courtesy of Rupali Guha)

Basu-da and Hemant Kumar on 21 January 1978 at Sun-n-Sand Hotel, with Sonali Chatterji and the groom, Dr Ashok Bhattacharya (courtesy of Rupali Guha)

G.P. Sippy, Ramesh Patel of Film Centre and Basu-da (courtesy of Rupali Guha)

With Anil Dhawan (courtesy of Anil Dhawan)

Deb Mukerji, Narinder Singh and K.K. Mahajan (courtesy of Rupali Guha)

Jeetendra, Basu-da, Rajesh Roshan and Rakesh Roshan (courtesy of Rupali Guha)

Ranjan Bose, Deb Mukerji, Anil Ganguly and Basu-da (courtesy of Rupali Guha)

Sanjeev Kumar, Basu-da, Suresh Chatwal, Raj Tilak and Vidya Sinha (courtesy of Rupali Guha)

Rotary Club meeting (courtesy of Rupali Guha)

Shabana Azmi, Hema Malini, Gulshan Rai, Basu-da and Jaya Chakravarthy (courtesy of Rupali Guha)

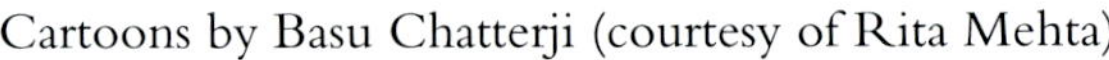
Cartoons by Basu Chatterji (courtesy of Rita Mehta)

Rain motifs in Basu Chatterji's cinema: Artist Mehnaaz Husain's impression of 'Rim Jhim Gire Saawan', *Manzil*

Mehnaaz Husain's impression of 'Cham Cham Barse Ghata', *Priyatama*

Mehnaaz Husain's impression of 'Pal Bhar Mein Ye Kya Ho Gaya', *Swami*

Mehnaaz Husain's impression of 'Kaise Din Jeevan Mein Aaye', *Apne Paraye*

Umbrella Art: Priyatama, Dr Jayati Sengupta

Umbrella Art: Chameli Ki Shaadi, Dr Jayati Sengupta

Prakash and Pratibha Dixit, the actual characters behind the story of *Sara Aakash*, 1969 (courtesy of Viraj Dixit)

Madhuchhanda Chakrabarty and Rakesh Pandey in *Sara Aakash* (courtesy of the NFAI)

A.K. Hangal, Tarla Mehta and Mani Kaul in *Sara Aakash* (courtesy of the NFAI)

Asrani, Vidya Sinha and Amol Palekar in *Chhoti Si Baat*, 1975 (courtesy of the NFAI)

A.K. Hangal and Amol Palekar in *Chitchor*, 1976 (courtesy of the NFAI)

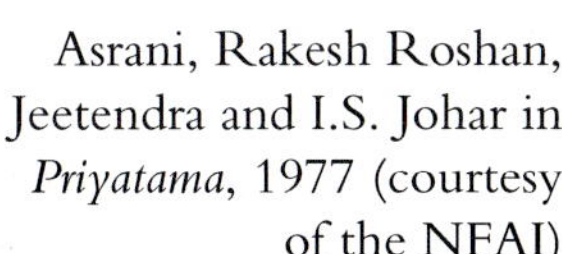

Asrani, Rakesh Roshan, Jeetendra and I.S. Johar in *Priyatama*, 1977 (courtesy of the NFAI)

Swami, 1977: Four FTII grads, including classmates Shabana Azmi, Preeti Ganguly and Ritu Kamal, and senior Dheeraj Kumar (courtesy of the NFAI)

Khatta Meetha, 1978, (courtesy of the NFAI)

Ranjit Chowdhry in *Khatta Meetha* (courtesy of the NFAI)

Pearl Padamsee, Tina Munim and Ranjit Chowdhry in *Baton Baton Mein*, 1979 (courtesy of the NFAI)

Moushumi Chatterjee in *Do Ladke Dono Kadke*, 1978 (courtesy of the NFAI)

Kiran Vairale debuting in *Jeena Yahan*, 1979 (courtesy of the NFAI)

Simple Kapadia and Rajesh Khanna in *Chakravyuha,* 1979 (courtesy of the NFAI)

Girish Karnad and Hema Malini in *Ratnadeep*, 1979 (courtesy of the NFAI)

Dev Anand, Tina Munim and Girish Karnad in *Man Pasand*, 1980 (courtesy of the NFAI)

Mithun Chakraborty and Subbiraj in *Pasand Apni Apni*, 1983 (courtesy of the NFAI)

Annu Kapoor and K.K. Raina in *Ek Ruka Hua Faisla*, 1985 (courtesy of the NFAI)

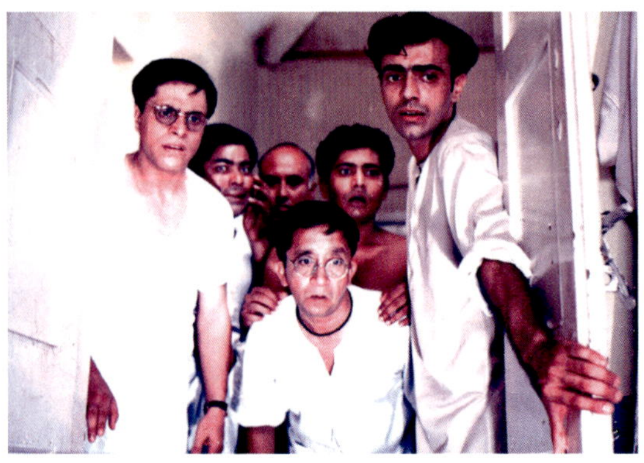

K.K. Raina, Suresh Bhagwat and Rajit Kapur in *Byomkesh Bakshi*, 1993 (courtesy of Rajit Kapur)

The team for *Khatta Meetha* was large by Basu's standards. Apart from the leads, the cast included lesser-known actors like Ravi Raj, Vimal Sahu and Devendra Khandelwal. Pearl's son Ranjit Chowdhry debuted in the film. Unaccustomed to the ways of Hindi cinema, Ranjit was initially a difficult customer to handle, till he compensated with a brilliant performance. Dinesh Shankar Shailendra recalls:[222]

> We were staying at a hotel in Panchgani. We did have initial issues with shoots, especially with Ranjit. One day I was asked to go and wake him up for his shot, to which he said, 'Tell Basu that I cannot. I have a hangover.' I started laughing. First of all, no one calls him Basu, it is always Basu-da. Secondly, such excuses are not tolerated during shoots.

Incidents like these were few. The general atmosphere was that of a happy family. Bindiya, who was one of the youngest in the team but a star by then, recalls:[223]

> I think the hotel where we stayed was named Dreamland, but I am not very sure. They had very good food. The entire cast and crew stayed over there.
>
> My mom used to be there with me. Mostly. Pearl [Bindiya's sister who was an air hostess with Air India] used to fly, so she would be there sporadically. My team—makeup man, spot boy, chauffeur, and hairdresser—were also there.
>
> Basu-da was a very destressing director. Never felt it was acting. A very family-family affair. I felt I was on a picnic. You are doing your shots, coming back, sitting, chatting, going back for a shot, all in a very planned manner. Night scenes were shot at night, day scenes in the day. We were shooting at people's bungalows, and that implied that we had to adhere to the timings as agreed with the owners. Having said that, the shooting, though conducted very fast, was certainly not rigorous.

There were continuity gaps though. In one of the scenes, Rakesh Roshan gets beaten up by goons hired by Mr Kerawala (Pradeep Kumar) during the night. In the next scene, he is seen coming home in the morning. In another, the jalopy which Fali Mistry (Ravi Raj) has sold off to help the family with some liquid cash is seen parked in front of his bungalow.

Continuity issues in Basu's films have been often spotted by filmgoers and film-makers. Arunaraje Patil discussed this in an interview with the author:[224]

> In cinema, there used to be a 'Continuity Girl' for years and years. Never a 'Continuity Boy'. Regarding the continuity of the saree, hair, earrings, props, etc., girls would normally be precise. They would tell you an actor was lifting the cup with the left or the right hand. Now there is no continuity girl. They are called Script Supervisors.
>
> Coming to Basu-da, we have lots of respect for him for how he managed the film society. While making films, he, though being an excellent storyteller, was impatient. This could have been a reason behind his continuity issues.

Not having a girl as the continuity person could be a reason for continuity lapses generic to Hindi films as well. Women probably are more detailed in their observations.

⋆ ⋆ ⋆

Minor glitches notwithstanding, *Khatta Meetha* had fine performances all around. Bindiya also recounts her memories of Ashok Kumar and Pradeep Kumar:[225]

> I used to be in awe working with Pradeep Kumarji and Ashok Kumarji. We were told to watch out for Ashok Kumar's timing. It used to be very precise. You do retake after retake, he used

to replicate the same thing as he did before. For example, the number of steps he walked. This impression of Ashok Kumar remained with me forever. With Pradeep Kumar, I was going back to the songs of *Taj Mahal* (1963) and *Bahu Begum* (1967), like 'Hum Intezar Karenge' from the latter; for me, that was a very romantic side of him and then I was thinking—OMG, this is that actor, and he is playing my father, and a father where we don't see eye to eye . . . how interesting. But there was no sense of fear, as Basu-da would make life very comfortable for us.

Talking of reshoots, I recall one more apart from my first shot. My marriage scene. The Parsi community, which vetted the film pre-release, said that we were sitting on the wrong side of each other. Custom demanded the bride to sit on the left. Hence, this had to be reshot.

Basu-da was not impatient though. We used to know whether we have done the scene well or not by the quantum of his handkerchief he had crumpled. He used to always carry a white handkerchief which he used to either bite the tip off or keep on rolling in his hand.

Arup Gangoly adds:[226]

Basu-da was not an actor. But he knew a lot about acting. He would only pick up those actors who he thought would convey these characters correctly. He would discuss the personalities with the actors and tell them what he wanted them to do. You can do it in your style. Just follow the lines and understand the character you are playing. He knew that these were good professionals, and they would do their jobs properly. Of course, the chief assistant would be with the actors with their lines. But he would be there and also speak to them. In a very soft manner.

One of the key players in the film was Arup Gangoly's youngest sister Preeti Gangoly, another FTII grad to join Basu's team. While people would laugh at her obesity, she used it to her advantage and made it her strength in the film. Basu also had his favourite Master Raju, the first actor to win the National Award for a Basu Chatterji film. Raju won it for *Chitchor* (1976).

The other National Award-winner K.K. Mahajan had dropped out of *Khatta Meetha*. One more National Award winner, Apurba Kishore Bir, had joined the team as cinematographer. KK had become busy. Also, he would be in Calcutta for Mrinal Sen's films. KK's chief assistant Ajay Prabhakar was in his hometown of Kanpur when *Khatta Meetha* happened, as a result of which Bir joined the team and would work with Basu for four films. Going back in time, he talks about his road to a Basu Chatterji film:[227]

> A promising cricketer in my youth, I was preparing for the Orissa Ranji Trophy team when I joined FTII in 1966. Prabhakar was my classmate, as were Balu Mahendra and Naresh Bedi, who later became a famous wildlife photographer. When I came to Bombay, the whole filmmaking culture was radically different. Commercial cinema was too dominating. I got a National Award for my very first film, *27 Down* (1973). Awtar Kaul, the director, wanted close shots of the characters with dialogues too. I used a handheld Arri camera retrofitted with a car battery, which was very heavy. I also used a 'block lens' and not a telephoto lens as it has better resolution. I did not use any light.
>
> Based on my work [it could be the work with a handheld camera inside the train which heavily impressed Basu], Basu-da called me at his Worli house. I was young, and naturally excited. The first film I signed with him was *Prem Vivah*, but *Khatta Meetha* was made and released earlier.
>
> Basu-da used to be very thorough with his script. And extremely spontaneous during execution. He used the zoom very often. He would keep instructing us where to go and to zoom in, zoom out, pan, tilt-up, etc. He would keep you on

> your toes. His script was so well laid-out that there would be little discontinuity in his work.
>
> *Khatta Meetha* was a film I enjoyed doing. It is my favourite film by Basu-da.

The fascination for zoom had also earned Basu the name Zoom Chatterji.

★ ★ ★

Khatta Meetha also changed Basu's perception of a film song. He used the songs as applicable in a musical. All the songs, barring the incidental 'Tumse Mila Tha Pyar' were essential to the film. A.K. Bir recounts how he shot them:[228]

> Basu-da would have a basic layout in his mind for all the songs which he would share with us. Shots would be segmented as per his convenience, considering the actors, location, lighting, etc. He would be careful to make adequate use of a lighting setup, thus minimizing setup time and cost. Actors would also be trained to understand the emotions needed for effective role-play.
>
> During 'Roll Roll Mako Nisa', Dadamoni (Ashok Kumar) was driving the vehicle. He used to keep asking me what light I would use, and I had to tell him how I would balance the camera depending on the light condition. Even the jerks in the van were giving a different feel to the camera movement. Dadamoni was thrilled. We also took some shots inside the vehicle. And from another van following the van. It was difficult, as there was quite some crowd on the streets of Panchgani.
>
> For 'Thoda Hai Thode Ki' and the title song, the outline was done before. The shooting was on the spot.

> The sequence of Preeti Gangoly dreaming about Amitabh Bachchan was later shot inside a studio and added to the song. As was the marriage song.

It is probably Romu Sippy who got Amitabh to do the cameo, says Dinesh Shankar Shailendra, and continues:[229]

> Basu-da had planned the song in all possible detail. There was no confusion at all. Shots were scheduled for Khandala, and the Amitabh Bachchan shots, etc., were planned for Bombay. The song was written with the edit in mind.
>
> I was the clapper boy during *Khatta Meetha*. I was standing outside the door of the bungalow in Panchgani. Suddenly, a car arrived. Raj N. Sippy, Rajesh Roshan, and a couple of other friends arrived. Rajesh Roshan knew me, and asked, 'What shoot is on?' I said, 'The title song.' 'Where is the music?' Rajesh Roshan asked me. 'Ask Basu-da, he is the director,' I replied.
>
> Basu-da had it all in his head. Rajesh Roshan, initially piqued, was probably happy seeing how his song had been shot.

Rakesh Roshan and Arup Gangoly concur. Gangoly further adds that 'Roll Roll Mako Nisa' was 'organized chaos'; a stunt driver was specially hired to manoeuvre the vehicle through the congested by-lanes of Panchgani.[230]

> *Adda* and informal partying would rule the evenings, like most location shoots of Basu-da. Not all the staff, but the assistants, the sound recordist, the cameraman, etc., we all used to sit together, eight to ten of us, and drink. Basu-da drank whisky but was not fascinated by single malt. In Bombay, we used to do a lot of editing together after the shooting too. Mr Mayekar, the editor, would be there. Mr Gul Anand, the producer of *Khatta Meetha*, would be there almost all the

time, even in the editing room. He did not have a production house; hence he had used the Sippy banner.

The post-shoot informal partying would be enjoyed by all, with sound man Arun Chakravorty's parodies of popular Bengali songs being a prime attraction. The happy feel was infectious, so much so that the last shoot at Panchgani had Ashok Kumar doing a boisterous, merrymaking scene despite being seriously ill.[231]

Khatta Meetha, like some more films of Basu, got its censor certificate in December. Released a week later on 6 January 1978, it was given a very 'meetha' reception around the country, especially in the west and south, though Basu was flummoxed by its failure in the north.[232] Dara Kotwal, the booking clerk at Dreamland Theatre on Grant Road, Bombay, remembers it running for thirty-five weeks during the matinee show.[233] A handful of critics, like the one from *Sunday*, Calcutta, panned it for reasons which they failed to justify. For them, it was a case of 'khatta' grapes.

For most, *Khatta Meetha* was nostalgia. And lots of it. As Bindiya puts it, almost forty-five years hence:[234]

> Do you remember the scene where we have been thrown out of the house as my father has this house vacated leading the entire family to sleep out on the patio? The sequence was so beautiful. We used to start shooting early in the morning, and it happened exactly like that. Between shots, we used to relax on the sofa, and the mother giving us *garam* chai (piping-hot tea), it was all so real. That moment of shooting is very close to my heart. It was like the song, which was being shot, in the words of Gulzar:
>
> *'Thoda hai, thode ki zaroorat hai / Zindagi phir bhi aha khoobsoorat hai'*

Rajesh Roshan, too, is nostalgic about the song:[235]

> 'Thoda Hai' is my most favourite song from the catalogue of Basu-da 's films. Gulzar Saab and I worked together for the

> first time in this film. We both were at our creative best. The songs happened spontaneously and at lightning speed. I regret not having done many films with him after that. This song was marvellously picturized too. Basu-da was an expert as far as working with newcomers was concerned. Nobody has that knack even till today.

★ ★ ★

Hrishikesh Mukherjee had introduced the concept of a funny title song in middle-of-the-road cinema in *Biwi Aur Makaan* (1966). The attempt was a failure then. *Khatta Meetha* reinstated the form, but with matching shots to familiarize the viewers with the faces they would see for the next two hours. It was a huge success, though one is not sure if it provided Mukherjee the stimulus for the title songs of his next two comedies, *Gol Maal* (1979) and *Naram Garam* (1981).

A few months before *Khatta Meetha*, Basu, probably inspired by fellow Bengali film-makers Bimal Roy and Mukherjee, was giving the final touches to a film based on a story by Sarat Chandra Chatterjee.

Bengal Stories

From Mini to Saudamini

Approximately three and a half years after Basu wrote the screenplay of *Rajnigandha*, he went back to Mannu Bhandari, soliciting her views on a novel by Sarat Chandra Chatterjee he was planning to adopt for the screen. And in the process, he forged a partnership with her, where Bhandari put in a clause: any help with the scenic treatment was subject to her being given total autonomy.

To paraphrase Bhandari from her autobiography:[236]

> Basu-da was making the film at the request of Hema Malini's mother. He had certain reservations about how the story had been written and reached out to me for re-writing the screenplay. [Basu had received a screenplay from another film-maker, something which is discussed later in the chapter.] Shocked I was; overwriting Sarat Chandra was blasphemy, something beyond me. On unswerving doggedness from Basu-da, I deciphered that the main theme was extraordinary, however, the storytelling could do with some modifications. Basu-da gave me complete freedom to interpret the story in my style and make additions or deletions which I would feel were necessary.
>
> Meanwhile, Basu-da had become like family to me, so much so that his wish had become my command, provided I liked the theme, which was the case with *Swami*.

> Forced into an unconsented marriage, Mini despises Ghanshyam [spelt Ghanashyam in this book as per Bengali pronunciation], but as she bears witness to his silent suffering at the hands of a tyrannical stepmother and her family, she finds herself taking his side, which gradually blooms into affection and finally into respect and unconditional submission. This cause-effect theme, represented by an evolving equation between a husband and wife, was the crux of this story.

This happened around September–October 1975. The final phase of the shooting of *Chhoti Si Baat* was at Khandala. Jaya Chakravarthy, Hema Malini's mother, helped fast-track the filming of 'Janeman, Janeman', which wrapped up the shoot of *Chhoti Si Baat*.

While Basu and Bhandari redid the story, cutting out the flab, they stuck to the name as given by Sarat Chandra, *Swami*. This would be Basu's first release in 1977, almost a year [362 days] after *Chitchor*.

★ ★ ★

Basu's middle-of-the-road saga came at a time when Hindi cinema had embraced romcoms in picture-postcard environs. Propelled by colour and fuelled by incredible romanticism, the heroes, barring stray exceptions, no longer donned the national dress. Neither did the heroines wear plain cotton, except in arthouse films. Even the weekly waged labour had to be a style icon; Amitabh Bachchan as the underpaid longshoreman in *Deewar* wore a designer jeans shirt tied at the lower front. As meticulous as he was, Basu was not a stickler for perfection; he had a *chalta hai* attitude when it came to dates, costumes or props. He was part of the generation that personified the 1970s, with women in chiffon and men in shirts often discordant with the social stratum they represented. Having said that, he would impose a few guidelines and follow them up in a manner most nagging. For example, the leading lady in Basu's common-man films was rarely seen endorsing branded merchandise. The research scholar in *Rajnigandha* habitually wore full voiles, Bengali *taant*, chiffon prints and the one-off south Indian silk. The officegoer in *Chhoti Si Baat* wore printed and plain chiffon with short-sleeved and small roundneck blouses, a few of them with closed necks, slightly puffed sleeves, and with lace trimmings, probably inspired by vintage Bengali blouses. The village belle in *Chitchor* would be asked by her mother to wear the best her father, the modest headmaster, could afford: printed cotton, georgette/chiffon, and a cotton saree with applique work and embellished border. The heroes were city-bred, and while Sanjay in *Rajnigandha* and Arun in *Chhoti Si Baat* stuck to simple apparel made by the friendly neighbourhood tailor, Vinod and Sunil Kishan wore designer clothes in *Chitchor*. The 1970s teen might recognize a particular variety of Elpar shirts that were very popular then. Costume in Basu's cinema was more a generational thing. It was not specific to the story, in the sense that there was little to demarcate between the Vidya Sinha of *Rajnigandha* and the Vidya Sinha of *Chhoti Si Baat* if clothing was the parameter. Vidya wears heavy silk during the cinema hall sequence in *Rajnigandha* though, a pointer to the dreaded winters of Delhi. Basu, apparently casual with details not very integral to the script, had the locale in mind this time.

Take *Swami*. Basu's engagement with the film happened just after *Chhoti Si Baat*. It was not an extension of the common-man tales. It was an attempt at interpreting Sarat Chandra, whose stories have been the toast of film-makers from the 1930s through to the next millennium. Shabana Azmi, playing the lead in a Basu Chatterji film for the first time, took it upon herself to select the attire which would suit her character. In an interview with the author, she says:[237]

> I remember when we were creating the character of Saudamini (aka Mini), Basu-da said he wanted me to look authentic. And so, I got one of these saree-walas, you know,

> the kind who move from house to house carrying their wares on their heads, and I picked up about 10–12 sarees. They were very inexpensive, ranging between Rs 30–40 each. I showed them to Basu-da; he was very happy that despite working in mainstream cinema, I had the good sense to understand what he meant by authentic. He asked for the saris to be soaked in water to take away the starch so that they looked like they'd been used and worn several times. This was a small detail but was important coming as it did at a time when the costumes of mainstream actors had to be brand new irrespective of which class of society was being represented on screen! The sarees became very popular—as they were very different from the ones the heroines would wear then—they came to be called 'the Shabana Azmi sarees'. Basically, *cotton tangails* that were easily affordable.

In this context, it also merits mention that Shabana, playing the nineteen-year-old Mini, wore the sarees exactly as a Bengali girl would. Especially with the *pallu* draped over her left shoulder, something which was the opposite of how women would do in the western part of the country where she belonged.

Mini's village, unnamed in the story, was christened Madhupur by Basu. A carryover of the memories of *Chitchor.* Her in-laws would be from Chitor, a nondescript village in Dinajpur district in the northern part of the state. The village is still there. The nearest town is Raiganj, and it finds mention in the original story as well.

Incidentally, Shabana was not the first choice, according to Vikram who played Naren Majumdar, the only son of Bipin Majumdar, the zamindar of the village. As discussed with the author:[238]

> The film *Julie* (1975), where I was the male lead, as you would know, was big during its time. Lakshmi and I were considered a hit pair then. Jaya Chakravarthy, actress Hema Malini's mother, got in touch with me as she wanted to do a film repeating

the pair of *Julie*. At that time, I was playing one of the leads in *Sankoch* (1976), which was based on a Sarat Chandra story, as a result of which one more story of Sarat Babu was on my mind. My role was not a big one, but I believed in the strength of the role.

I was an FTII grad of 1972, and Basu-da had a fondness for FTII grads. When Mrs Chakravarthy told me to look out for a director, I had two in my mind. Both Bengalis. Hiren Nag and Basu Chatterji. Hiren Nag I was unable to contact. Basu-da I did, and I discussed Sarat Chandra's *Swami* with him. It was a woman-oriented story, something like Bimal Roy's *Bandini*, which had gone into history.

Things between Jaya Chakravarthy and Lakshmi did not work out as expected. I was searching for a replacement, and the options were Smita Patil or Shabana Azmi. I was closer to Smita but could not contact her. Basu-da reached out to Shabana.

I am not sure why Lakshmi walked out of the project. I had a good equation with her. However, what went on behind the doors between her and Jaya Chakravarthy is something I never asked.

Indrakumar Bahl, Hema Malini's manager then, has a slightly different version. As he recounts to the author:[239]

> Jaya Chakravarthy, Hema's mother, was after me for quite some time when I used to work for Hema. She wanted to produce a film. We met for tea and there she told me—go ahead and get the project rolling. I want to do the muhurat fast. I asked her—who is the director, what is the story? She said—I leave it all to you.
>
> Basu-da was riding high on the success of *Rajnigandha* then. He was also doing films which became successful, both aesthetically and commercially. We met him, and it was decided that he would direct a film to be produced by Mrs Chakravarthy.

> There used to be a producer named Madan Mohla who made films with Hema in the lead [*Shararat* (1970), *Raja Jani* (1972), *Dus Numbri* (1976)]. He was then working on a subject called *Swami*, to star Hema in the titular role of Mini, and to be directed by Bansi Chandragupta, the famous art director. This project did not work out. We took over the rights from Madan Mohla, for whatever he had done so far. And then Basu-da reworked the entire script. We were sure that Hema would star in the film. That is how the project was launched. Later, Hema was not considered for the role. Most of the decisions were taken by me and Basu-da. Lakshmi had been thought of as the lead, there were some discussions with her. But we felt that someone more grounded and typically Indian would suit the character better. And we went to Shabana. This myth about Lakshmi walking out I think is not correct. You only walk out of a film when you have signed the contract and then refuse to do it.

It appears that memory played truant with Mr Bahl. As per Basu's interview, and a documented one, it was art director Sudhendu Roy [not Bansi Chandragupta] who wanted to make Swami. The printed sentence was: 'When I was making *Piya Ka Ghar*, Sudhendu Roy was planning *Swami* with Hema Malini and Manoj Kumar. At that time, I wished I had that subject. You see, I am fascinated by the process of change in a human being. In *Swami*, for instance, how the girl who didn't like her husband came to like him. As luck would have it, five to six years later it came to me.'[240]

Shabana goes back in time:[241]

> If my memory doesn't fail me, Basu-da and I used to meet during international film festivals in Delhi where both of us were regulars. Every now and again he would recommend a film to me and inevitably I would like it. He was very knowledgeable about international cinema.
>
> One day he came along with Ms Jaya Chakravarthy, Hema Malini's mother, to my house, Janki Kutir in Bombay.

> She was venturing into film production and had signed Basu-da to make *Swami* based on Sarat Chandra's novel. This was perhaps in 1976 or 1977.

Like most of Basu's films of the early 1970s, *Swami* was also the story of a girl who has two men in her life. Basu needed one more male lead, possibly a new face to play Ghanashyam Mukherjee, Mini's (Shabana) husband. Says the near-nonagenarian I. K. Bahl:[242]

> Basu-da did not want a known face as most had a defined image with which the crowd would associate them. He knew Girish Karnad, also, that he was the erstwhile principal of the FTII. So, the consensus was—let's try.

Basu knew Girish right from his IPTA days. Contrary to perception, his Hindi was not bad. There was no difficulty as such in his dubbing. Basu, the ever-reticent communicator, had a basic guideline for him: 'It's enough if you manage to express the maturity that you conveyed in *Samskara* (1970).'[243]

Other male members in the film included Dheeraj Kumar, who played Girish's half-brother Nikhil Mukherjee. 'Both Vikram and Dheeraj were young and very enthusiastic,' mentioned I.K. Bahl to the author.[244] Dheeraj recalls Basu's first conversation with him which had Basu saying—'Heard praises of your acting skills. But in my film [*Swami*], don't act.'[245]

With Mini wearing Bengali sarees, the onus was on the male members of the village, especially Ghanasyham, and Nikhil to wear traditional Bengali attire. Dheeraj Kumar, an FTII grad of 1964, has a vivid recall of how they were made to wear dhotis in Bengali style. While Girish had never worn one, Dheeraj had some idea, but it was courtesy of a Bengali dress man which helped them adjust to the change. Dheeraj later became an expert on wearing the dhoti.[246]

Born Puroshottamdas Kochar, Dheeraj Kumar, along with Rajesh Khanna and Subhash Ghai, was one of the three male winners of the United Producers-Filmfare contest in 1965. His career as a Hindi film hero commenced with the 1969 film *Raaton ka Raja*. Later, he gravitated towards negative roles till he made a name for himself on television. *Swami* was a film that gave him some visibility.

The rest of the cast would comprise people Basu was comfortable with, including Preeti Gangoly and Ritu Kamal. *Swami* was Sudha Shivpuri's debut and probably her most remembered role in Hindi cinema. Shashikala's act as the widow of the late Radha Binod Mukherjee would remain a fascinating footnote in her career.

Vikram mentions to the author that he suggested Utpal Dutt's name:[247]

> Utpal-da had played my father in *Julie*. During the casting phase for *Swami*, I told Basu-da, 'I know somebody who would fit the role of Mini's mama.' 'Who? Dadamoni?' asked Basu-da. I said, 'No, Dadamoni is in my heart. But for this role, I would suggest Utpal Dutt.' 'You just echoed my thoughts,' Basu-da said.
>
> I used to have interesting chit-chats with Utpal-da. I deciphered that he used to stretch his lines at times, saying something like *Achhhaaa* . . . and in the meantime, would try to recall the next line. He laughed when I told him this, asking me not to reveal his secret.
>
> The *Julie* success of Rajesh Roshan also worked in his favour; he too joined the team of Basu-da with *Swami*.

The story was based in 1920s Bengal, where urbanization was limited to small pockets in places like Calcutta, Dacca, and Burdwan. Sal, palash, simool, piyal, banana, mango, blackberry, jackfruit, krishnachura, varieties of jasmine (jui and beli), gardenia (gandharaj), siris, palm, and coconut trees, Rangoon creeper (Malatilata and Madhabilata), streams, water bodies, rains, alluvial soil, etc., would mark the canvas of Bengal then. The thought of relocating to Bengal for the shoot however came with the baggage of additional costs. For a first-time producer, this was not a commercially viable proposition, and the task at hand was to find a location resembling rural Bengal.

* * *

Chene Creek (locally referred to as China Creek) is today a weekend tourist spot in Thane West. To reach the place from Bombay, you need to turn right after Meera Road, till you reach Ghorbanda Road. Today the place has many buildings, including a few resorts as well. In the 1970s, it was a *kaccha* (unpaved) road. Few would use it. Chase sequences would be shot there then, mentions Vikram to the author:[248]

> I said to Basu-da, why not check out a location that would look like Bengal? I can show you a place which might meet your requirement. You would get the atmosphere you want. I took him to China Creek. Basu-da said, 'This looks very nice. I feel we can shoot here.'

Chene Creek, as the name suggests, also has a creek, and it would serve as one of the pivotal settings for a particular scene. Sarat Chandra's story had the houses of the zamindar and Braja babu (Mini's mama) separated by a brook, which the lead pair had to cross—when it was in spate after a downpour—by walking on a tree trunk. Vikram continues:[249]

> You would remember the scene involving me crossing the *nala* with Shabana. The tree trunk crossing happened as an improvisation. Basu-da asked, 'Can you walk on the trunk?' I checked and was fine with it. Shabana was very scared. She said, '*Pakka? Hoga toh* (Are you sure it can be done)?' Basu-da replied, 'If you can cross it, it would be excellent.' K.K. Mahajan was there. He shot the scene very beautifully,

> and in a manner that it is difficult to understand how it was shot.
>
> Basu-da was rarely fussy. He could turn a shortcoming into an advantage. During the shooting at China Creek, suddenly there was rain. Any other director would have stopped the shoot. Basu-da's attitude was, why bother? Let's shoot the rain.

The advent of monsoon triggering the first flush of love would be a recurring motif in Basu's films. *Swami* had the additional advantage of the countryside as the backdrop. Mr. Bahl agrees. 'We were in luck, you see,' he mentions. The rain came suddenly, and Basu-da kept shooting.[250]

Shabana too echoes the same thought:[251]

> During *Swami*, the monsoon scenes were shot during the monsoon as well. This was quite remarkable, and you need to give a huge thumbs-up to KK as he did it without any additional lighting. Particularly during the song 'Pal Bhar Mein Yeh Kya Ho Gaya'.

The starting notes of this ethereal melody were inspired by the opening bars of Olivia Newton John's 'Sam' (1974). From there, the tune took a diversion, and it is sheer poetry, not only to the ears but also the eyes, with the shots catching the world of Mini from her dreamy solitude to her kohl-laden eyes meeting those of Naren.

The song is about Mini sifting through priceless moments frozen in time, capturing her vulnerable side. Rajesh Roshan, then a new composer, in an interview with the author, says:[252]

> 'Pal Bhar Mein Yeh Kya Ho Gaya' is one of the finest rendered songs by Lataji for me. Interestingly, we hardly spoke to each other during the recording. That she had grasped the song to a T goes without saying. I never did get a chance to rehearse with her. She used to come to the set, learn the song and

> then render it there and then. Genius! She and Kishore-da (Kumar) became working partners with me. The three of us had a perfect silent understanding! Every time we recorded, it turned into magic.
>
> For this song, there were stalwart musicians like Hariprasadji (Chaurasia) on the flute, Shiv Kumarji (Sharma) on the santoor, and Charanjeetji (Singh) on bass guitar. All the stalwarts worked with me off and on.

Banya Barua, then a kid, remembers going with Basu to the re-recording of the monsoon sequence in *Swami*.[253]

> He was there with the recordist telling him all the sounds he wanted. Put some thunder there. A strong breeze. Feet paddling in the water. Soft rain. Torrential rain. Let's have some sound of the rain hitting the ground. Follow it up with the sound of dripping water from the shed. Add the sound of crickets . . .

And then there was Mini. Savouring the rain with her body and mind, in a manner almost 'Durga-esque' (as in *Pather Panchali*). Shabana shares the spirit of Mini as under:[254]

> I think Mini is a beautifully etched-out character. She is strong-willed, loves books, spends hours having intellectual arguments with her mama (Utpal Dutt) much to the chagrin of her mother (Sudha Shivpuri) who mutters that nothing good will come of it! It was a refreshing character to play.
>
> When she moves to her husband's house, she doesn't turn into the docile *Sati Savitri* which was what happened routinely in Hindi films. I remember a shot where her husband Ghanashyam (Girish Karnad) says, '*Hum Vaishnava hain. Hamare yahan Swami ke saamne kabhi jhoot nahin bolte.*' Mini turns around and says, '*Hamare yahan toh kabhi kisi ke*

saamne jhoot nahin bolte.' She was a spirited person, who could hold her own.

I used to find it a bit difficult to accept why her mama would choose Ghanashyam for Mini knowing that she was in love with Naren. But, in the end, it turns out that Ghanashyam is the better choice for Mini because he was the perfect foil to Mini's impulsiveness.

Mannu Bhandari, who was otherwise satisfied with the film, had her reservations with the volte-face which marks the climax:[255]

The title *Swami* had a deeper subtext—an analogous transition from agnosticism to theism. As much as the success of the film was due to Basu-da's deft direction, it was also because of stellar performances by Shabana Azmi and Girish Karnad. Not only did the film enjoy a silver jubilee run, it also won a few awards [three Filmfare awards—Basu Chatterji for direction, Shabana as best actress, and the late Sarat Chandra for best story]. What struck a sour note for me was that towards the end of the movie, Basu-da had chosen to digress from my story and had shown Mini falling at Ghanashyam's feet!

We had a huge fight over this. Why did she have to touch his feet? She could have fallen into his arms, as I had visualized it.

Initially, Basu-da tried to brush aside my disapproval and disgruntlement by saying, as if in jest, 'Why! A woman should be at her husband's feet, it is her rightful place!' But once he noticed my increasing annoyance, he put forward his rationale behind the same. 'Don't forget that it is Sarat's story! And what was the social standing of women in Bengal of those times? Weren't they mere doormats for their husbands?'

I wouldn't agree. 'How the women of Bengal were during that period is beside the point. Mini's character was different. She was a rebel, a brave heart, someone with self-respect. Someone who could take a stand. By making such a woman cower in front of a man, you have not done justice to her character,' I told him. But Basu-da wouldn't back down. He countered, saying, 'You're right. Mini is that kind of a woman. As much as she is capable of leaving home, on being subjected to mistrust and insult by her husband and his family, she also has the heart to fall at his feet on realizing that she was wrong!'

Anyway, we both had our points of view, but the fact was that the movie had already been released and much applauded, and nothing would come of these creative differences now. But Basu-da's statement, even though he supposedly said it in good humour, still rankled. Why is the male ego not satisfied by a woman touching their feet? Does she have to grovel as well?

In our country, there are several rituals where the wife has to touch the husband's feet, and the husband, even the educated and apparently liberated—who otherwise waxes eloquent on equality of sexes—will proudly stick his feet out for the same. When called out, they will profess their irreverence towards these customs and claim that they do it for the happiness of their wives. Well, I, for one, have seen many of these husbands to be wife-beaters. Some women put up with physical abuse and some with mental torture, as if this was a wife's destiny!

Shabana, while agreeing with Mannu's point of view, prefers to use a rider.[256]

As a feminist, I found it difficult to accept Mini touching her husband's feet and asking for forgiveness but I realized that applying today's lens for incidents in the past doesn't always work.

I used to enjoy working with Basu-da—his dialogue was conversational and free from bombastic language and the grammar he used was refreshing. He was a good editor and kept his scenes short. Of course, we didn't realize then that *Swami* would become the huge success it did, both financially

> and critically. I was really pleased when I got the Filmfare Award for Best Actress for it. In Filmfare, you were competing with mainstream performances, and yet, this, which was in no way mainstream, came up to match that. The feeling was very rewarding.

Swami, among the finest adaptations of a Sarat Chandra story not only in Hindi cinema but in Indian cinema, unexpectedly had a few technical bloopers. Multiple shadows during daytime being one, a case in point when Mini's uncle leaves for the residence of the prospective groom. Continuity was another. In the scene where Mini comes down from the terrace to meet Naren, she wears a green Tangail saree which she had put on the sling to dry a few minutes ago.

Was *Swami* a period drama? One does not know. The story is set in the 1920s, but there was nothing in the film to suggest that it belonged to a particular decade. The pedestal fan was a 1950s-model, the decades of the alarm clocks are difficult to identify, and the transistor radio set probably dated back to the 1960s. A gold chain was priced at Rs 1000, indicating that it could possibly be set in the early 1970s. Naren wore thick belts and bell-bottoms, which were popular in the 1970s. The car used during the wedding sequence looked like a 1965 Ford Mustang convertible. Basu's *Swami* was a 1920s story reworked to fit in with the early 1970s, about people from two small villages where the divide between the rich and the poor was wide.

For the final sequence, Vikram, who was also doing some production work, had ordered a steam locomotive. The railway authorities goofed up and sent a diesel locomotive—which was a rarity in the North Bengal area then. Vikram wanted to send it back but sensing that it would amount to losses for the producer, Basu let the filming continue.[257] The fact that he willingly took risks at the cost of his reputation earned him the sobriquet of 'producer's director'.

Swami was not a literal adaptation of the novel. Avoiding over-dramatization, Basu had relieved the viewers from the twists and tangles which marked the climactic phase of Sarat Chandra's story. He made it simpler, shorter and more cinematic. The film had some remarkable imagery not commonly seen in Hindi cinema. In the scene where Mini's uncle passes away, the camera focuses on an incense stick burning in the background. Ashes to ashes, dust to dust, as the saying goes.

* * *

On 7 June 1977, *Swami* opened to a near-disastrous response. Things fell in line after a week, as recounted by Bahl:[258]

> The budget for *Swami* was a paltry Rs 11 lakh. We released it through Rajshri. We also had to make multiple compromises during the release to satisfy distributors from various circuits. Firstly, we had agreed on a single-hall release. A new theatre was coming up then. There was some issue with the civic authorities who wanted to stall the construction of the theatre in Worli as the management of the adjoining CEAT Tyres office had objected to the same. To circumvent any problem that might have cropped up, we released the film on a Wednesday.
>
> Initial issues were many. An unknown star cast. Nobody knew Girish Karnad. Vikram was not very famous either. Shabana was still not the great actor she would become. Rajesh Roshan had just one or two popular films behind him.
>
> You see, a new theatre, an unsung release, that too on a Wednesday, a Basu-da film which was not a comedy—resulted in a very bad opening. Most people were not aware of the release of this film. Or the theatre. [Author's note–the inauguration of the theatre happened at the hands of Chief Minister Vasantdada Patil a day before the official release of *Swami*. The guests included Jaya Chakravarthy, the producer, Hema Malini and Dharmendra.]

> I decided to put up a Housefull board to which the management of Rajshri objected, citing that they had never done this. If a film is not doing well, it is not doing well, that's it. I said, 'Give me one week. After that, I will agree to whatever you say.' Then, from the next Wednesday, the film picked up. Till that day, people would ask me, 'Sir, why are you wasting your time and money? People go out in the interval and do not come back.' On day two I was sitting with a prospective distributor on the balcony. There were four people in the auditorium. It was very discouraging, but that is something I took upon myself.
>
> Word of mouth helped. From next Wednesday, the Housefull board was for real. Then, there was no stopping. A full-page ad was sanctioned for *Screen* with the ad line, 'Now winning plaudits at Bombay's newest luxury cinema house Satyam (Worli)'.

The completion of *Swami* had coincided with Basu shifting to a new house. Henceforth, West Avenue Road, Santacruz, Bombay 54, would be his address. The film would prove to be lucky for him, and the reclusive film-maker reached out to the press: 'I like the way it has shaped out. It means a lot to me because I generally have one-line subjects like *Safed Jhooth*. In *Swami*, for the first time, I have attempted a good, solid subject.' He mentioned that he was not happy with the addition of a Dharam-Hema song in the film. But that move was obviously to toe the line of distributors.[259]

Besides helping him retain the sobriquet of the director with the Midas touch, Basu was also invited as a juror at the Moscow Film Festival, where he travelled with his wife in July 1977. Accompanying him was fellow film-maker Mrinal Sen. Apart from rubbing shoulders with film personalities from around the world, Basu also met Tarla Mehta and her husband there.

* * *

Swami celebrated a silver jubilee at Satyam, which was later expanded to be part of the multiplex Satyam-Shivam-Sachinam. The film became a huge success across the country, including in small towns where it was exhibited in regular shows, not restricted to Basu's 'balcony-class viewers'.

The film also received the National Award for the 'Best Feature Film with Mass Appeal, Wholesome Entertainment and Aesthetic Value'. The citation mentioned terms like 'a taut script, restrained, matured, and dignified performances (especially by Girish Karnad), etc.'. Jaya Chakravarthy was awarded a Swarna Kamal (22-carat gold medal) and Basu a Rajat Kamal (silver medal).[260] Girish Karnad would later remember *Swami* as a movie that 'astonished the film world and proved a triumph both at the box office and in the eyes of critics.' He continued, 'Even if I wasn't a star in Hindi cinema, I knew I could be a successful actor at least. The trouble was that I hadn't the slightest interest in acting. What I really wanted with a passion was to be a director like Satyajit Ray. So, I turned my back on Bombay.'[261]

Basu did not buy the argument, and henceforth, Girish would be a regular feature in his films, though he would never achieve the level of success he did in *Swami*.

The Salvation

Sarat Chandra's stories were a pet subject for film-makers down the years. In Bombay, Bimal Roy had followed up *Parineeta* (1953) with *Biraj Bahu* (1954), and almost immediately with *Devdas* (1955). Hrishikesh Mukherjee's *Majhli Didi* (1967) failed to be a matinee favourite but enjoyed critical acclaim during its time. Despite excellent music and the star values of Jeetendra and Hema Malini, Gulzar's *Khusboo* (1975) was not a commercial success, but that did not deter him from announcing *Devdas* in the late 1970s which he, unfortunately, could not complete.

Basu found Sarat Chandra a safe bet, acknowledged pan-India.

Most of Sarat Chandra Chatterjee's stories were about people in the villages of Bengal. The context occasionally shifted to Calcutta, as Bengalis took to the legal profession like fish to water. *Niskriti* was one such tale. A joint family, an orchestrated schism, Calcutta, a court case, and the village house—all essential components. Basu found the tension within the Calcutta household interesting, the sense of entrapment worthy of filming.

★ ★ ★

After *Piya Ka Ghar*, *Swami* had the first full-fledged set that Basu commissioned. It was set up at Filmalaya Studio. Made by Bansi Chandragupta, there was little to demarcate between a Bengali home and Bansi's impression of the same. Especially the red-coloured cement, the part-louvered doors (aka *kharkhari*), cast-iron make vertical prison bar-styled window grills, the setup of the kitchen, the tube well in the courtyard, and a few trees in the backyard . . .

The set design would get extended to Filmistan Studios for *Apne Paraye*, Basu's variant of *Niskriti*. Shabana had a twenty-one-day schedule in *Swami*. Here, the duration of her engagement was slightly longer, as she, Amol Palekar and Utpal Dutt had an outdoor schedule in Bengal. The first time Basu shot there was near the Ganges delta where the river was at its widest. Onlookers remember the cast getting down from the boat and walking from the bank to the road carrying their chappals in their hands.

Why Basu travelled to Bengal is not known. Maybe the financiers were willing. Maybe he wanted to get the texture of rural Bengal. Once you left Calcutta and ventured south via the Sealdah line, it was like heading back to a world that had failed to change over time. Apart from the occasional electric locomotive, and the uncouth sight of people hanging from the rankling buses which plied on the ill-maintained highways, the refugee encampments were the only sore sight in the all-encompassing greenery. The vegetation, comprising coconut and banana trees, was complemented by the ponds—belonging to the zamindar or the influential people in the village—and the *char-chala* huts, something unique to the state.

Also, the countryside gave Basu the opportunity to have a greater depth of field and perspective. In *Swami*, it symbolized freedom. In *Apne Paraye*, it would be used to signify claustrophobia as the story would unfold.

★ ★ ★

While the shoot of a Basu Chatterji film was mostly fun, *Apne Paraye* had tense moments too. Samir Samanta, son of film-maker Shakti Samanta, was Basu's assistant for three films, his assignment starting with *Apne Paraye*. As he mentions:[262]

> Mushir and Riaz, the producers of *Apne Paraye*, had produced father's *Mehbooba* (1976). I knew them, and when they used to come to the sets of *Apne Paraye*, I would sit with them. That gave me some comfort as Basu-da would be very charged up and irritable as he had to deal with a huge cast. He was very upfront. His scripts were brilliant. If you read one, you will feel that they are more entertaining than the film. His style of writing, his narrative, etc., was so precise and in so much detail that it presented intricate visuals of who is doing what and how. There were occasions when the actors would fall short of expectations that Basu-da had from them.
>
> I remember Basu Chatterji as someone very sharply focused and direct, whose humour was exactly like that. With a poker face, he would just say something, and it could be very sarcastic. And it could be directed at you as well, but you just couldn't help admiring the man for his comic timing.

There were times though when Basu's fast ones would ricochet off the young lot with sharper tongues. Shabana, who played Sheela (Shailo in the original story), the central character in the film, married to the simpleton Ramesh Chatterjee (renamed Chandranath in the film) recalls one such incident.[263]

> I remember shooting for *Apne Paraye* at Rajkamal Studios, and an aspiring actress hung around on the sets till she pinned him down and showed him her photographs. Basu-da, in his usual curt manner, said, '*Nahin, tumhare daant bahut bahar hain* (No, you have buck teeth).' She turned around and said, '*Aapke heroine ko dekho, uske daant kuch kam bahar hain kya*?' 'But she knows acting,' Basu-da replied. 'Unless you give me an opportunity, how can you know if I can act or not?' the girl hit back.
>
> Basu-da was stumped, and shot a look at me. I laughed out loud and instead of being offended, like the assistants on the set feared, I put my arms around her, commended her for her spirit and offered her a cup of tea.

Of aspirants, Basu had many in *Apne Paraye*. One was Bharti Achrekar, daughter of Hindustani classical singer Manik Varma, and daughter-in-law of the famed art director M.R. Acharekar. She had started her association with the camera as a producer at the age of twenty-three at Doordarshan on 2 October 1972, the day Doordarshan was born. Bharti's role as Naintara was to work with her husband, advocate Harish Chatterjee (Girish Karnad), to proselytize her sister-in-law Siddheswari, played by Ashalata Wabgaonkar (billed as debutant Ashalata Naik in the film), in a role previously refused by veteran actress Raakhee. Bharti goes down memory lane:[264]

> Basu-da was a regular visitor at Shivaji Mandir, Dadar, where Marathi plays would be staged. Ashalata Wabgaonkar and I were working in *Hamida Bai Chi Kothi*, a play directed by Vijaya Mehta, head of NCPA. She was a big name in Maharashtrian theatre. Basu-da had come to see the play. I am not sure if he knew Marathi, but I'm sure he could understand through the expressions. Many people who did not understand Marathi, like Kanhaiyalal, would also come and see our plays. After the play,

> Basu-da met us backstage. Everybody knew he had come. He was a very big name then. We had seen his films like *Chitchor*, etc, which were not only big but also very nicely made. We were extremely excited when he met us backstage. But he did not mention anything about offering us a role in his cinema then. He called both Ashalata and me later through someone I do not remember. He spoke with me in a mix of Hindi and English.
>
> The studio shoot of *Apne Paraye* was completed in 20–22 days, or at the most twenty-five days. We were very happy that it was so tightly managed. I was very impressed with the whole thing.
>
> The characterization in the film was extremely good. I was very surprised when he asked me for a negative role in the film. It was not my genre. My genre was comedy. He knew that. But still, he asked me, as he felt I could do this role. *Unhone chun chun ke sabko nikalein* (He selected us based on what he felt we could do). Interestingly, all of the cast [which also included Amol Palekar, Utpal Dutt and Girish Karnad] was from theatre, except Shabana. Basu-da had high respect for theatre artistes. He did not tell us what to do. He gave us dialogues and the freedom to express ourselves the way we wanted. Then he used to arrange the camera.
>
> *Apne Paraye* was a very good film. I sincerely do not know why it did not do well then. It was a film which you could see with the family. Now, this film is a huge favourite with most.

Shabana echoes these thoughts while discussing Utpal Dutt (playing advocate Girish Chatterjee, the head of the family) and the most poignant scene of the film, where she breaks into a paroxysm of tears, no longer in a condition to endure the severe mental duress of the fabricated blame, her resilience questioned the only time in the story.[265]

> Utpal Dutt was always a great delight to work with. He was very irreverent, had lots of stories to tell, would make light of

> his work in Hindi cinema but there was never any doubt that he was a very fine actor. He was involved with the politics of the era and was very engaged with that. Sometimes we would have some discussions around that, but you know those days you hardly ever worked in a film in a continuous schedule. I remember I was shooting during the 7 a.m. to 2 p.m. shift, and after that, for another film, in another studio during the 2 p.m. to 10 p.m. shift. One did not get the time to bond in the way one does during outdoor shoots, or when we work continuously on a film at a time.
>
> The last shot between Utpal-da and me was on the lawns of my home Janki Kutir. That's the genius of K.K. Mahajan. I just love that film, the characters . . . it is vintage Basu-da. The fact that Bansi Chandragupta did the sets also lent that kind of authenticity to the film.

Another aspect that had the stamp of authenticity was the music. Like *Swami*, it added great warmth to the situations and the characterizations. There was a minor difference though. The songs of *Swami*, barring the Bhairavi thumri 'Bajuband Khul Khul Jaye', were created after taking certain artistic liberties. This included 'Ka Karun Sajni', the most popular song of the film, which was more of a chord-based progression and less the well-known thumri. And while Kishore Kumar's 'Yaadon Mein Woh', Lata Mangeshkar's 'Pal Bhar Mein Yeh Kya Ho Gaya', and the Yesudas-Asha Bhosle duet 'Bhag Jaungi' were exquisite compositions, especially the first two, they had little to do with Bengal, its ethos or its folk music. It is here that *Apne Paraye* added additional value. *Disco Dancer* (1982) had not happened, and during 1979–80, Bappi Lahiri, the composer of *Apne Paraye*, was associated more with quality music than with quick-fix tunes that he had prioritized in *Suraksha* (1979).

In an interview with the author on 24 August 2021, Dheeraj Kumar mentioned that the shoot of 'Ka Karun Sajni' was extremely memorable. This was not only for the excellent melody and picturization but also because he made a minor blooper during the lip-synch, something Basu let go of and did not reshoot.

[Author's note: Basu had cut to a shot of Shabana Azmi in the line which had this slip-up.]

The late Yogesh went back in time recalling his work with Bappi Lahiri:[266]

> I had never worked with Bappi Lahiri before. My association with Basu-da implied I also did a few films with Bappi, of which I enjoyed *Apne Paraye* the most. He used a lot of Bengali folk songs for the film, and this extended to the background score as well. Being a tabla player, Bappi knew a lot about rhythm, and the addition of an expert like Sudarshan Adhikari to the team helped. My lyrics were not based on the original Bengali songs, but I was given the outline by Basu-da. Think you are writing for a Vaishnav who would be singing on the streets and begging for alms. The trick helped.

Bappi Lahiri, who had been christened the 'Poor Man's R.D. Burman' for his similar style and emphasis on rhythm, probably had S.D. Burman in his mind when writing the music of *Apne Paraye*. The background score would have snatches of the traditional Bengali kirtan 'Rai Jago Rai Jago Bole'. 'Rai Jago Go', another traditional kirtan, would have its Hindi counterpart sung by Yesudas as 'Gao Mere Man'. Pandit Sudarshan Adhikari, originally from Midnapore district in West Bengal and one of the last exponents of the *khol* (a rhythm instrument used by itinerant kirtan singers in Bengal) in Bombay, played the instrument for the songs and the background score as well. Adhikari was very close to SD, who would have tasks specially cut out for him, like playing the *khol* in 'Aaj Sajan Mujhe Aang Laga Le' in *Pyaasa* (1957).

The rare occasion of Amol Palekar singing the first phrase of an SD kirtan—'Madhu Vrindavan E Dole Radha'—was also used in *Apne Paraye*.

Apne Paraye had a title song—'Kaise Din Jeevan Mein Aaye'—sung by Kishore Kumar, and was used midway through the film. The use of recurring long notes and Kishore's bass would make you think that Basu-da probably wanted the Rajesh Roshan sound, something which Bappi reproduced well. The song, the only one used in the background, has remained a rare gem that connects the listener directly to a dramatic moment in the story. And to Bengal, the gloomy pre-monsoon sky, the Ganges, its languid gait, the *Pansi* boat, the sailed *Sultani* boat,[267] and the music of the fishermen. Talking of music, Shabana, who is a decent singer herself, goes down memory lane reminiscing about the songs which were featured on her, and about music in general.[268]

> 'Pal Bhar Mein Yeh Kya Ho Gaya', written by Amit Khanna and music by Rajesh Roshan, from *Swami*, has been popular over the years. The *lori* in *Apne Paraye* is also lovely. It was interesting that Basu-da found the space for songs in his film and didn't cock a snook at them as the new films do. I feel film songs are integral to storytelling in Hindi cinema. Lip-synching to songs is so endearingly Indian, and when you look at the films of Guru Dutt, Mehboob Khan, or Raj Kapoor, I can't imagine them without songs. Songs can say many things that sometimes scenes cannot. I yearn for them to hold centre stage once again.

* * *

Having the blessings of a big producer like Mushir Riaz helped *Apne Paraye* in getting good publicity. A full-page ad with the picture of Shabana dominating the layout was published in *Screen*.

There was some footage too in terms of the storyline and stills. The release was also timed perfectly, on 8 August 1980, exactly a week after the publicity material with the blurb 'Your Story . . . And Mine!' reached the readers of this widely circulated tabloid, and almost immediately after the film got its film certificate on 4 August 1980.[269]

Released at Amber Theatre in Bombay, the response across mainstream media—from the *Sunday Standard* (reviewed by Iqbal Masud) to the *Trade Guide*—was unanimous. *Apne Paraye* was heart-wrenching and true to life, something which resulted in the film being released in more theatres in Bombay.[270] Unfortunately, the film failed to recreate the commercial magic of *Swami*. An upset Basu would later lament that while *Apne Paraye* was one of the best films he ever made and one which was sold all over India within a week of its release in Bombay, it did not live up to expectations, leaving him saddened.[271]

Thanks to cable television, the revival happened some twenty years later. Time is perhaps kind to the deserving. As they say in Hindi—*Der aaye, durust aaye.*

Failure with Superstars

'And all at once, summer collapsed into fall.'

—Oscar Wilde

The Daydreamer—1

'I remember it rained for three days continuously,' reminisces Moushumi Chatterjee, going back in time about a milestone in her career.[272]

★ ★ ★

Married on 10 March 1972, in Calcutta, the Bombay reception of Jayanta Mukherjee and Moushumi Chatterjee was held at Khar Gymkhana on 18 March. Moushumi's Bengali debut *Balika Badhu* (1967) had been a roaring success; she was getting offers by prospective producers even before she arrived in Bombay. Her first shoot at Bombay happened during the period 22–24 March. It was for the song 'Sunri Pawan Pawan Purvaiyaan' (*Anurag,* 1972). Many of the directors who signed her up were there at the reception.

Basu Chatterji, who was awaiting the release of *Piya Ka Ghar,* was there too. He was working on a few scripts then, two of which were *Rajnigandha* and *Us Paar.* Another one was based on Mrinal's Sen *Akash Kusum* (1965). A surprisingly mainstream film by Sen, the story was about failed ambitions, of an existence which was funny yet tragic. The ending was characterized by the dark boundaries of Calcutta where hope was discouraged. Basu, ever-optimistic, had revised the script to suit the buoyancy of Bombay. He had reached out to a few rookie producers as well. One was Raj Prakash Gupta, married to Lalita Pawar, whose son Jai from her first husband Ganpatrao Pawar would be one of the producers of the film as well. Rajiv Suri, Suresh Jindal's production manager, would join the team. The trio of Prakash, Pawar and Suri had produced *Parwana* (1971).

Like Basu, all were hopefuls.

Suri passed away during the first wave of COVID-19 in 2020.

By the time the four joined hands, Moushumi had signed a film with a little-known Amitabh Bachchan. It was in July 1972, for Narendra Bedi's *Benaam* (1974). Basu announced the second Moushumi–Amitabh venture in October, and the *muhurat* happened with the recording of 'Rim Jhim Gire Saawan' by Lata Mangeshkar. The film was named *Manzil*.

Moushumi, who was new to Bombay, did not take decisions on film selection then. Dilip Mukherjee, her '*mesho-shoshur*' (husband of Jayanta Mukherjee's maternal aunt) would play the role of the negotiator. He was Basu's friend, and both had after-shoot soirees where they discussed everything over whisky, from politics to cinema. He was also one of the co-producers of *Us Paar*.

The main driver for onboarding Moushumi was her smile, which partly mirrored Aparna Sen's, the leading lady in the original. Moushumi would remain one of Basu's favourite actors for comic roles—along with Neetu Singh and Amrita Singh, as mentioned to the author.

Basu found Amitabh—his original choice for the common man—gentlemanly. His height helped. Soumitra Chatterjee in the original was tall too. Kiran Kumar, a 1971-batch FTII graduate, was signed for the role of Amitabh's friend Prakash Beriwala. He was as tall as Amitabh, and both would have to share the same suit as per the demand of the story.[273]

By the end of December, six reels of *Manzil* had been canned. Basu had shot many scenes involving Amitabh, Moushumi, Satyen Kappu, Lalita Pawar, A.K. Hangal, and Urmila Bhatt. Kiran Kumar had failed to land up at the shoot, and Basu had to hurriedly summon the services of Rakesh Pandey who was four inches shorter. He obliged.

Akash Kusum had a short sequence depicting rain. Basu decided to take it ahead further, and a song was written. Little did Basu, Yogesh the lyricist, RD the music composer, KK the cinematographer, or for that matter anybody else realize that this would remain a favourite romantic fantasy even after fifty years. Consequently, capturing the rain became Basu's metier.

'Rimjhim Gire Saawan' would become the melody of fairytale moments, of sharing the shiver of rain and the mystery of haze, of adolescent dreams, and everlasting memories. Including Basu's own. It was his tribute to 'Pyar Hua, Ikraar Hua Hai' (*Shree 420,* 1955), a souvenir of the romanticism that was typified by the hope of the migrant-turned-dweller. Like Raj in *Shree 420*. Or Shailendra, Yogesh, and Basu.

★ ★ ★

Moushumi goes down memory lane:[274]

> I remember the day we first shot 'Rimjhim Gire Saawan'. It was raining cats and dogs, and it was difficult to walk. I had to keep pace with Amitabh who was very tall and hence matching his steps was a challenge too. I think these three to four days were the only time it rained in Bombay that year.
>
> Filming a rain song came with an intrinsic challenge—where and how to play the song? The inevitable happened. The song was not played during the shoot. Thankfully, Basu-da had made us listen to it time and again so that we understood the feeling and the gestures which were needed.

> He would play a portion of the song to us and say, 'I will shoot this stanza. I will drop you at that location. After the shot is complete, a car will pick you up.'
>
> A man standing by would signal with his hand to start and finish. Amitabh would see that and start walking or emoting, whatever was asked. We knew that the camera was running. The eyeliner I was wearing would melt in all that water, with the colour dripping all over my face and body. Amitabh would constantly ask me to wipe it. The saree I was wearing was chiffon/synthetic. It started bleeding; the turquoise colour coming out and sticking to my body. It did not wash off for days.
>
> Basu-da used to fix the camera somewhere in the dry. KK had it covered with protective material. Despite meticulous planning, there were retakes. There was no way we could have had lunch, as continuity would be lost if the rain stopped. So, after a few shots, we used to go to a cafe near Colaba that served tea, coffee and snacks. And be back for the next round of shooting.

Praba Mahajan, who was there with the cast and the crew, recalls the café:[275]

> I used to see movies at Tarabai Hall near Marine Lines. Near that, there's a flyover that crosses from the Marine Lines Station to Marine Drive. In 'Rimjhim Gire Saawan', there's this amazing shot—zoom, I guess—taken from a café near the flyover showing the actors Amitabh and Moushumi on the rain-swept stretch of Marine Drive. I saw KK taking the shot.

Ajay Prabhakar, who was assisting KK, adds:[276]

> Most parts were shot from a car. We had hired an old Chevrolet; hence the shock was less, and the transitions were smooth. There were some static camera placements too. The song was

> shot for over two to three days. The final shape which you have seen on the screen came through the editing.

Seeing the sequence, it is difficult to make out that the camera was handheld in many places. Some of the long shots were taken from far-off places, widening the expanse. The camera captures an eclectic panorama, a montage of South Bombay—Gateway of India, Sachivalaya, Oval Ground, Rajabhai Clock Tower, Queens Road with the Art Deco buildings, Marine Drive, Chowpatty Flyover, Churchgate, Flora Fountain . . . one would just keep on drooling for more. Of a rain-drenched weekend when life was simpler and the city a lot cleaner. The song was a celebration of our childhood when jumping in a puddle of water and running around in the rain was cool. Nobody objected, not even stern parents.

Neither did the audience when the song became a huge hit on television. Today, if viewed with a critical eye, the cutting has a few rough edges. The route followed by the lead pair is not logical either; Gateway of India to Flora Fountain via Marine Drive is a peculiar path to take, especially when the couple has been shown crossing Oval Ground. One might also notice the Worli Sea Face masquerading as Marine Drive during the last few seconds.

Nonetheless, these become incidental. Nobody cared, as long as the melody was siren-sweet and the frames stunning. And it even became a 'Find Basu' exercise for the viewers.

'I was there at the Flora Fountain controlling the crowd, and I accidentally came into the viewfinder. So that became my cameo,' said Basu to the author.[277]

But was that unintentional? Basu was also captured before in the song, walking down the Queens Road with an assistant, a shared umbrella providing relief to the duo. Maybe the presence of two Basus in the song made it the phenomenon it is today. Actors believed that a Basu cameo was a good omen.

'Rimjhim Gire Saawan' was the first sequence that signified Basu's fascination for rain, articulating an obsession that would act as a leitmotif in his cinema. The intimacy, almost graphical, of the couple in the rain in Bombay was set up as a sharp contrast with the manner in which a couple conducted themselves during a purported visit to the theatre in the small town of Agra. Different towns, different social strata, different cultures.

Marking his debut during the shoot was small-towner Shailendra's Bombay-bred son Dinesh Shankar Shailendra, who recalls:[278]

> I was part of the crew when Amitabh Bachchan was shooting at Marine Drive during *Manzil*. It was a Sunday. Offices were closed. We had been granted permission to shoot on a Sunday. The camera was in the car, or handheld at times. We did not have Steadicams at that time. I just attended one day of shooting at Marine Drive. This song was shot for more than one day though, and I did not attend the full shoot.
>
> After that, I was an assistant to Basu Bhattacharya for four films, out of which only one was released. But he taught me a lot as far as direction goes. I started as an apprentice in *Anand Mahal* (1977) and got promoted to an assistant during that time. The other three were *Madhu Malti* (1978), and the incomplete *Asampta Kavita* and *Teesra Pathar*. During this phase, I was informed that Basu Chatterji wanted me at BR Sound and Music Studios where he was doing the dubbing of *Swami*. Basu Bhattacharya had started shooting *Grihapravesh* (1979) with Uttam Kumar around that time.
>
> I reached BR Studios to find Basu-da dubbing with Shabana. I sat down at the side. Shabana had got stuck with some dialogue and had requested the grammatical explanation of a sentence she had to speak. Basu-da told me, 'Babloo, I am a Bengali, and I have issues when it icomes to Hindi grammar. Can you explain it to her?' I knew very well that Basu-da's Hindi was much better than mine as he was from Mathura. I understood it was a test, and I did the necessary corrections

> to the sentence. I was then asked to come to Natraj Studios where he had started the shooting for *Dillagi* (1978).

In the meantime, any further shooting of *Manzil* had to be cancelled. Indefinitely . . .

Misfired Banter

Friendships in the film industry are fragile. Mostly. Basu and Dharmendra were good friends in the early 1970s. Dharmendra also worked in two obligatory cameos for Basu, lip-synching songs, of which one became widely popular. The friendship led to Dharmendra asking Basu to make a film for him.

And *Dillagi* happened, interestingly, on the rebound. Pramod Chakravarty—who had till then religiously onboarded the pair of Dharmendra and Hema Malini as the lead in three films: *Naya Zamana* (1971), *Jugnu* (1973) and *Dream Girl* (1977), and in a guest role in *Barood* (1976)—was offered the film. He was busy with another Dharam-Hema production called *Azaad* (1978), and Basu, who shared the office of Natraj Studios with Pramod, took it up.

Says Dinesh Shankar:[279]

> *Dillagi* was Dharmendra's home production, where he had left almost everything from the selection of the story to the cast to Basu. Contrary to his style, Basu had to shoot most of the film at the studio [Author's note: At RK Studio, Mohan Studio, Chandivali Studio, and Natraj]. Initially, most of the work was supposed to happen in Mysore. However, out of a fifteen-day schedule, only three or four days were productive due to an unfortunate accident. It included a song featured on actress Kajri, which was shot on the banks of the Kaveri. The rest of the shooting had to be arranged in the studios. A few scenes were shot at Bhavans College in Bombay too.
>
> Something I learned from Basu Chatterji: never go to the floor without the script and dialogues. Bhattacharya

> never taught me that. Basu (Chatterji) always had a complete screenplay with dialogues. Hence, even during eventualities, he would manage to recover. He scored over his contemporaries because he was very planned in his approach, and even a Dharmendra-Hema Malini film did not take more than 40–45 days to shoot.

The rewriting of the script and dialogues of *Dillagi* was done by Arup Gangoly.[280]

> Basu-da's handwriting was small. Mine was large, hence, he gave me the task of rewriting the fair version of the script. I used to carry a portable typewriter then, hardly weighing two kgs. I would use that to type the script in English. The dialogue part I would write in Hindi.

Despite an amusing story complemented with a score by Rajesh Roshan that was partly reminiscent of the music of *Swami*, the characters did not mesh well. There were too many of them, including a slew of aspirants. Apart from the lead pair, prominent members of the cast included Shatrughan Sinha, Mithu Mukherjee, Kajol Mukherjee aka Kajri, Asrani, Deven Verma, Shobhna Shah, with Basu regulars Ritu Kamal and Preeti Gangoly among others. In the end, one came out of the theatre confused; what were so many people doing in the film? Asrani and Kajri were probably cast as a pair to capitalize on their popularity in *Balika Badhu* (1976). Unfortunately, the chemistry was missing in *Dillagi*.

The bottom line was that this romantic comedy did not work. Unlike *Chitchor* or *Khatta Meetha*, the characters were not developed well. The interactions between them were synthetic. Objectivity and timing are critical to the narrative of comedy. Halfway through the film, the objective was lost. By the time the plot terminated in a climax which was difficult to sit through, Basu could probably see the writing on the wall. 17 November 1978, the day *Dillagi* was released, did not augur well for Basu or Dharam. The verdict was not in favour of the tepid love story.

Suffering losses, the producer blamed it all on Basu.[281] Never mix business with friendship, as they say. Dharmendra and Basu did not collaborate again, though Jaya Chakravarthy, who managed her daughter's costumes and finances, had no issues working with Basu.

The Unsolved Labyrinth

'I am a fan of Billy Wilder. He was a great storyteller. So was Hitchcock.'

Thus said Basu Chatterji to the author in 2015. He failed to remember why he made *Chakravyuha* (1978) though, his only attempt to recreate a Hitchcockian thriller called *39 Steps* (1934). In later years, it transpired to be something he had forgotten he had made. It was his only work with the first superstar of India, Rajesh Khanna. Though, in a volte-face, it was Rajesh Khanna who needed Basu Chatterji and not the other way around. In the early and mid-1970s, directors would wait at his door for days to sign on Khanna. Misjudging many a proposal, Khanna would end up signing films, the redeeming feature of which today remains only the music. Khanna needed a few hits then and was producing *Anurodh* (1977) around that time. He produced *Chakravyuha*.

Arup Gangoly, who worked as an assistant and knew Khanna from the time he was a college student, recollects some anecdotes:[282]

> I knew him from his college days. He was called Jatin then. He was a few years senior, and used to do Hindi theatre. I used to do Hindi and English theatre. We had a common director called V.K. Sharma (Vinod Kumar Sharma), who made a couple of films like *Savera* (1972), also did small roles, and wrote dialogues in films. Sharma used to direct plays in colleges and call us for the shows. I had been to see a play at HR College, where I found that eggs and tomatoes were being pelted when Rajesh was on stage. It was so bad that

the curtains had to be pulled. It was the first and the last time I saw this happen. Later, I heard this was orchestrated by an anti-Rajesh Khanna group inside HR College. For me, it was highly insulting and humiliating. Those days, reactions like these were unheard of. The anti-Rajesh gang wanted to disrupt his play. It was even more regretful as Rajesh Khanna was a good actor.

After a few years, I came to know about Rajesh Khanna from the ads of *Baharon Ke Sapne* (1967). I found that he had changed his name. He was no longer Jatin; he was Rajesh. And with time, he became very big.

Chakravyuha was signed when Rajesh Khanna's popularity was on the wane. He wanted to work with somebody who could give his career a fillip. Post *Chhoti Si Baat*, Basu Chatterji was very famous. Anybody and everybody wanted to sign him. '*Aare, jo paisa hai do,* Basu Chatterji *ka film hai* [Give whatever money you have, it's a film by Basu Chatterji].' The idea behind this was that a Basu Chatterji film would not fail. Basu-da had lots of scripts too, and he must have picked up *Chakravyuha*.

[Author's note: Rajesh was a student of KC College which is 50 metres away from HR College. Arup was a student of Jai Hind College and used to go to HR College to see plays. The anti-Rajesh feeling could have stemmed from inter-college rivalry. Yasser Usman, Rajesh Khanna's biographer, mentions that Rajesh was a regular at the HR College theatre circuit.[283]]

As the story was about an innocent man on the run, the shooting started on the highways near Bombay. The sequences were lengthy, and the place would change every day. Morning scenes were shot during the 7 a.m. to 2 p.m. shift, while evening and night scenes would mandate 2 p.m. to 10 p.m. and 10 p.m. to 6 a.m. shifts, respectively. The entire team would assemble as per schedule at the identified locations, as Basu would make maximum use of the setting and the light conditions. However, the dynamic nature of the story mandated movement on the road, something that added to the lead time due to multiple setups. The shooting happened for a prolonged period, and there was a phase when KK was in Calcutta for around a month and a half for a Mrinal Sen film, during which Ajay Prabhakar handled the camera.[284]

Waiting for Rajesh Khanna was a given. Despite being the producer, Khanna would never reach the location before 11 a.m. during morning shifts. By 2 p.m., Khanna would be gone. On many occasions, the crew would get the news that Khanna would not be available for the shoot. In the absence of mobile phones and handsets, the news of Khanna's absenteeism would arrive with the food vendor.[285]

Prabhakar recalls, 'Often, we got to know that he was not going to come at 2.30 p.m. But he was magnanimous enough to have the food delivered. We would eat a good lunch and return.'[286]

Frequent breaks in the shoot led to loss of continuity too.

For example, one of the props was a hard-bound copy of the Gita that Amit Narayan (Khanna) was carrying in his pocket. Midway through the shoot, the Gita was lost. The replacement was larger, and the orientation of the text on the cover was different. The saving grace was that most of the film had only Rajesh Khanna; hence, continuity lapses were minimal. Neetu Singh, who played the heroine, had six or seven shifts of shooting, including the popular song 'Shaadi Karne Se Pyaar Kam Ho Jaata Hai' (Kishore Kumar and Asha Bhosle), where she had to change her clothes thrice—something she did in minutes, unlike leads of her time. Others, like Dina Pathak, Om Shivpuri, Pinchoo Kapoor, A.K. Hangal, and Pradip Kumar, had work that was completed in a day or two.

Rajesh Khanna was a recurring face in almost every sequence.

Basu knew how to handle him, and thankfully, Khanna's famous mannerisms were found missing in *Chakravyuha*. Prabhakar recalls:[287]

> Rajesh Khanna was more natural in this film than usual. There was a shot when he was eating and wanted to lift his hand to give more expression. Basu-da asked him not to move his hand. The next shot had him holding hands with Neetu Singh, below the table, and only the shot of their hands was taken. Rajesh Khanna said, 'Dada, had you told me this before, I would have given more expression.' Basu Chatterji said, 'I did not want any extra expression. Hence, I did this.'

Arup Gangoly agrees:[288]

> He was a director's actor. During his heyday, he would want the camera on his face, even during non-speaking shots. He wanted to display his reaction to a line of dialogue spoken by someone else. He used to dictate terms to the director as he was in a position to do so. When he came to Basu Chatterji, his popularity was fizzling out. Rajesh Khanna listened to Basu-da and did precisely what was asked of him.

'Rajesh Khanna was very fast. If Basu Chatterji was a fast director, Rajesh Khanna was an equally fast actor. He could imbibe the essence of the scene and complete eight hours of work in four. He had that quality,' mentions Narinder Singh to the author.[289]

However, despite Khanna's ability to close shoots at a speed that was very fast by industry standards, distributors showed little faith in *Chakravyuha*. Receiving the film certification on 22 July 1978, and released sometime later, Basu had to reshoot part of the film, including a few fight sequences, to ensure a re-release which happened almost a year later, on 22 June 1979. The makeover did not help.

The only acclaim *Chakravyuha* got was critical and more for Khanna's restrained performance than for anything else. The film was plagued by a complete absence of drama, aided in no little measure by a narrative that was leisurely and tame. This was fine for

Rajnigandha, but certainly not for a spy thriller where tension was a necessary ingredient.

Basu's predicament was like Alfred Hitchcock's, who had mentioned, 'If I made *Cinderella*, the audience would immediately be looking for a body in the coach.' A potboiler, and a relatively meek one, was not what the viewers expected from Basu. Marriage and the process leading to the consummation of the same, at times comical, was why people would flock to see his films. Basu had subtly touched upon the subject though, through the desires of Chhaya (Neetu Singh), who finally marries Amit, and Nandita (Simple Kapadia), whose love remains unrequited.

Reincarnated . . . or Better Dead

Septuagenarian Siraj Syed, apart from playing many parts in the film industry, is also a great raconteur. In a tête-à-tête with the author, he goes back in time recalling a funny incident involving Basu:[290]

> From 1974 to mid-1977, I was the chairman of the film society called Cine Circle. From the late 1970s till 1980, I was the chairman of another film society named Film Circle. By virtue of my position, I was made part of the executive committee of the western region of the Federation of Film Societies of India. One of the top office-bearers of the federation was Basu Chatterji. Basu Bhattacharya was the president for some time. Satyajit Ray, Chidananda Dasgupta, Vijaya and Suhasini Mulay, et al, were associated with the federation. The headquarters, usually, was in Calcutta.
>
> One of the activities of the federation was approving foreign films for viewing at the film societies. Bombay was the port where the films landed. It was followed by a review by the committee. Selected films would be sent to film societies across the country. I was part of the Customs screening committee. Basu-da was another member. A total of five members were there, and another one whose name I remember was Suresh

> Gohil. We all were once previewing a set of films at the auditorium of the Prince of Wales Museum. Unfortunately, the films being shown at that viewing were terrible. But we had to sit through them as we were the committee. Midway through the session, I turned back to discover that two of the five had left. After a few more hard-to-bear films, Basu-da, who was sitting in front of me, pulled three or four chairs together, lay down on them and dozed off . . .

Little did Basu know that one of his films would be subjected to similar treatment—*Tumhare Liye*. In hindsight, it was difficult to believe that it was a Basu Chatterji film. Even Sanjeev Kumar, arguably the best lead male actor in Bombay cinema at that time. looked confused. Probably Basu too was. Love stories transcending deaths have an appeal that lasts for generations. Case in point, Bimal Roy's *Madhumati* (1958). Forget generations, Basu's improbable tale of a failed romance through successive rebirths in *Tumhare Liye* did not even have the basic atmosphere essential to sustain the interest of the audience for even half an hour. The Lata Mangeshkar song 'Tumhe Dekhti Hun', composed by Jaidev, drew people to the theatre for some time. There were multiple instances of viewers walking out after this sequence.

One wonders how the maker of *Sara Aakash* and *Rajnigandha* could even contemplate making a film about unsatiated souls and multiple reincarnations. The only palpable reason could be money. Or his relationship with the B.R. Chopra family, the producers. Peers were surprised. Hrishikesh Mukherjee would advise Basu to go slow. Basu, in an almost apologetic tone, had confided to the press that he did sign films left, right, and centre to make up for the money lost during *Us Paar*. This led to a few shelved films as well, like *Heere ki Chori*, announced in mid-1975 with Shashi Kapoor and Moushumi Chatterjee in the lead roles. He was working on a two-shift pattern during the mid- and late-1970s. Dinesh Shankar recalls Basu coming to the office and asking for the file, not sure about which film he was supposed to shoot.[291] In Basu's own words, sourced from multiple interviews:

A director has no business to work in so many films at a time. I could not help it because I had produced a film called *Us Paar,* which flopped badly. I was in debt and I had to accept several directorial assignments just to pay off my creditors. But I'm almost in the clear now and I do not intend signing any more films till the present lot is completed.'[292]

A lot of money was coming my way those days. The themes of the films offered to me were appealing and soon I was working on twelve films at a time. They (*Chakravyuha*, and the disastrous duo *Dillagi* and *Tumhare Liye*) were good subjects. But I made a mistake in not realizing that the producers would expect me to deliver the films pretty fast and that I could not do justice to the themes. I am to be blamed for the films having flopped. I would not blame their failure on the producers or the cast.[293]

In 1981, while writing for a special publication of DFFI, Pearl Padamsee had described Basu thus:

Basu Chatterji is, without doubt, India's most prolific and speedy film director. A late beginner, he has so far established an average of three films a year, made at lightning speed, each within a span of forty shooting shifts. Obviously, he does not believe in the long haul of sporadic shootings. Built into his thinking are several vital factors that give shape and energy to his work. True to his motto—speed is the essence—he practices an economy of time invariably allowing an economy of budget. In truth, Basu Chatterji is now the master of the low-budget feature film.[294]

The issue was that the producers in the cases of *Chakravyuha*, *Dillagi* and especially *Tumhare Liye* were moneyed people who came to Basu as they were among the captive audience of his films. Basu could have bargained for more shifts and resources. The investment of time, money, and heart was completely lacking in these films. While *Tumhare Liye* was delayed for over a year due to unavoidable circumstances, Basu, it is agreed by most, was not the type to do a big, commercial film. This is echoed by Amit Khanna, who was producing his version of *Pygmalion* to be directed by Basu Chatterji.[295]

And to think that Basu had to forgo the brilliant *Pati, Patni Aur Woh* (1978) to do *Tumhare Liye* for the same production house . . .

The Botched Musical

Amit Khanna was probably one of the first graduates of St. Stephen's College to join the film industry. Before him, the only well-known one was Parikshit Sahni. Later, more people, namely Kabir Bedi, Shekhar Kapur, Benjamin Gilani and Siddharth Kak, found their calling in Bombay.

After graduating, Amit joined Dev Anand. His introduction to Basu happened through common friends like KK, Arun Kaul, Gogi Anand, et al. Not someone to toe the sentimental line, Amit does go back in time recalling his time with Basu-da.[296]

> Basu-da was a simple guy. He loved to keep to himself, even when he was drinking. He savoured his whisky. He used to call me a boring man, as I was, and have remained a teetotaller. I think I met him around 1971–72. He had two qualities that do not find mention in normal conversations. He was a very keen observer of life. Sometimes, during a conversation, he would make a very profound statement, which you would realize later. He was not very outgoing, but he often went out to help many unsung people. He never took names.
>
> If he had a paper and pencil around him, he was always doodling. Even during meetings, he would doodle. His knowledge about global cinema was phenomenal. Especially about Czech and Polish cinema. Krzysztof Kieślowski and Andrzej Wajda were among his favourites. The moment he had some expendable money, he would go abroad to see new

films. We had travelled together a few times; I remember being at Cannes together once.

My direct contribution to a Basu-da film started with writing lyrics. This was courtesy the success of my lyrics in *Chalte Chalte*, whose songs were recorded in 1973, but released late in 1975. I worked with Basu-da first in *Swami*. This was during the time that I decided to become a producer. The directors I had in mind were Basu-da and Surinder Suri, the latter one a gold medallist from FTII. Suri was making a film for children named *Rikki Tikki Tavy*, based on Kipling's book. I started *Naya Johnny* with him, which unfortunately remained incomplete after 9–10 reels of shooting. Around six or seven songs had been recorded too. Kishore Kumar had sung four of them.

Basu-da and I met very briefly for a film discussion. I was keen on taking Dev Sahab (Dev Anand). Basu-da too was happy as he had not worked with him. So, we were talking. I said let's make a musical. Then he asked me about *Pygmalion*. We watched *My Fair Lady*. There was a play written by Shama Zaidi's mother Begum Qudsia Zaidi called *Aazar ka Khwab*. There was a Marathi play *Ti Phulrani* which we saw. These three-four screenplays were in our mind when doing the screenplay for the film.

We had Salil Chowdhury as a script consultant. Basu-da had a few meetings with him as it was a musical. By then, I had decided to go with Rajesh Roshan as *Swami* had started.

In the final run, Salil Chowdhury was not acknowledged in the titles. Parts of the background music of *Manzil* sounds like creations of Salil, though there has been no official mention of the same.

Amit did not have to buy the rights to the book. In 1975, *Pygmalion* was beyond the copyright act. To be on the safe side, Amit found out the address of Alan Jay Lerner, the writer, and the lyricist of the musical *My Fair Lady*, and wrote to him mentioning that he was making a film based on *Pygmalion* where he would like to use some of the sequences of the film as well. Jay Lerner replied in the positive, expressing his happiness that India was doing a version of his play. There was no question of any money. They were not aware of India's market, and an Indian version was good news for them.[297] Thankfully, they were not aware that the play had already been adapted once for Hindi cinema—some twenty-five years ago, as *Nili* (1950), where Suraiya played the role of the poor girl who transforms herself. Incidentally, Dev Anand was Bombay's answer to Professor Henry Higgins in *Nili* as well.

* * *

Though the decision to make the film was taken in 1975, Basu was preoccupied with a few films then. Dev Anand was busy too, predominantly with the silver jubilee films for Navketan. *Man Pasand*, as the film was named, could start only in late 1977. It was again delayed as by that time Basu had become very busy, working with all the big stars—Amitabh Bachchan, Rajesh Khanna, Dharmendra, Sanjeev Kumar and Hema Malini. Dev was in London with Tina Munim for *Des Pardes* (1978). Hence, the schedule shifted by one more year, till 90 per cent of the film was completed by 1979, after which it became a challenge in terms of synchronizing dates. Tina was shooting for *Karz* (1980), Dev Anand was shooting *Loot Maar* (1980) where Tina had a major role, and Basu was doing two or three films as well. Amit had to put up the set for Dev's house twice, leading to additional costs.[298]

Vikas Desai, in an interview with the author, mentioned that he and Arunaraje Patil had thought of making a Hindi version of *My Fair Lady* before Basu made *Man Pasand*. Sanjeev Kumar was supposed to be the Indian version of Professor Henry Higgins, and Jaya Bhaduri was the chosen one to play a 'Gawalan', whose livelihood was selling dung cakes. The duo was also thinking of engaging R.D. Burman for the music. Like many projects, this too did not materialize.[299]

Man Pasand had quite a big star cast for a Basu Chatterji film. Getting them was another challenge. Girish, as India's answer to Colonel Hugh Pickering, was back. Mahmood from Dev's camp was there. A host of character artistes were onboarded too. Last-minute changes, inadvertent ones at that, happened. For example, the role of Champa, Kamli's (Tina) friend, was being played by someone who did not return after the first day. The scene, which was done at Panvel, had to be reshot with Madhu, who had acted in some Rajshri film before.[300]

Amit says:[301]

> For the train scenes, the first shoot happened inside a train. The rest we recreated at Mehboob Studios. We got an old bogie from the Railways. A scrapped one. The bogie was of an extended local which went to Virar, so the windows were like that of a third-class compartment.
>
> Basu-da was very economical with shot-taking. If he wanted an actor to underplay a scene, he used to say, '*Hey, paanch paisa kam kar do*' (tone down the overacting slightly). Or during a recording, '*Isko dus paisa badha do yaar sound ko*' (increase the volume marginally). He was the only film-maker apart from Hrishikesh Mukherjee who never took extra shots. If the cameraman suggested another take, he would say, 'Come on, it's all OK. Why do you want to waste time?'

> Likewise, he did not fritter away time during song sittings or recordings. He could extract the best out of the lyricists and the composer in just one or two sittings. He would narrate the situation and the song would happen. He would come to the recordings but would hardly interfere.
>
> 'Rehne Ko Ek Ghar Hoga', sung by Meena, was to be dubbed by Lata Mangeshkar. However, the version by Meena was retained to establish the contrast between Tina's voice before and after training. Meena used to sing in Marathi films. She has sung as part of the chorus. My favourite song from the film remains 'Main Akela Apne Dhun Mein Magan'. The film is my favourite, musically.

While the dazzlingly photographed 'Main Akela', sung by Kishore Kumar, is the showpiece of the film, Mohammed Rafi sang his last song for Dev in the film—'Logon Ka Dil Jeetna Hai Toh . . .'

Continues Amit:[302]

> I was happy with the result of *Man Pasand*. It was quite an economically made film, even with those stars. I had only one regret. The scale at which I wanted to pitch it did not happen. I had put up large sets. Basu-da, by temperament, was not a director who exploited locations and sets. He used to say, 'Don't spend money.' For example, we had put up a huge *bustee* set at Film City. He said, 'Why this, we could have shot this in a *chawl*. Why spend so much?' One day, KK said during the post shoot adda, '*Yaar, Basu, tum toh bara picture banata hi nahin hai. Bara picture ko bhi chota kar deta hai* (Basu, you never make a big film. You treat even big films like small films).'

Rajesh Roshan recalls an interesting incident about a song by Lata Mangeshkar in *Man Pasand*:[303]

> While we were recording the song 'Honthon Pe Geet Jaage', the atmosphere became mesmerizing. Mr Bansali, the

> recordist at Famous, Tardeo, who has recorded innumerable hit songs, became very excited, got up from his chair and recorded the song standing.

The premiere of *Man Pasand* happened on 11 July 1980, at Satyam, Worli. The blurb accompanying the publicity material was, 'Not the biggest, but the best.' The reaction of the crowd was neutral. It became very popular on the re-run circuit though—on TV. Basu, though, remained thoroughly dissatisfied with the film and would later say to the press that the Bengali version *Ogo Bodhu Sundari* (1981), which was made around the same time by Salil Dutta (which became Uttam Kumar's last acting venture), was much better than his interpretation of *My Fair Lady*.[304]

While Basu's statement was an act of self-deprecation, a similar benchmark was used a year before for another of his films.

The Daydreamer—2

While Basu was working with Rajesh, Dharam, Sanjeev, and Dev, *Manzil,* his film with Amitabh Bachchan, was still stuck. It was finally cleared by the censor board on 14 May 1979, and the release, an inauspicious one at that, happened seven years after the film was launched: 1 October 1979, at Sachinam. It was a Monday.

Viewers were dismissive. The naiveté of the Bengali story did not gel with Amitabh's superstar looks, and the inconsistency between the visuals resulting due to the break in the shooting was too conspicuous, almost in-your-face. A poor cousin of *Akash Kusum,* at best.

The reason behind the inordinate delay is unclear. Some say that after *Parwana* flopped, investors refused to pump in money for an Amitabh Bachchan-starrer. This made little sense. *Manzil* was launched a year after *Parwana.* Hence the flopping of the former could not have had a bearing on something which had the buy-in of the same set of producers a year later.

Another theory mentions Amitabh refusing to give dates after his sudden superstardom that began after mid-1973. This logic does not hold much water as Amitabh is known to honour his commitments.

A third angle, and an unexplored one, is the release of *Bandhe Haath* in early 1973. Anticipated to be a huge hit, the disastrous performance at the box office might have prompted financers to stop investing in Amitabh starrers. And while the same financiers came back to him after *Zanjeer* and *Abhimaan* (1973) became major successes, Amitabh was too much in demand to spare dates. Basu anyway was doing a lot of films then.

Whatever be the reason, *Manzil* remained a destination difficult to reach. It was through the efforts of the crew that it could be completed. Lalita Pawar also helped. She was playing Amitabh's mother in the film. Both her son and husband were among the producers.[305]

The gap of six years between the two phases of the shoot was the main reason why the film looked uneven. Amitabh's appearance had changed. The trademark glow and the superstar hairstyle were permanent features by then. He no longer looked the lower-middle class hopeful; the middle-class hopefuls now aspired to look like Amitabh.

Also, though Basu re-shot a few key scenes, including the climactic court scene, many scenes from the previous shooting spree remained. The final mix was very uneven.

Moushumi, the newlywed of 1972, was a mother of a four-year-old when the reshoot happened. Her face was fuller, and she had gained considerable weight. To bring the script more in line with the times, Basu re-wrote a few scenes, including the first meeting between the lead pair, borrowing the narrative from the real-life story of Lata Mangeshkar meeting Kishore Kumar on the way to Bombay Talkies. It probably was Basu's tribute to the singers of the famed tandem 'Rimjhim Gire Saawan'. Kishore's version, recorded much later, was filmed in a day and a half,[306] and became immensely famous on the radio and multiple compilations, starting with the HMV Album *Memories That Linger* (1980). When questioned about his work with R.D. Burman, Basu summed it up with a one-liner: 'Ah, what a song he created.'[307]

BOOK 3

Finding Oneself

'Maybe you are searching among the branches
for what only appears in the roots.'

—Rumi

The 9.10 a.m. Churchgate Local

Spread over 300 km, the parallel lines of the Bombay local trains have been crisscrossing the lives of millions for over a hundred years. Witness to innumerable stories of people cutting across all economic groups and social strata, especially the poor and the middle class, Bombay and its suburban train service are inseparable.

As was Bombay and the Western Railway line to Basu. Mentioning this to the author, he said:

> I have never written my autobiography. I had tried once but gave it up as the content could have hurt many. Neither have I made autobiographical films. But yes, one or two are reflections of my life. Like *Baton Baton Mein*. It is partly my story.
>
> During my early days, I would be riding the local train from Borivali to Churchgate. On average, it used to take an hour and five minutes. I had a fixed seat. The position of the seat could change, but the seat number would remain unaltered. You see, there are three seats per side on a local

> train. The unwritten rule was that four people used to sit on the three-seater wooden plank. I would always be the fourth passenger, sitting on the edge.
>
> I made my hero Amol Palekar sit in the same fashion in the film. I made him a cartoonist, just like me. I also made him wear glasses.[308]

While the origin of Amol's beard is nebulous with conflicting reports, one of which says that Basu based his looks on Mario Miranda, the great yesteryear cartoonist, there is little ambiguity about the character Tony Braganza played by Amol. A modern-day Basu who, like him, doodles during his train journey, but unlike him, finds his prospective bride in the process. For Tony, it was 'marriage at first sight'.

Similarly, there is little doubt about the milieu Basu wanted to capture. He does this rather tellingly, though the film's story—by C.J. Pavri of the BR Films Story Department—was not compelling enough to sustain the interest of the viewers. Fortunately, like most of Basu's films of that time, the innocence of the 1970s of the middle class comes through strongly, creating a sense of nostalgia, endearing the film to most of that generation, or for that matter, the Gen Y and Z as well.

★ ★ ★

The opening shot picks out the cross at the head of Saint Andrew's Church, Bandra, almost as a prayer to the Almighty to invoke his blessings for the success of the film. The camera bathes in the upscale suburb, the montage sweeping past the Light of Bandra restaurant, Jolly Dry Fruits Store, (the good old) Binny Textiles shop, the Raymond garment shop, a sugarcane juice vendor, shop signages elbowing each other trying to catch the customers' eye, and people, people and people . . . without a word of dialogue, the opening credit roll tells us that *Baton Baton Mein* is mostly about the Bandra suburb. Through the camera's fleeting eye, we see the announcement of an exhibition that tells us that the story starts somewhere in late October or early November.

The soon-to-unfurl saga is about a Christian family.

One morning, over a mug of coffee, the middle-aged Mrs Rosy Pereira has a woman-to-woman talk with her pretty twenty-something daughter Nancy, 'You know, dear, we, the Pereira family of Bandra, used to be very wealthy. In 1932, your grandfather built this stately two-storeyed Pereira Mansion with an expansive garden in front. But fortunes changed and our wealth dwindled as your father passed away young. I know it irritates you, but my singular priority now is to find a suitable boy for you at the earliest. Look, he must earn more than you because I want you to live a comfortable life.'

Thankfully, there was no scene like this. And that is what made *Baton Baton Mein* the film it is. If Basu Chatterji had used the above scene and dialogue, he would have employed what Robert McKee calls 'forcing words into a character's mouth to tell the audience about world, history or person'. Instead, Chatterji does what McKee advocates—'show, don't tell'. A low-angle opening shot in soft focus shows the two-storeyed Pereira mansion with a spread-out garden located in a leafy locality of Bandra. The number 1932 inscribed prominently on the road-facing wall is so typical of old houses those days. And the connect with the audience is formed. With a lost look in her eyes, Nancy (Tina Munim) is listening to an English song on a gramophone player while her brother Saby (Ranjit Chowdhry) is playing his violin. And we see that the Pereira family is musically inclined.

'We shot at this old bungalow in Bandra. Between Carter Road and Sea Rock Hotel (now defunct), there is a small area that had a row of small bungalows belonging to only Christians. Christians were given this area perhaps. Gradually, most of the bungalows gave way to buildings; but this bungalow was thankfully there when we were shooting for *Baton Baton Mein*. The road was very narrow with little traffic desecrating the silence, making the shoot easy,' recollects Arup Gangoly, who was an assistant to Basu for the film.[309]

The house was like a set. Maintained moderately well, and serving as a flashback to the doors, latches, cupboards, washbasin and switchboards, which can now be termed as vintage accessories. The paint on some of the inner walls of the house had chipped off, though. As Nancy and her elderly uncle, Tom (played by David) prepare to leave for Bandra station to catch the 9.10 a.m. local, we observe that the garden is green but a tad overgrown. The old boundary walls of the house are moss-covered due to lack of maintenance.

Once again, images do the storytelling.

Baton Baton Mein had a flavoured cast too. And most of them—Amol Palekar, Pearl Padamsee, David, Piloo Wadia, Arvind Deshpande, Sobhini Singh, Tina Munim and Ranjit Chowdhry—looked their character in the film. Ditto for Uday Chandra, who is till day remembered for his five-minute appearance. In an exclusive interview with the author, he describes how the role of Henry, the frail-looking softie whose love for Nancy goes unreciprocated, happened.[310]

> You know, I wanted to do Indian classical music, and on the advice of my friends, joined the FTII. One of my friends from St Xavier's, Bombay, was Shabana Azmi who helped me get into FTII. She was a year senior to me at the institute. I graduated in 1974, and after some struggle, landed the film *Khel Khilari Ka* (1977). A couple of years later, one evening, at around 8.30 p.m., I got a call. Shabana was on the line. She said, 'Can you come to Basu-da's?' I landed up there, and as I was walking up the stairs, Basu-da, who was sitting on the sofa and watching, burst out laughing. It was a peal of very endearing laughter. He knew in his mind that I was the actor he was looking for. Looking back, I recall he had mentioned the role to Shabana who must have told him that she had just the guy in mind.
>
> Basu-da asked for three days of my time. '*Teen din ka kaam hai*. I will pay you [this] money. Come down tomorrow, I need to get your costume stitched.'

> We used to shoot in a bungalow behind St Andrew's Church. One of my scenes was to walk along the road to the house. I knew the place rather well; as a child I used to take the road to school. This shoot happened almost in a jiffy.
>
> On the set, I was very nervous, to the extent that I had to take out my hanky and wipe the sweat off my face. '*Isko rakho, rakho, aise hi karo* (keep doing it, don't stop),' exclaimed Basu-da. My nervousness was a prerequisite for the scene at the bungalow. The entire scene was like a small tea party. Very beautifully done. I felt I was meeting a real family. Ranjit (Chowdhry) became a friend.

The onboarding of Ranjit Chowdhry, if some reports are to be relied upon, was based on a suggestion to Basu by Ranjit himself. Doesn't Nancy need a younger brother?

★ ★ ★

Baton Baton Mein was the second instance of the mother and son duo essaying their real-life roles on screen. By that time, Pearl had polished her Hindi. Ranjit had done a few plays and was more screen-friendly. As Saby, Nancy's scruffy-haired younger brother with schoolboy looks, he is like the common man in R.K. Laxman's cartoons, the silent observer, if at times of the mocking variety, perhaps laughing his pants off in the privacy of his room at this hullaballoo about Nancy's marriage. Every time Rosy's worry becomes vocal, Saby waltzes into the room with his violin like a bard, rendering a hilariously soulful tune signalling his meddlesome mother to stop making heavy weather of bright mornings. His satirical and bittersweet reaction is a great stress-buster, keeping the Basu Chatterji variety of comedy running through the fabric of the film.

Traditional, good-intentioned, inter-family banter also raises its head, sparingly, as in Marie's (Uncle Tom's wife, played by Lulu Patel) comment about Rosy to Tom: '*Kabhi akal se kuch kaam kiya ho toh, aakhir hai toh tumhari behan*' (Has she ever used her head? No wonder. She is, after all, your sister).

There are a few other interesting characters as well—old Philomena Aunty (Leela Mishra) from Versova, who often lands up and claims that she wants to leave immediately but ends up staying for two to three days. She is the quintessential family elder who alludes to her decades of experience in being able to discern Tony's dubious intent. She is always sceptical, pretending to be pragmatic, and plonks herself down as an informal marriage broker.

If Tony Braganza is often buttonholed by Nancy's mom for his indecisiveness, at home he has his mother Mrs Braganza (Piloo Wadia), the mother of all control freaks, to contend with. Refusing to let her son as much as select his safari suit, she is convinced that she, and only she, has the right and the capability to select the right bride for her 'little boy' and that Tony has no business seeing any other girl. Poor Mr Braganza (Tony's father, played by Arvind Deshpande) hides behind the morning newspaper at his wife's routine onslaught.

But it is an inanimate object which is the main character in the film: the Churchgate local.

Matches, they say, are made in heaven. In *Baton Baton Mein*, it was made on the local train. The 9.10 a.m. local is witness to the love story created by the master of ceremonies at Filmfare Awards, David Abraham. Basu Chatterji also plays a passenger, as if observing the proceedings, and one gets to see his white tuft of hair and glasses for a split second from behind in two successive sequences.

Arup Gangoly describes how the train sequences were shot:[311]

> We had hired a train for a few days. The shoot would start at 11 a.m. and continue till 4 p.m. when the main crowd was not there. It was a normal local train, given to us by Western Railway, and we would be travelling from Churchgate to Dahisar and back. A lot of junior artistes were used to fill the compartments. We had been allocated the fast track to prevent

> people from boarding. The train had make-up rooms, change rooms for costumes, etc. Food was also organized inside the train. The train shoot was completed in two to three days. It was planned meticulously. Basu Chatterji was extremely organized. While he did not do storyboards, he would sketch the shots when needed. On the script, which I would type out for him, on the margin, he would make a small frame, suggesting how the shot would look on the screen, things like the man on the left-hand side and the girl on the right-hand side, etc.
>
> There were instances when he would shoot based on ideas he had in his mind. In absence of the shot documentation, we would get confused and ask, 'Basu-da, what is this supposed to be?' To which he would reply, 'We'll see.' Later, in the editing room, we would realize that the shot was for a song sequence.

A.K. Bir, the cinematographer for *Baton Baton Mein*, was a master of train shoots, having burnt his fingers shooting inside the train in *27 Down* (1973). No additional light other than sunlight was used.

Another character in the film is the suburb. Barring the bustle, which is the local train travel, Basu's Bombay is a cosy hamlet, especially for the young lovers who hang out at the Bandra Bandstand, the locale a kilometre away from Bandra Fort, made famous by the pair of Archana and Navin Nischol in Hrishikesh Mukherjee's lovable comedy *Buddha Mil Gaya* (1971). Unlike *Piya ka Ghar, Rajnigandha,* or *Chhoti Si Baat*, Basu's Bombay in *Baton Baton Mein* doesn't take us to the traffic-burdened arteries. The regular meeting place of Tony and Nancy, at the rocks at the fag-end of the island city with the sea crashing in, is not very far away from where Nancy lives. *Baton Baton Mein*'s Bombay is a calm and quiet one. The associated traffic with the emerging vertical structures was not a nagging problem yet.

★ ★ ★

Going back forty years in time, one interprets *Baton Baton Mein* as a story about well-meaning but insensitive elders forcing their decisions on their children who would abhor being taken for granted. Even Uncle Tom (David), who is otherwise an adorable old man, is bent on extricating the precise details of the breakup between Nancy and her ex, Peter (Deb Mukerji). His mindset—despite the good intentions—fails to respect the privacy his darling niece deserves. Like his sister Rosy, he too is indifferent to the aspirations and goals of the new generation. Thankfully, Tony and Nancy do not jump off a rocky cliff, nor do they elope. Neither do they mind breaking into a song when the situation demands.

Talking about songs, Shyamal Mitra had first been entrusted with the task of writing the music for the film. He had also composed the title song, though the recording was yet to happen.[312] Fate was unkind to him, and he had to be replaced by Rajesh Roshan who was a more saleable name in Bombay. Roshan did not disappoint. Though he had become very busy then and was left with little time to devote specifically for the film, two songs became blockbusters: 'Uthe Sab Ke Qadam' (sung by Lata Mangeshkar, Amit Kumar, and Pearl Padamsee[313]) and 'Suniye, Kahiye' (sung by Kishore Kumar and Asha Bhosle). With time, the other two, 'Kahan Tak Yeh Man Ko' (Kishore Kumar) and 'Na Bole Tum Na Maine Kuch Kaha' (Asha Bhosle and Amit Kumar), both written by Yogesh, have become popular too. Amit Khanna, who wrote the lyrics for the two songs mentioned earlier, also recollects that Basu shot *Baton Baton Mein* during the phase he was doing *Man Pasand*. He completed the shoot in one month flat, while *Man Pasand* was delayed for quite some time.[314]

Serious film buffs looking for life-changing equations in a film would have an issue with *Baton Baton Mein*, as, like most Basu's films, it had no message to be driven home. As a storyteller, Basu also remained on the side of conservatism, advocating the importance of marriage not only as a necessary landmark in life but also as a certificate of a long-term commitment. But that was Basu. A believer in simple solutions to complex problems, he hardly ever broke basic paradigms which set social revolutionaries discussing poverty, socialism and mass struggle in spas and five-star coffee shops.

Do spare a thought for poor Asrani—always losing out in the last mile to the altar. Playing the role of Francis, he lands up confidently on a Sunday at St Andrew's Church, all set to marry Nancy. Only to find out that Nancy and Tony are having their wedding photograph clicked.

A Bit of the Sky

Baton Baton Mein, released on 13 April 1979 at Regal, a premier theatre in Bombay that incidentally was where R.D. Burman's love story began in 1964,[315] had a moderate run. But it was the re-runs during noon shows, on cable TV and OTT platforms that imparted to the film its longevity. The reason for this strong recall was a function of Basu's vision. The characters, all of them, were nicely drawn. They had shades of grey. They were people who came right out of our families, friends and acquaintances. Basu's mantra for the characters of Tony, Saby, Rosy and Uncle Tom, among others, was to be attentive to places, people and situations he had got to know.

Uday Chandra recollects that he has remained in the public consciousness courtesy of the film. This is interesting, given the fact that few remember his name. Christened Dhruv in his first film *Khel Khilari Ka*, the titles of *Baton Baton Mein* credited him as 'Uday'. Nearing seventy, this Pune-based dramatist goes back in time to something pleasantly surprising for him.[316]

> *Baton Baton Mein* is the only film I am remembered for. I was more visible in the film as a character. Thirty-something years after *Baton Baton Mein* was released, I was invited by Shabana for Javed Akhtar's sixty-fifth birthday party at Hyatt, Santacruz.

> Tina Munim, by that time, was very big. She had quit films and married Anil Ambani who was a leading industrialist. A few years ago, I had sent across a request to her to attend my mother's art exhibition. She did not come; maybe the note did not reach her. I just let it be. Anyway, Tina was one of the guests at the party hosted by Shabana. In the course of the party, Tina, when she saw me, was almost zapped, to the extent that she shouted, 'Henryyyyyy!' with her mouth remaining that way, open, for about half a minute.

Cleared by the censor board within four months of *Baton Baton Mein* was a Basu film that incidentally did not enjoy the joyride of the Amol-Tina starrer. A film with a difference, in the sense that Basu would question the building blocks of a traditional mindset.

Jeena Yahan (1979) was Basu's attempt at displaying solidarity towards the city he chose to live in. Somewhat like Hrishikesh Mukherjee's *Anand* (1970) that was dedicated to the city which he called his home. While the logic behind *Anand* being dedicated to Bombay was its indomitable spirit, Basu's focus in *Jeena Yahan* was a comparison setup between the city and his village of dreams, Madhupur.

⋆ ⋆ ⋆

Basu's 'Bombay' background was set with outdoor montages; shots of pedestrians walking heel-to-heel at peak hours, the overflowing local trains which, like in *Baton Baton Mein* and *Piya Ka Ghar*, is a private-public place for personal conversations without the worry of being overheard. Lekha (Shabana Azmi) and Shekhar (Shekhar Kapur), the lead pair, somehow scramble to get into the local train, an indication that local train travel was one of the many challenges of Bombay. Basu draws heavily from the problems faced by people in the city—not limited to Bombay, though.

Like the problem of Sushma (Zarina Wahab in a short role), whose father (Abu Sivani) would not approve of her alliance with

Dinesh (Amol Palekar), a singer in a drama troupe. Not the job a strict father would approve of.

There are more friends, with problems of their own. Shipra (Vidya Sinha), a widow with a little daughter, is opening a kindergarten and has enrolled twenty-five children by campaigning door to door, and she is highly anxious, wondering if at all there would be a decent turnout at the inauguration. And there is yet another friend of Shekhar called Verma (V.K. Sharma) who has run up huge domestic debts because his factory has been under lockout for months now. Union leader Subhas (Arup Gangoly) is a fighter, and is bullish about the workmen running the factory.

Chatterji cements the fact that the core of Bombay is all about struggle. The duet, 'Hum Nahin Dukh Se Ghabrayenge' (sung by Lata Mangeshkar and Yesudas) echoes the struggle, as in the words of Yogesh:

Hai nahi sukh zara sa
Charo taraf hai nirasha
Phir bhi chhodenge na aasha
Har dum muskurayenge

Composed by Salil Chowdhury, the tune goes back almost a decade when it was used as part of the background score in *Anand* (1970). Was it a conscious decision by Salil and Basu for the tune to serve as a tribute to Hrishikesh and Bombay? One would never know.

The layers of helplessness are, however, not limited to a particular generation. Sushma's father's frustration at his daughter's choice stems from the fact that the middle-aged man has been unemployed for a year or more. He knows which side the bread is buttered, and therefore, his forceful dissuasion of his daughter's choice of Dinesh is well-meant, after all. Like in most films of Basu, the city woman is a pillar of strength, exemplified by Sushma's mother, in a short but brilliant portrayal by Sudha Shivpuri.

It is in the spirit of Bombay that all of them—Lekha, Shekhar, Shipra, Dinesh, Sushma and Verma—appear happy hanging out together and coping with their struggles without grumbling. And most importantly, united. As Dinesh says, '*Yahi to Bambai hai. Ye bheed, yeh garmi, yeh ghutan, phir bhi sari takleefon ke bawajood sab yahin tikey hain. Pata nahi kaun si kashish, kaun si asha ki kiran hame yahan baandhi hui hai* (This is Bombay. The crowd, the heat, the congestion. Despite all this, a ray of hope makes us want to cling on here).' Words similar to the dialogue in *Piya Ka Ghar*. This dialogue is the voice of the film-maker. Bombay is the city of water rationing, houses with scarce ventilation and natural light, a peep-of-the sky, and measured timings. But Bombay is also the gateway to a world of opportunities.

The initial reaction of a 'Mumbaikar' tired of Bombay's bustle was a getaway. Where they went was of not much importance. Getting away was all that mattered. Basu brings a delectable contrast between the calmness of the rural world and the simmering tension inside the house. And the exact opposite in Bombay's city life where the external world is a churning cauldron but there is an oasis of peace inside the house.

★ ★ ★

However, sticking to a formula can be counterproductive. The Bombay of Basu is stylistically almost indistinguishable from his previous Bombay-based films. The only separator, apart from a few establishing shots by KK, is the tenor. *Jeena Yahan* had a sombre one.

One wishes that Basu had been more subtle and relaxed in the exposition of his characters, as he had been in his other classics. He appears to be in a hurry to narrate their stories within the first thirty minutes. Moreover, after the first thirty minutes, apart from Lekha, none of those characters are to be seen, except in the last scene. So, the character arcs remain incomplete.

Flaws in logic crop up too. Shekhar advises Lekha to take a break and enjoy her holidays at his ancestral house in Madhupur. There is a big gap in the story here. Shekhar married Lekha without his family's approval. Would it not be natural that he accompanied her on her first visit to his home? Further, gauging from the instant familiarity and the spontaneous warmth with which her in-laws welcome her to their run-down village house, has Lekha already been to her in-laws' place earlier? When was that? Adding to the confusion is the comment by Shekhar's mother (Dina Pathak) that Shekhar and Lekha have been married for two years.

These missing pieces confuse the viewer. And Basu doesn't go deep enough into the backstories either. There is a hurry to shift from scene to scene, in comparison to the relaxed deportment which marked most of his earlier films.

The film also suffers from weak characterizations compared to most of Basu's films, barring the odd one like *Tumhare Liye*. While the village seems to be an escape from the aggravations of city life, the characters in the household are cardboard cut-outs. Not only do they behave predictably, but individuality is strictly exorcised. We witness a classic power struggle, a standoff between generations where the older generation, earmarked as grumpy old hags, give the young ones no leeway. A rare case of miscasting hits you too; the villagers, all of them including Deena Pathak, Arvind Deshpande, Rajeeta Thakur, Ranjana Sachdev and Devendra, look city-bred and forcibly implanted in a village, though one would agree with the selection of Kiran Vairale who made her debut in this film. She is bubbly, positive and inherits no mannerisms from her stage work. Her naivete is natural. Her sequences with her sister-in-law (Shabana Azmi) are nice, though Basu's indulgence in pan-and-zoom restricts the visual grandeur, something which could have been exploited better.

Akhola-born Kiran Vairale, now an entrepreneur shuffling between homes in New York and Cape Town, has an interesting take on the use of light in the film. And she shares the same in an interview with the author:[317]

> You see, I feel that there's a philosophy behind the use of shades of darkness in *Jeena Yahan*. It begins on a cheerful note. Bombay is shown to have a lot of sunshine. Gradually, the darkness takes over. When Shabana goes to the village, it's all so bright and sunny and so on, till darker hues make their presence felt in the dingy house. So, there's a lot of internment in the minds of people there, which is in sharp contrast to the outward lustre of the place. And when she returns to Bombay, her house has a fresh coat of paint and is visibly livelier. In a nutshell, the use of light is in direct relation to the heroine's state of mind.

Jeena Yahan was started before the Janata Government came to power. We find Coca-Cola being consumed during the function organized for the school inauguration.[318] A major part of the shoot was completed during the Emergency, and the film was scheduled for an August 1977 release. Among the distributors roped in was Shashi Kapoor, who had bought the rights for the Bombay region. Unfortunately, the film got stuck for over a year and a half. Though the film marked the debut of Kiran Vairale, it became her third film. The actress who won a lot of hearts in the late 1970s and the early 1980s discusses her journey in cinema with Basu Chatterji:[319]

> In 1976, I was in my second year at St Xavier's College, Bombay, when one day, Utkarsh Mazumdar, the famous theatre actor who was then at Xavier's too, told me about a group called IPTA and that Satyadev Dubey was casting a play with five female roles. He was looking for a lot of girls and asked me to just go and do a script reading. The play was *Sambhog se Sanyas Tak*. I got cast as the Sutradhar, in one of the main roles. My co-artistes included Ratna Pathak, Sushma Tendulkar (Vijay Tendulkar's younger daughter) and Naseeruddin Shah. The romance between Naseer and Ratna started there.

Dubey was writing the script for *Bhumika* (1977) then. After the rehearsals, he would always drop us home. One day, with our permission, he took a detour and went to a studio where the dubbing of Shyam Benegal's *Manthan* (1976) was going on. Smita Patil was there. I knew her as both our fathers were politicians, and we started chatting. Shyam Benegal and Dubey were also chatting, and one of them said, 'Do you think it will work?' Then they made me and Smita stand side by side, trying to figure out if we would look like mother and daughter. And in no time, I was offered three scenes as Smita's daughter in *Bhumika*.

Two or three days after I said yes to Benegal, my phone rang and the person at the other end said, 'I am Basu Chatterji. You know, there is a role in one of my films, and I would like to meet you.' *Rajnigandha* was a big sensation then, and I was sure that the caller at the other end could not have been Basu Chatterji. I thought that one of my friends had found out that I am doing three scenes in *Bhumika* and was playing a prank on me. So, nonchalantly, I replied, 'Oh, sure. I am doing a play at Chhabildas High School, Dadar. Why don't you come there?' Chhabildas is in a very crowded area, and you had to climb up three or four floors via a rickety staircase to reach the hall. I was sure that someone of the stature of Basu Chatterji would not come to a crowded area to watch a play starring me, Amrish Puri, Sunil Shanbag, et al. And to put things in perspective, I had also forgotten about it, assuming it was a prank.

When the play started, someone came up to me and said, 'Kiran, Basu Chatterji is here to meet you.' I was dumbfounded. 'Yeah, he is among the audience in the hall,' the man replied. Dubey was there, and he helped me regain my composure and accompanied me when I went to meet Basu-da after the play. As we met, I told him that I was sorry, I had assumed that someone was joking, else I wouldn't have made him come all the way. 'No, no, I enjoyed watching the

> play. And I am serious,' he replied. Apparently, Mr Tendulkar's daughter who was in the play had put in a word to Basu-da about me when he was searching for a young girl for a role in his forthcoming film.
>
> So, while I verbally agreed to play Smita's daughter first, I first faced the camera at Rajkamal Studio where Basu-da had put up a set of the village house. The shot was welcoming my sister-in-law (Shabana) when she arrives at our home.
>
> My college classes used to finish at 1 p.m. For *Jeena Yahan*, I would be taken to the 2 p.m.–10 p.m. shift to the studio. I was given printed cotton sarees to wear, and my shoulder-length hair was augmented by a 'gangawan' (wig made of natural hair). This was used to give me the look Basu-da wanted. For the outdoor shoot in Mysore, he waited for my summer holidays. My mother accompanied me there.

One of the reasons why *Jeena Yahan* had a delayed release could be attributed to an interruption in completing the remaining part of the shoot. Breaks in the film would add up to continuity issues as well. In the case of *Jeena Yahan*, fragmented logic.

* * *

Basu would, from time to time, mention that *Jeena Yahan* was close to his heart. He probably saw a slice of his fight in the film. Unfortunately, distributors were not enthused by Basu's stories of struggle. A Filmfare Critics Award for Best Film of 1979 notwithstanding, the film failed to be part of the normal distribution network. It was only through select theatres, and that too years later—like Nandan in Calcutta—that the film would reach the masses. Another reason for the film's lack of popularity could be the excessive use of indoor shoots. In effect, it looked more like a telefilm. Thematically, it was significant, as Shabana Azmi puts it to the author. '*Jeena Yahan,* I feel, is a very underrated film. It is an important film and can be made even today.'[320]

Mannu Bhandari was not so generous. Her take was surmised thus: 'Basu-da had also made a film on my story *Ekhane Akash Nei*. The film was neither well made, nor did it do well commercially.'[321]

* * *

Ekhane Akash Nei has an interesting backstory. The base material was sourced from Bhandari's experiences as a schoolteacher in Calcutta. The events go back to the mid-1950s when the film *Shapmochan* (1955) had become a rage in Bengal. Starring Uttam Kumar and Suchitra Sen in the lead, the film saw the Hemanta Mukherjee-Uttam Kumar partnership flower. One of the songs of the film, 'Shono Bondhu Shono, Pranheen Ei Shohorer Itikatha', was about the lack of human values in the city called Calcutta. 'Ekhane Akash Nei', the fourth line of the song, gave the story its name.

Bhandari's story was about the Calcutta of the 1950s. Basu transposed it, almost in its entirety, to Bombay and the late 1970s. The fitment did not happen. A black-and-white period film with Calcutta as the epicentre might have worked better. And surely with more visuals and fewer dialogues.

* * *

Visuals were the toast of *Ratnadeep* (1979). Shot in Mysore within the premises of the Lalitha Mahal Palace Hotel, this was Basu's most ornate work. However, despite the meticulous use of colour, decorative set design, low light photography, and controlled acting, especially from Girish Karnad, the film fizzled away from public memory.

The reasons were many, of which the comparison with the 1951-released bilingual by Debaki Bose is one. Bose's version was taut and dramatic. Taking liberty with the original story by Prabhat Kumar Mukhopadhyay, he had altered the ending, making it a hopeful one. In the original, the heroine dies; death was considered a respectable option for a widow in the early twentieth century. Basu stuck to the original ending but made an uncalled-for modification that robbed the screenplay of the dramatic element. The tension in the original story was augmented by the hero's dilemma; apart from being an imposter, he is caught in the web of two women: his purported wife and his estranged wife. Basu made the hero a bachelor, in the process sacrificing a major part of the tautness that was the strength of the plot.

The film was witness to incidents purely trivial, one of which was Hema Malini's questioning of A.K. Bir's competence in lighting the set. The lighting was also innovative for its time. Bir recollects:[322]

> For additional shoots, Basu-da had put up a set at Film City. We had arranged the lighting in such a manner that both day and night scenes could be shot back-to-back just by switching on/off a few lights. The shift was so fast that the actors would get frustrated . . . 'I've just finished one shot, and you are back with another immediately?'
>
> At that time, we mostly used incandescent lights, solar or tungsten halogen lights. The studio had these lamps, and we had to specify the specifications and quantity so that they could be blocked. The more, the merrier.

The grapevine was also ripe with rumours about Hema Malini and Girish Karnad having an affair. In his biography, Girish mentions the backstory:[323]

> After the spectacular success of *Swami*, Jaya Chakravarthy began work on the film *Ratnadeep* and paired Hema with me in it. One evening, when we were shooting in Khajuraho [*sic*], Hema asked me to accompany her on a walk and asked the important question. She said, 'The press is saying we are going to get married. How do you feel about the idea?' I said, 'Thanks. Look, I don't give any importance to what the press says. My reason for saying no is that I am engaged to someone in the United States.'

Basu reused his lucky mascot—Prabha, this time played by Nandita Thakur. All these bits and parts did not add up to the potential which the story had. Today, 'Kabhi Kabhi Sapna Lagta Hai' (sung by Kishore Kumar and Asha Bhosle to the music of RD and Gulzar's lyrics) is probably the only reason someone might express an interest in the film.

★ ★ ★

Around that time, to harmonize Bengali stories or stars with the Bombay milieu, Basu had delivered a few more turkeys. Prominent among them were *Do Ladke Dono Kadke* (1978) and *Prem Vivah* (1979). Produced under the banner of the Sippys and financed by Jayanta Mukherjee, son of Hemant Kumar, *DLDK* was a comic disaster. It was verbose, had too many characters resulting in confusion, and became a drag fest with the viewers losing interest in the plot. Which was flawed, anyway, as Basu had taken the risk of adapting the story of *Sadhu Judhishtirer Karcha* (1974), which, despite the pair of Robi Ghosh—who was the story writer, director and one of the two leads—and Chinmoy Roy, proven comics both, had suffered calamitous commercial consequences.

> *Sadhu Judhishtirer Karcha* was Jaya Bhaduri's last Bengali film till she came back to do a few more decades later. This is one of the many films which is lost. Permanently.

Having the Sippy banner came with the saving grace of excellent background music, recorded previously for films like *Abhimaan* (1973). *DLDK* was the only professional partnership of Hemant Kumar and Basu, and a particular song—'Chanda Ki Doli Mein'—a honey-laden duet between Asha Bhosle and Yesudas became moderately popular, though the Bengali original by Lata Mangeshkar in *Sanai* (1977) is more evocative.[324]

Popularity did not trouble *Prem Vivah*. Despite Utpal Dutt's funny act of wallowing around in confusion, and the excellent chemistry in real life between Bindiya Goswami and Asha Parekh (who played Bindiya's elder sister), the film was completely lacking in drama cohesive enough to catch the fancy of the viewers. Mithun Chakraborty, then almost new to the industry, was known to Bindiya from the time he was a dancer using the pseudonym Rana Rez. He was her brother Rajiv's friend and a regular visitor to her house in Bandra, Bombay. This was his first film with Basu, who would later mention to the author that he had difficulty in getting Mithun on board as producers did not want to cast him. Dark skin, they would say. 'I was happy he proved them all wrong.'[325] The producer initially also refused to get the costume stitched for Mithun. Basu refused to shoot unless he was provided the necessary ones.[326]

Despite the failure, Basu considered *Prem Vivah* to be a stepping stone to a few more projects where he would use Mithun's services.

★ ★ ★

Conceived in the late 1970s but released in early 1982 was another film where Bindiya had Utpal Dutt as a co-star, playing her father-in-law. *Hamari Bahu Alka* (*HBA*). Based on Manoj Basu's 1940s story *Ekoda Nishith Kaale* and inspired by *Ek Tuku Basha* (1965), Tarun Majumdar's Bengali film on the same story, this was as tame as a sheep and as trackless as the sea. The strength of Basu's simple and often timid stories was the sudden introduction of a character. It would often change the complexion of the story. Examples are many—Naveen in *Rajnigandha*, Nagesh in *Chhoti Si Baat*, Ghanashyam in *Swami* or Sunil Krishan in *Chitchor*. *HBA* had none. Devoid of any surprises or drama, *HBA* flattered to deceive. The only takeaway is that Alka Yagnik had her first known break in Hindi cinema, about which Rajesh Roshan mentions, 'Alka once came to my music room and sang 'Yeh Raatein Nayi Purani' (*Julie,* 1975). I was highly impressed and decided then and there to give her a break. She was living in Calcutta; I called her and said that there is a song waiting for you.'[327]

HBA was the first Basu film to be shot in an air-conditioned environment. One assumes it was Seth Studio, which had its boundaries with Natraj Studio. Arup Gangoly, who had a reasonably long role in this film, bid adieu to cinema after this film. It was Rakesh Roshan's last film with Basu, as was Bindiya's.

Bindiya remembers Utpal Dutt with great affection, especially as he would exude sparkling fun all the time. As she mentions to the author:[328]

> Utpal-da was an actor I enjoyed working with. Because he used to have us in splits before shots after shots and also during shots. So full of the smile; and that chuckle of his. When we did *Prem Vivah*, we used to keep chuckling because he is in love with me. And I am in love with Mithun-da, trying to set up Utpal-da with my elder sister played by Asha-ji. It was also very funny. It was kind of a quadrangle, you see. During a song sequence, we had to go and shoot in the middle of Marine Drive, where the Queen's Necklace is. There we had to go inside the sea to do some boat shots, and we had to show that we are laughing and cracking up, and I remember him making us laugh by saying numbers. For example, he used to say, 'And then, 78!' We would crack up. The boat did not capsize, thankfully; could have been disastrous if it did, as I do not know swimming. Our chemistry in *Hamari Bahu Alka* was also great; even my daughters wonder why this film did not do well.

And so did another Bengali, who probably made the greatest comedy in Hindi cinema ever, a film which starred Utpal Dutt and Bindiya as father and daughter.

> Noted author, scriptwriter, and dialogue writer Kamleshwar, whose voiceover in *Chhoti Si Baat* is quite well-known, played a cameo as a television presenter in *Prem Vivah*. He was called Kamleshwar in the film.

Middle-of-the-Road Cinema . . . or End of the Road?

'For after all, the best thing one can do
when it's raining is to let it rain.'
—Henry Wadsworth Longfellow

For Twin's Sake

Middle-of-the-road cinema came with its roadblocks. Despite their immense popularity, the leads remained small-time stars. In a country where cinema was still viewed as an alternative to the circus, acting skills were weighed with parameters and aesthetics very different from art. Perhaps it was with this in mind that Hrishikesh Mukherjee would go ahead and write a sequence in his film *Gol Maal* (1979) where the leading man Amol Palekar would become Amitabh Bachchan. It was a dream, and not an aspiration. It could never happen. The big star was larger than life. The next-door-boy actor would have to bask in fancied glory. Mukherjee tipped his hat to Basu as well, as we find Deven Verma mentioning a Basu-da film, a fictional one, *Meri Ma Kaun Hai*. Basu was the small film-maker who, in his way, had become big.

Mukherjee probably had no idea that *Gol Maal* would be a game-changer. Amol Palekar's transformation from a simpleton to a city slick had been initiated by Basu in *Chhoti Si Baat*. With *Gol Maal*, the transition was complete. The contributing factors included polyester shirts with psychedelic prints, a right-side hair parting (something in vogue in the western world), an attitude that went along with the twin who was not there, the stereophonic voice of Kishore Kumar, and the brass-driven music of Rahul Dev Burman with album covers of Bread, Elvis, George Baker and Gordon Lightfoot staring at you.

Amol Palekar did not become Amitabh Bachchan. But *Gol Maal*, probably the most amazing comedy in Hindi cinema ever, raised the bar for the middle-of-the road cinema. Drama became an essential component; simple stories about people we encounter in our day-to-day lives were gradually passé. The Asiad in 1982 in a way marked the urbanization of the country, and to quote Javed Akhtar, the people who gravitated from villages to cities became the first-generation middle class of the 1980s.[329] The expectation from cinema was high-voltage stuff. No wonder that Mukherjee, in *Naram Garam* (1981), his brilliant follow-up film to *Gol Maal*, failed to create the magic of the former. Only Sai Paranjpye's *Chashme Buddoor* (1981) and *Katha* (1982), with unassuming stories told in a manner most lucid and picturesque, kept the banner flying. These are acknowledged as classics and are among the most in-demand films on OTT platforms. Like Basu, Sai also had a very strong technical team headed by 1976 FTII graduate Virendra Saini, who considered K.K. Mahajan as the first star from the institute. KK by then was working less for Basu, and it was with a Goa trip that the partnership would run into rough weather once more after *Tumhare Liye*.

Despite being extremely well-made, *Gol Maal* too had bloopers. The exhibition match between New York Cosmos Club and Mohun Bagan was on 24 September 1977. The first Test between India and Australia which Ram Prasad (Amol) mentions to his sister happened on 2 December 1977. The hockey match between India and Pakistan at Bombay happened on 9 February 1978. Mukherjee confuses the timeline, the three are mentioned as simultaneous events in the film.

Gol Maal was inspired by the Bengali film *Kana Machi* (1961) with Anoop Kumar impersonating his non-existent twin and romancing Sabitri Chatterjee. Gautam Banerjee, son of actor Bhanu Banerjee, mentions that the negative of the film was hired by Hrishikesh Mukherjee. On the return trip, the first reel, which had the titles, was lost in transit. Another print of the film was at New Theatres Studio, and that too was lost as the reels melted due to heat. Tara Burman, the producer, was not interested in restoring the film. 'This was very disappointing for me as my father had received the Ultorath Award for Best Comedian. His role was done by Utpal Dutt in Hindi.'[330]

Utpal Dutt would be a prominent member of the Goa trip as well, in a film that was Basu's tribute to his technicians.

The Libidinous Trio

Real-Life Inspirations

Inder Raj Anand, among Hindi cinema's prominent script and dialogue writers of all time, had, in the early 1960s, at the insistence of Subhash Desai, planned a film titled *Chhoti Si Duniya*. While the technicians who were signed included Subrata Mitra, the star cast kept on changing, from Soumitra Chatterjee and Sharmila Tagore to Raj Kapoor and Nutan. The film was never made; Desai had signed too many films at the same time to accommodate one more. But in the process of the interaction with the Calcutta-based technicians, Anand befriended Satyajit Ray's art director, Bansi Chandragupta. It was either courtesy Anand's or his son Tinnu Anand's recommendation to Rajinder Bhatia (or his sons) that Bansi landed a film in Bombay. This was the late 1960s. Once Bansi came to Bombay, he gave his house keys to Tinnu who was going back to Calcutta to work with Satyajit Ray in *Aranyer Din Ratri* (1970).[331]

In Bombay, Bansi was put up at the North Bombay Society in Juhu. Despite appreciation from the very best in the industry and approval of the film festival crowd, Bansi could never become a big producer's art director in Bombay. He remained an integral part of Rajinder Bhatia and Basu Chatterji's cinema only. 'Bansi was a very honest man. And you can't survive in a cut-throat industry if you are honest. He was such an honest person that he would not allow any corruption in his department, something that did not suit many people around him. The managers would make money in the form of commissions from suppliers. Bansi would just not allow that,' Tinnu tells the author.[332]

In 1981, Bansi had just been signed for Basu's *Shaukeen* when he passed away after suffering a massive cardiac arrest in New York on 27 June, R.D. Burman's birthday. A bachelor, Bansi would often paint and take still photographs during shoots. He had a peculiar habit of switching his glasses from time to time. One for reading, and the other for long-distance vision.

In this act of Bansi, Basu found his Om Prakash Chaudhry.[333]

* * *

He was an outlier. In a fraternity that prides itself on the use of colloquialism and the vernacular, he spoke English with a convent-educated accent. Intending to join the army, he ended up passing out of the institute with a gold medal in 1966. His first film took him from Japan to Lebanon via Iran. One of the rare sound engineers to have worked with James Ivory, Mrinal Sen, Mani Kaul, Kumar Shahani, Satyajit Ray, Basu Chatterji, Gulzar and Sai Paranjpye, among others, his manner earned him the nickname 'Etiquette' by fellow technicians. While Narinder 'Etiquette' Singh had stopped working for Basu starting in the late 1970s, Basu found the traits of his personality a good fit for the character of Indra Sen, proprietor of Anderson Travels.[334]

* * *

An early morning visitor to Basu's flat at Santacruz would be greeted by the familiar sight of the director sitting on the floor, working on his scripts. As his daughter Rupali recalls:[335]

> One of my earliest memories was seeing him in the living room, spectacles perched on his head, seated on the ground using the square green sofa as a table, mouth moving slightly as if he was chewing a piece of gum, and writing. Writing vociferously on white A4 sheets—day in and day out. This visual greeted me every morning, irrespective of what time I woke or when he slept. He would wake every morning before 7 a.m. and begin to write. This discipline, this steadfastness, this sincerity, this commitment to his craft added with dollops of creativity with an insatiable urge to read literature is what defined the man.

On most occasions, he would be bare-chested, with a visible midriff countering his intelligence and concentration. This was the image he had in mind for the persona of Jagdish Bhai, building contractor and moneylender.

The habit of changing glasses, the emphasis on protocol, and the look of a barechested man lost in thought were the three drivers for the main characters in Basu's forthcoming comedy, *Shaukeen* (1982). It was as much a tribute to his technicians as it was to Billy Wilder.

An unsavoury incident was the precursor to the genesis of the idea for the film though. Ramesh Gupta mentions the same to the author in an interview:[336]

> You see, I was signed by Ramraj Nahata—father of present-day film critic Komal Nahata—to make a film on Billy Wilder's *The Seven Year Itch* (1955). He was producing two films at that time, one for Basu Chatterji (*Prem Vivah)*, and the other for Hiren Nag (*Saajan Mere Main Saajan Ki,* 1980). Ramraj Nahata had also signed Sanjeev Kumar and Rekha for the pivotal roles in my version of *The Seven Year Itch*. Somehow

Basu got wind that I was making this film, and took it further ahead with Ramraj Nahata, expressing a desire to make the film as he loved the subject. In the meantime, both the films by Nahata flopped, and he was in no position to produce film number three. But he talked to Sanjeev Kumar, seeking his nod if Basu Chatterji was the director. Sanjeev Kumar refused as he had already committed to doing the film with me. During the housewarming party of K.K. Mahajan at Four Bungalows, Basu and I had a great debate over this incident. KK helped us cool down.

But incidentally, he made *Shaukeen* just after this debacle. I feel it was partly inspired by *The Seven Year Itch*.

The Making and the Response

Gautam Banerjee goes back in time:[337]

> Nirmal Mitra, the director of films like *Rajdhani Theke* (1958) and *Kanchanmulya* (1961), told me a very interesting story after my father had passed away. I was very close to Mitra; we used to meet at his place near Ganja Park, Bhowanipore, where actress Mala Sinha had a house.
>
> In the early/mid-1970s, Nirmal Mitra wanted to adapt Samaresh Basu's story *Ramnaam Kebalam* for the cinema. They were friends and used to drink at an outlet near Dharmatala (Esplanade in central Calcutta). *Ramnaam Kebalam* was probably inspired by a Hollywood film [it was *Boys' Night Out* (1962)]. Samaresh Basu would write stories based on Hollywood films as well. One I recall is *Kuhak* (1960), which was written exclusively for the screen, inspired by *Night of the Hunter* (1955).
>
> Samaresh Basu sold the rights of *Ramnaam Kebalam* to Mitra, who was planning to make the film with Utpal Dutt, my father, and someone else. My father was very sick at that time. Utpal Dutt was not convinced about Mitra's abilities,

and requested him to part with the rights, mentioning that Basu Chatterji was interested in doing the film. He said, 'You won't be able to justice to it as compared to Basu.' Nirmal Mitra was not getting sponsors either. Manab Roy, his main financier, who used to stay near Jagubabur Bazaar, had passed away. Mitra's earlier film financed by Roy was *Pratham Basanta* (1971). It had flopped, and prospective moneylenders were reluctant to take the plunge.

The rights were then sold to Basu Chatterji.

Hema Malini's secretary I.K. Bahl, who was associated with the film as a production controller, has many memories as well:[338]

We knew a man called S.N. Mitra from Bengal [I am not sure about the exact name now], who was directly or indirectly related with a chit fund. He was in Bombay for some time, and I was working for him. His wife wanted to make a film. We listened to five or six stories from various people but none of those interested us. Then we discussed with Basu-da. He was like—if he had to meet a producer, and there was no car or driver, he would jump into an auto and ask the driver to step on the gas. Basu-da told us the story of three lecherous men, and we agreed to do the film. A.K. Hangal's onboarding was controversial. Dadamoni and Utpal Dutt were natural selections. For the third oldie, I was more interested in Madan Puri, to which Basu-da said, 'I have two fat men. I don't need any more of them. I want to settle it with a lean and thin guy.' Hence Hangal did a role most unconventional.

Our first trip to Goa was for location scouting. We had put up at the Taj Fort Aguada beach resort, which was the only five-star hotel then. I was sharing a room with Basu-da. One day I got up around 4.30 in the morning and found that he was writing the script. That was the kind of obsession he had with his work.

He wrote the script in Hindi. At times interspersing it with notes in English. Interestingly, Basu-da was not very comfortable with five-star hotels and said, 'Let us now shift to a hotel of my choice.' We shifted to a smaller hotel called Flora.

The initial part of the shoot happened in Goa, mostly in Panaji, Dona Paula and on the Miramar beach. K.K. Mahajan was the cameraman during this phase, after which Ajay Prabhakar took over. In a sense, it was his first independent assignment for Basu. A man with an excellent memory, he shares his experience with the author:[339]

> During *Shaukeen*, I started working independently as KK had to go abroad on work. After the location shoot at Goa, the outdoors, especially the car sequences, were shot on the outskirts of Bombay. We selected roads which had very little traffic.
>
> We were having problems during the shooting of the car song ['Wahin Chal Mere Dil', sung by Suresh Wadkar], as the sky was getting reflected on the windshield. Especially when the camera was moving in sync with the car, the polarisation of the pictures was not happening to our satisfaction. I suggested removing the windshield. Basu-da thought that the public might notice this. An assistant also felt it would be kind of obvious and agreed only after we assured him that it needed to be managed on the editing table.
>
> The indoor shots were mostly in Bombay. The producer Devika Mitra had a flat in Bandra, and the shots of Ashok Kumar dancing to his brother's (Kishore Kumar) rendition of 'Jab Bhi Koi Kangna Bole' was shot there. The outdoor depicting the quaint little bungalows happened in Goa. The indoors for the same were arranged at Dr Sood's bungalow in Bombay which he would rent out for shoots.

> The two dance numbers featuring Rati Agnihotri as the crooner were shot at Juhu hotel, a favourite destination for film-makers. Sun-n-Sand, a costlier alternative nearby, was also a place sought after by film producers, but Basu-da was reluctant to spend on production costs.

Samir Samanta, who had graduated to a position higher than his first film with Basu, nods in agreement:[340]

> Despite writing such brilliant scripts, Basu-da, who I used to call Basu-Kaku outside the precincts of the studio, used to always do films with frugal budgets. His shortcoming, maybe? That's why the production values felt short. The general feeling was that it is such a fabulous script, but technically, cosmetically and aesthetically, it falls short of what it could have been. The ancillary departments weren't commensurate with the kind of writing he had. His kind of script deserved much more by the way of production values, unfortunately.
>
> Coming to acting, he was, again, very thorough. He would give very clear details. For example, Mithun Chakraborty was someone who couldn't smile very easily at the camera. He had his own expression, but Basu-da would ask for a different countenance to accompany his laughter. *I want to see your teeth.* Mithun would have to give a laboured, artificial smile, as he would be forcibly made to. *Smile more, more.* Basu-da would go into all those particulars. He was a scriptwriter, so he wanted to have the visuals as per his vision.
>
> Utpal Dutt, Dadamoni, and Basu-da had a great rapport. Between shots, they could carry on interesting discussions. It was a privilege to sit beside them and hear them talk. The ponderings were both intellectual and humorous and included jokes and riddles. The overall atmosphere was very enlightening. Utpal Dutt was a very educated man. Dadamoni was a genius anyway. He was like an encyclopaedia. Basu-da was very intellectually inclined. They had great vibrations

together. I experienced that in *Shaukeen*. An experience of a lifetime.

Producer Debika Mitra was intellectually inclined as well. Sister of author Subodh Basu (of Bimal Roy's *Naukri* fame), and trained in Hindustani classical music, she had sung on AIR Calcutta after her marriage in 1954. In the late 1970s, she floated a film production company named Senmit Movie Visuals. *Shaukeen* followed, with Rati, then new to the industry [*Ek Duuje Ke Liye* (1981) was yet to be released], and Mithun, who Basu would describe as 'most volatile and intense among the new generation of box-office stars in this country'.[341]

The film ran into rough weather after some time, with the producer being accused of being part of a Ponzi scheme. Basu bought the film during the auction which happened, as mentioned by Dharmanand Joshi, Basu's one-time accountant and friend.[342]

Released on 23 April 1982, *Shaukeen*, publicised as 'Join Us on a Unique Flirtious Trip', was completed under a budget of Rs 18 lakh,[343] a pittance for a film with location shoots with multiple stars. Ajay Prabhakar remembers that many of the crew accompanied Basu to the first show at Bandra Talkies. Like *Chhoti Si Baat*, the film started with a commentary. Minutes into the film, the public loved the build-up and started whistling. Basu got up and said, 'Let's go. I just wanted to see if this was needed to be kept or edited, as my gut feeling was that the commentary part might drag. Fortunately, it has come out well.'[344]

The commentary was also accompanied by the song 'Jab Bhi Koi Kangna Bole', a composition which RD had based on his father's song 'Nitol Payer Rinik Jhinik'. Interspersed with an interlude borrowed from the *asthayi* of a Rabindra Sangeet 'Gram Chara Oi Ranga Matir Poth', this Kishore Kumar solo has remained one of the main attractions of the film.

★ ★ ★

Shaukeen was Basu's first film to be given an Adults Only certificate. Old men craving for curvy young things was deemed taboo; enforcement of moral policing had to happen. But apart from the theme which had an adulterous spin, *Shaukeen*, at the most, had some cleavage show limited to the shots of Jayashree T. Skin show in *Shaukeen* was nothing as compared to what would be paraded in the 1980s in the name of mainstream Hindi cinema, especially of the Padmalaya Studios variety.

At another level, *Shaukeen* was a bold film, in the sense that it is optically secular. All its key characters, including the desirable women, are Hindus. Film-makers in the 1970s would normally have fancy Christian names for kinky women. Fewer would attempt doing sex comedies, and that too with actors with very lovable and saintly images like Ashok Kumar and A.K. Hangal. In fact, the only other film which announced itself as a sex-comedy before *Shaukeen* was Hrishikesh Mukherjee's *Sabse Bada Sukh* (1972), which was a disaster. Basu broke a taboo. The film became a major hit and was talked about among teenagers, most of the lot who had been denied entry due to age restrictions. Subsequently, cable TV transmissions yielded a huge fan following.

Shaukeen also marked the last playback of Ashok Kumar. The song 'Hum, Tum Aur Yeh Nasha' had been sung by Sapan Chakravarty and Chirasree Bhattacharya[345], till Ashok Kumar put his foot down and refused to lip-sync the same. A new song had to be written and composed in a short time, which was hurriedly done by Yogesh and RD.[346] 'Chalo Haseen Geet Ek Banayein' remains one of the most endearing moments in the film.

The Downward Slide

Shaukeen had a Basu cameo where he is seen as a customer inside the office of Anderson Travels as if silently observing the proceedings. Unfortunately, the few films which followed *Shaukeen* had Basu almost as an observer. A popular film-maker, when questioned about the sudden drop in the quality of his films, had replied tangentially—the very reason why the maker of *Sara Aakash* is making *Pasand Apni Apni* (1983).

This is an interesting observation, as *Pasand Apni Apni* was not exactly a bad film. It was among Basu's better works in the 1980s. The images captured the manner of the also-rans in a big city, and overall, the film had a feel-good tonality. This statement made by the popular film-maker was more of a generalization, an assertion about the downward graph of Basu's cinema, the departure from the realistic norms he espoused in *Sara Aakash* or *Rajnigandha*. In short, his films were no longer different from the run-of-the-mill variety he detested.

Another angle had emerged from the narrative. Basu, one of the main advocates for the use of literature in cinema, had completely fallen back on the indigenization of foreign cinema, getting into the habit of frame-to-frame copies of classics, some famous, some lesser-known. He had previously done the same with *Chhoti Si Baat* and *Khatta Meetha*, but these were films where the blending of India with the west was more organic. In 1984, Billy Wilder's *The Fortune Cookie* (1966) ended up as *Lakhon ki Baat* (1984), the failure of which was primarily attributed to the new face Anjali Sen, who had replaced Sarika, the original choice.[347] While Sen certainly was not a revelation, the film had stalwarts like Sanjeev Kumar and the early 1980s common man Farooq Shaikh. Basu was extremely satisfied with Sanjeev and was more than just generous in appreciating his acting skills and would mention, 'I remember how Sanjeev Kumar won my admiration by delivering a lengthy speech which required 300 feet of film exposure. The speech was delivered perfectly, with the right pauses and nuances, just the way I wanted it. Not an extra foot of film was needed. I have worked with professionals like Amitabh, Rajesh Khanna, and Dharmendra, but even they required a little assistance at some time or the other. This never happened with Sanjeev.'[348]

The issue with the film was—despite a few typical Basu touches like a cameo and the comical acts involving a sobbing mother going back to stories with absolutely no relevance to the context—that it needed to be made with better production values. There was too much restriction on the movement of the camera as well, and most of the shooting was indoors. Music, something strongly embedded in his work even when songs were used sparingly, had become devoid of colour. There is hardly any recall of the songs from films like *Lakhon ki Baat.*

Pasand Apni Apni was an adaptation of *Happy Go Lovely* (1951), based on a story going back to the 1930s and made into many films in languages more than one, including commercially successful ones in Hindi as well, like *Sajan* (1969) and *Jhoota Kahin Ka* (1979). Basu's film, where the tamasha was a figurative character, was the most realistic one of all the Indian adaptations. He repeated the successful pair of Mithun and Rati, and this remains, along with *Shaukeen*, one of their films that still has a recall value. But the real value adds came from Utpal Dutt, his employees, and his creditors, in the form of Javed Khan, Subbiraj, et al. In a sense, they were like the trio of Agha, Keshto Mukherjee, and Mukri in *Piya Ka Ghar*, the real leads.

Talking of leads, a new pair had to be replaced soon.

* * *

Basu had a symbiotic relationship with the B.R. Chopra camp. BR, apart from producing a few of his films, would often lend out the small studio at Khar for dubbing. When Basu pitched the idea of making a film on a small budget starring rookie Rashmi Chauhan with Tapas Paul of Bengal, fresh from his huge success with Tarun Majumdar's *Dadar Kirti* (1980), they had no objection. Around this time, Basu had started functioning as a surrogate producer, in the sense that he would take up a film like a project within a given budget. He made this a practice, and all his films henceforth were made in turnkey modes. This film was named *Nilami.*

By the time *Nilami* was completed, in 1986, the leads had been replaced by Raj Babbar and Padmini Kolhapure. The finally agreed-upon title was *Kirayadar* (1986). Deepak Qazir recalls that he had shot for two days but was never called back for dubbing.[349] Could be time, could be differences within.

The thing about a film, a literary work, or a musical composition is that one can easily tell whether its creator was emotionally invested in it or not. The thought that crossed the minds of viewers when they watched *Kirayadar* was, 'Surely this can't be a Basu Chatterji film.' But it was. Ironically, the only passable feature of the film was Bappi Lahiri's music. Bappi had a blink-and-miss appearance in the film too, conducting the orchestra for his composition 'Dil Liya Dil Diya'. Probably having Bappi as part of the cast was considered a good omen. The huge success story of Bappi's 1980s music, for whatever it was, had started with *Himmatwala* (1983) where Bappi had a cameo too. Not surprisingly, one of the ads of the film in the periodical *Screen* was promoted with mugshots of B.R. Chopra and Bappi Lahiri, and with the blurb—B.R. Chopra and Bappi Lahiri team up for the first time in BR Films' *Kirayadar.*

A weak premise, a complete lack of rhythm, and an assortment of abysmally bad acting—something rare for a Basu Chatterji film—all came together to create the disaster *Kirayadar* was. The court scene with Chowdhury's lawyer Desai's (Chandrashekhar Dubey) theatrical extended monologue with no counterarguments and cross-questioning looked like a spoof of the standard Hindi masala scenes. Coming from someone who would adapt the courtroom drama *Twelve Angry Men* into *Ek Ruka Hua Faisla* (1985) quite commendably while working on a parallel track during *Kirayadar*, one was visibly quizzed. Basu's worst till then? Surely. Even *Tumhare Liye* had Sanjeev Kumar and the picturesque Rajasthan.

★ ★ ★

Almost on the heels of *Kirayadar* was released *Sheesha* (1986), another production that was delayed for more than two years. The film triggered great interest in Bengal, mainly because of a rumour which mentioned that it was based on *Teerandaaj*, a 1984 story by Mani Shankar Mukherjee (popularly known as Shankar in Bengali literature). While the rumour propagated by a vernacular daily might have added momentum to the sales of the book, the film was actually based on another novel of Shankar, *Maan Samman*, published in November 1981. Till 2006, it has had 88 editions, and quite a few of them have the names of Basu, Moon Moon Sen, Mithun Chakraborty and Mallika Sarabhai in the acknowledgments section.

Sheesha was a disappointment. For viewers used to the comforting and familiar motifs where everything from a smile to a sigh would be underplayed, *Sheesha* was melodramatic. Furthermore, the chemistry between the leads—Mithun Chakraborty and Moon Moon Sen—did not work.

The reason for the debacle was the inordinate delay in getting the film completed, mentions Archana Shourie, daughter of producer Sattee Shourie.[350]

> *Sheesha* was made to launch Moon Moon Sen in the Bombay film industry. Basu-da was everybody's choice of a director then. I have very nice memories of him. He completed our project despite the difficulties faced. I recall that Mallika Sarabhai was also very cooperative. The film had overshot its budget because of somebody's issues and flamboyant lifestyle, and I distinctly remember Basu-da waiving his last payment. Mithun-da (Chakraborty) waived off Rs 1 lakh, a big sum in those days. And in fact, Mithun-da was the reason the film was completed. He supported us throughout the film, and said to my mother, 'Sattee Ji, doesn't matter, we have lost money; let us work together to release the film.' And thanks to him and Basu-da, the film was released. It did not do well.

★ ★ ★

Frustrated with the proceedings of *Sheesha* and attempting to turn the tide, Basu, around the same time, had another failure in *Zevar* (1986). Contemporizing a Sarat Chandra story (*Darpachurna*) in 1985 was not a very bright idea. And that too with minimum focus on outdoors. It was sad to observe someone who had almost institutionalised location shooting fall back on the option of shooting inside bungalows for a story that needed the ambience of a sub-divisional town in Bengal.

To cut a long story short, the final result was so depressing that Rakesh Pandey, who had a short role in the film, is still not sure if *Zevar* was at all released.[351] Basu's only association with Gulzar as the screenplay and the dialogue writer did not augur well for the film.

Notwithstanding Basu's failures, the temptation to act in a Basu Chatterji film was high, and Tariq, the singing-dancing star of *Yaadon Ki Baraat* (1973) and *Hum Kisise Kum Naheen* (1977), was more than happy to oblige. As he mentions to the author:[352]

> I had acted in some films in the 1970s, because of which I used to be invited to film functions like Filmfare awards, etc. I had met Basu-da a few times, and it was all a formal namaste-type of interaction. During one such party, we were both seated at the same table. It was then that I asked him for a role. He said, 'See, your image is that of a modern guy. My films are about the common man, not stars.' To prove that I was not just a glamour-laden, no-good actor, I gave him the example of a serial I was doing, *Kahan Gaye Woh Log*, where I was cast as a revolutionary from Bihar. Basu-da then asked if I would be interested in a small role in a film that was on the floor. I was told it was a film on a shoestring budget about a printing press and was asked to bring my attire. 'If you have a suit and a tie, bring it. We'll shoot straight away.'

> I was thrilled that he considered me worthy of working in his film. The production people then called me to a mill (printing press) near the passport office at Worli where the shooting was on. I was given my dialogues there.
>
> He paid me a nominal amount, but the cheque was disbursed right after the pack-up. He had the reputation of always paying on time and the promised amount.

Though it received its certification on 29 August 1986, *Zevar* failed to get a proper release. The sudden disappearance of subtle romance and light humour from Basu's cinema was gradually suggesting a fundamental reassessment of his work not only by the critic fraternity but also the viewers. The verdict was that Basu had underestimated his audience. Also, the complete tilt towards a graphic depiction of vulgarity in mainstream Hindi cinema had practically alienated the second- and third-generation middle class, who were gradually getting glued to their black-and-white TV sets, especially in metros and state capitals.

That's when Basu decided to move.

His Last Hurrah

'When ambition ends, happiness begins.'
—Thomas Merton

The Small Screen

Fire, Feminism and Other Stories

When Sabita Bose arrived in Bombay from San Francisco in mid-March 1985 with Sharmila, her daughter, and Abhik, her six-week-old grandson, she was witness to an unusual sight in the living room. There were lights, many of them, and an equal number of reflectors. Inside the labyrinth of wires on the floor was Basu Chatterji, his glasses perched on his forehead, directing a young lady. The young lady was Priya Tendulkar, playing the iconoclastic Rajani, whose address was the fourth floor flat at Shastri House on 19th Road, Khar West, registered in the names of Chittaranjan Bose and Sabita Bose. As Mrs Bose mentions:[353]

> I was in the US when shooting had started. But seeing the shoot happening in front of my eyes was a different experience. The area then was very nice. You could see a lot of sky from our house. Housings were few, we could also see the Arabian Sea, as we often would be witness to the planes taking off from the airport at Santa Cruz. The skyline, since then, has changed. A 22-storeyed apartment blocks most of the view that was part of our daily oxygen.

> During the shoot, there used to be a huge rush during lunchtime. I had instructed my maid to dash to the set when lunch would be served and grab our portion of the food. Due to the shooting, we were mostly confined in one room, with nothing much to do. No cooking either. The table in the kitchen was used to lay out the dresses for the characters. The dress man would be there, adding the final touches to the costumes. The shoot would happen in the hall and one of the two bedrooms. I find a disconnect with the class portrayed by the lead character though. Our house was a nice one. Bought in 1983, it was as good as new. Rajani represented the lower-middle-class strata who did not live in plush apartments.

Little did Mrs Bose realize that she was witness to the making of one of the biggest hits on Doordarshan of all time. Rajani was like the female reincarnation of Amitabh Bachchan of the 1970s. Though, unlike Amitabh, her anger did not build up to a point where it culminated in fistfights and gun wars. She did not believe in breaking the law. She challenged its misuse.

A point to note was that Basu had never held a TV camera in his life before. This was till S.S. Gill, the visiting secretary to Mexico in 1983, thought otherwise.

Ananth Mahadevan, in his masterly autobiography *Once Upon a Prime Time*, mentions:[354]

> Circa 1983. Mexico threw up other palatable attractions besides its tacos, nachos, and enchiladas. The discovery was effected by the visiting secretary for Information and Broadcasting, S.S. Gill. In fact, he shoplifted an entire idea. The soap opera . . . On his return from Mexico, Gill recounted the strange phenomenon he had witnessed with the excitement of an Archimedes. The serials were influencing Mexican society, even changing it. Gill extolled the concept of television shows on the Indian airwaves. It was a medium waiting to be reinvented and adapted for a

> wider section of society. Rounding up like-minded, middle-of-the-road film-makers like Basu Chatterjee, Gulzar, Sai Paranjpye, Kundan Shah, and others, he elaborated on how the format could be implemented to advantage here.
>
> Nothing was really trending until *Hum Log* came along, on 7 July 1984.

The DD serial and the India audience from then on became inseparable.

★ ★ ★

The first subject Basu was offered by Gill was *Mahabharat*. He ducked the offer. But the scale of a serial and the money associated with the same enticed him to take to the TV camera. A pilot on the lines of the American sitcom *Here's Lucy* was shot with Padmini Kolhapure, then a very successful film heroine, in and as *Rajani*. Filmed in 1984, it would have continued if Padmini had not decided to walk out fearing the weekly shooting spree, prompting a change in script. And the lead actress.[355]

The final idea of *Rajani* was developed in consultation with Mannu Bhandari at her residence in Delhi. Basu would grumble that Indians were happy with armchair activism, and few had the gumption to take it beyond the drawing room. He wanted to float the idea to the country through someone they could identify as one of their own.[356]

Preoccupied with work, Mannu Bhandari was unable to dedicate herself to the project. But she did chip in with a few stories, one of which was about taxi drivers.[357] It became a colossal hit, and within no time, Priya Tendulkar, who played Rajani, became a national icon. Immediately after the first few episodes of *Rajani*, director Ashok Chopra announced the release of his *Nasoor* (1985) with the blurb—'You have seen her in *Rajani*. Now see her in *Nasoor*.' Priya, daughter of famed playwright Vijay Tendulkar, was spotted by Basu at a party.

There was something in her which made Basu overrule his previous choice of Moushumi Chatterjee. Other actresses in contention included Anita Raj and Bindiya Goswami. Bharti Achrekar, who found Priya too soft-faced for the role, had harboured intentions of playing the titular character as well.[358] Basu was adamant about his choice. It was the overall demeanour of Priya that made him shift to the storyline of a housewife who could challenge the government machinery and its dysfunctional systems that mandated epic overhauls. Before Ramanand Sagar's *Ramayan* united the families in the mornings, *Rajani* could stake its claim of delaying everyone's lunch on Sundays. The telecast started around the summer of 1985. By the time the first thirteen episodes were aired, Priya had been roped in for a few commercials. Basu himself directed two of those, completing each ad in two to three days when the industry trend was a minimum of eight to ten days per ad. He consequently got sacked as the ad agencies felt that he was not working hard enough.[359]

Priya's rise, as Rajani, was meteoric. Suddenly she was being identified as a social worker. Unimpressed critics like Amita Malik, who found the serial 'no great shakes, artistically or content-wise, and the acting wooden', had to accept that the criticism of accepted loopholes in the public service touched a nerve. And a raw one at that.[360]

Rajani never had issues with sponsorship, though the limitations on the budget forced Basu to shoot mostly at his friend's house—a friend with whom he would sit down for a drink after work. It had become a daily ritual since the time Ranjan Bose and Basu were neighbours at Santacruz. The tradition continued. Bose and Shakti Samanta would join Basu almost every evening. The location would shift based on the convenience factor. In most cases, Basu would play the host.

The huge success of *Rajani* helped Basu buy a flat at Seven Bungalows, Versova. The taxi episode, one of the most remembered episodes in Indian television history, unfortunately riled the Bombay taxi drivers, who, unlike their kin at metros like Delhi and Calcutta would never refuse a customer. Pankuj Parashar, who was doing

Jalwa (1987) at that time, saw an opportunity there and requested Basu to play himself, only to be chased by taxi driver Javed Khan. This became Basu's most well-known cameo.

But *Darpan*, the serial Basu did almost on the heels of *Rajani*, has a story of struggle.

★ ★ ★

I.K. Bahl goes back in time:[361]

> The serial *Darpan* was my brainchild. I had thought of thirteen stories, each one from a different language, getting them translated in Hindi, and making episodes for them. The first episode was directed by Ashok Roy. It was rejected by those who mattered at Mandi House [where Doordarshan is headquartered]. After the rejection by DD, I met Basu-da with a request to take up this work. Preoccupied, he initially turned down my offer. I reiterated, '*Ek aadh kahani toh sun lo* [at least listen to one or two stories].' After the story sessions, he mentioned that he would like to direct them, but time was a major constraint. On the rebound, Kamleshwar and I went to Hrishi-da [Hrishikesh Mukherjee]. He patiently listened to the first story, and said, 'Kamleshwar *yaar*, sorry, I don't like the story.'
>
> It was then that Basu-da agreed to take up the work. He would be shooting two serials almost back-to-back. Each episode would be shot in two to three days. It was that fast. After the necessary dubbing, I would fly to Delhi on Saturday, get the approval from Mandi House, return to Bombay, and initiate the shoot of the next episode. For thirteen episodes, I had to travel to Delhi every week. We had a good mix of new and experienced actors—Annu Kapoor, Alok Nath, Pankaj Kapur, Navin Nischol, Rameshwari, Kulbhushan Kharbanda, Abhi Bhattacharya, Vidya Sinha, A.K. Hangal, Rohini Hattangadi, Ananth Mahadevan and Utpal Dutt, among others.

> The hectic pace of the shoot troubled many. Utpal Dutt, after shooting an episode, said, 'I'll never do a serial again, you made me work so much.'
>
> Kamleshwar would write the script. [As per Mannu Bhandari, she also wrote the script for 10 stories.[362]] Basu-da used to direct mostly at the studio. There was no time for location shoots. We would try to book Mehboob Studio, but we did most of the shooting at Famous Studios. We also shot at Natraj, where Basu-da had his office. Due to the weekly format, there was no way we could postpone a single shoot. The complete onus was on us; do whatever is needed, book whatever is available, but the cassette should fly to Delhi on Saturday. Thankfully, DD used to sanction on time. For pulling the shoots through, we had to reach out to ad agencies for the money. Geoffrey Manners, who made the famous Forhan's toothpaste, paid us through Clarion Advertising. They paid for the entire serial, and part of the money was received in advance.

Basu Chatterji considered *Darpan* his best work for television. The stories were about showing a mirror to society, something Basu was interested in. Ananth Mahadevan, who had received a call in 1986 from an apprehensive Basu offering him a role in one of the episodes, was more than happy even when he was paid only the modest sum of Rs 500. It was an honour to work with Basu.[363]

Darpan was also a challenge for Basu, as Bahl felt that the stories selected for the serial did not lend themselves to good visualization. He was on a mission to prove his friend and producer wrong.[364]

Talking of challenging missions, there was another one he had undertaken.

The Tele-Film

It was a time-bound activity that the twelve men were tasked with; the decision needed to be binary i.e., 'Guilty' or 'Not Guilty.' The jury had to be unanimous. There had to be a dozen of them with a mix of the rational, logical, irrational, unflappable and biased. They were not permitted to leave the room till they arrived at a unanimous decision. The room would get claustrophobic. There would be frayed tempers. There would be high drama. None of these foundational pillars of Sidney Lumet's 1957 classic *12 Angry Men* could change in an adaptation.

In an exclusive chat with the author, dramatist Ranjit Kapoor dwells on the history:[365]

> *Ek Ruka Hua Faisla* was my play. People knew (and I had not concealed the fact either) that it was an adaptation of the play by Reginald Rose, which was the source material for a film too. I had not seen the film then. I saw the film at the American Centre two years after I had written the play. And I was very happy that my adaptation was in no way inferior; rather, it had more dramatic moments. The original film was slightly dry, with no humour. Initially, the play was supposed to be staged in Bombay with Amol Palekar, Om Puri, and others but it won a big response in Delhi with several shows. It received good coverage in *India Today* too, with Anita Kaul (Basu) carrying my interview. Kaifi Azmi witnessed the play and expressed his keenness to stage it as part of the IPTA meeting in Bombay with Javed Akhtar and Shabana Azmi pitching in with the sponsorship.

And then followed the offers for adaptation into a film. Says Kapoor:[366]

> I received three offers for the play being dramatized for the cinema with the first one coming from Yash Chopra. But he got busy with his film *Mashaal* (1984) and suggested that I go ahead with other offers if any. I had two more offers; from Basu Chatterji and Raj Marbros. I was in a bit of a hurry as I needed some money and therefore struck the deal with Basu-da who bought the rights to my play and gave me an air ticket from Delhi to Bombay.

Basu Chatterji had the unenviable task of having to Indianize *12 Angry Men* as well as he could, having resigned himself to the knowledge that people would still dismiss it as a copy. However, it was a legitimate adaptation as Basu had purchased the rights to the Hindi play.

Curiously, the film *Mashaal* finds mention in *Ek Ruka Hua Faisla.* Perhaps this was Ranjit Kapoor's subtle 'trailer' to the back story that he held back, deciding to share the details only if someone were to ask him about it!

Maybe in anticipation of the accusation of *Ek Ruka Hua Faisla* being a copy, Basu made no attempt to pretend that his work was *not* an adaptation of another original. He went to great lengths to ensure that his creation mirrored the original, to the extent that the seating order of the jurors in *Ek Ruka Hua Faisla* was the same as that in *12 Angry Men.* The proceedings in the next three hours were identical too, as was the outcome at the end of the session.

So then, what was Basu Chatterji's contribution to the Hindi version?

Firstly, he got the title correct. Not all the twelve men were angry.

Secondly, Basu had to dig out the conviction from deep within himself that he could reverse the trend of his failures with Hollywood remakes in films like *Man Pasand* and *Chakravyuha.* What could he do differently? And here came what was arguably his biggest casting coup. Except for Subbiraj who had played the tailor in *Pasand Apni Apni*, none of the other jurors had played any significant role in any of Chatterji's films before *Ek Ruka Hua Faisla.*

Ranjit Kapoor shares some interesting information about the cast selection. Says he, 'Amol Palekar was part of the cast originally. But then I was clear that I needed to have a say in the choice of actors. Except for Subbiraj, all the rest of the cast was chosen by me, including Deepak Qazir Kejriwal [who had initially worked backstage on the play and played juror number four or seven when S.M. Zaheer or M.K. Raina were busy respectively],[367] who replaced the original choice of Bajju Bhai (Ram Gopal Bajaj). Only Subbiraj was Basu-da's suggestion; we needed a replacement for Vinod Nagpal who could not take time off from *Hum Log.* All the actors except him knew the scenes, dialogues, everything—before the film was made.'[368]

And thus, it was virtually a new cast for Basu.

One is not aware of any other film by Basu Chatterji in which the scriptwriter was so 'intrusive' to the extent of deciding the cast. Kapoor's involvement in the project went beyond the script and cast.

Said Kapoor,[369]

> I wanted the set to represent the decrepit judicial system—a character in its own right so to say. And therefore, I checked out courts in small towns and would find *paan* (betel) stains on the walls, wooden wastes lying around, and dirty and creaky staircases. Constrained by sparse funds, Basu-da rented a bungalow for the film instead of creating an elaborate set. The camera angles were all Basu-da's, as was the choice of background music. I did not have any say in those. For the end piece in which juror number three stands isolated against the other eleven, I had a difference of opinion with Basu-da on the shot. I wanted a composite shot to represent eleven men on one side, and one man on another. This was the formation I used on stage. But Basu-da went ahead and split the shots adding that he would manage during editing. During the dubbing at BR Studios, Basu-da admitted to me that he should have taken a composite shot as I had suggested.

The chemistry between Kapoor and Chatterji worked well enough to create a classic out of another classic. Summed up Kapoor, 'Basu-da said, "Ranjit, this is a labour of love for me." The fee for all actors was uniform. The schedule was from start to finish with no breaks, though Deepak Qazir had to go to Benaras for his brother's wedding and was a day late. The shoot was completed in 20–25 days. Cleared by the censor board in July 1985, the film was released on TV to a rapturous response by the young generation. The film became part of the course material in an MBA course in Delhi for its use of persuasive logic and persistence.'[370]

The one glaring error that both Kapoor and Chatterji failed to notice was the period. The jury system had been abolished in India in the late 1960s. *Ek Ruka Hua Faisla* was set in 1984.

Pulp Fiction: The Final Comedy

Wrestler Charandas was twenty-three years, three months, and seventeen days old when he met Chameli, the well-muscled daughter of coal merchant Kallumal and Champa, his wife. And he fell for her like a ton of bricks.[371]

Were these the two lines which prompted Basu to accept Prakash Mehra's offer to make *Chameli Ki Shaadi?*

Maybe. He also found the theme to be within his comfort zone.

It was of little surprise that, after weathering an indifferent patch, Basu Chatterji fell back on his tried and trusted elements of a young girl's marriage, romance, roadblocks-to-marriage and clean comedy in 1986. The result was the success called *Chameli Ki Shaadi* (CKS). Here, Chatterji also broke his jinx of 'failing with the stars' as *CKS* starred the box-office-safe-bet of Anil Kapoor. And Amrita Singh, fresh from her *Betaab* (1983) success.

There was another reason for his acceptance. Basu was an avid reader, and nothing escaped his eyes, from classics to pulp fiction. *Dhadkanein*, a social satire by Om Prakash Sharma, was written almost like a scenario. The backdrop was a suburb near Delhi. The dialogues were in a dialect Basu had grown up with. And then there was Sharma himself, who was happy when Basu came with the idea of filming his novel. The idea for the spoof came as part of the bucket list of Satyendra Pal Chaudhari, who was Prakash Mehra's financier for quite some time. Satyendra was from Meerut, which was Sharma's place as well. After working in Delhi, he had settled down in Meerut, where his sons founded Janapriya Prakashan Mandir, a publishing house. Basu came down to meet Sharma and shared his screenplay. The deal was signed.[372]

Bharti Achrekar, who did a brilliant job as the uneducated Champa, tells the author:[373]

> This was a Prakash Mehra production. We were surprised that Prakash Mehra produced a film that had a total disconnect with the stuff he would do. He also gave a free hand to the director. He did not want to make an in-your-face commercial film. Maybe because of his respect for Basu-da.
>
> The shooting was great fun. You see, most of us, Annu Kapoor, Pankaj Kapur, Satyen Kappu, me, and some actors, all came from a theatre background. Amrita was also very good. She was a star, but very cooperative. As I said, it was like a family. The entire set was made in Chandivali Studio.
>
> I had a great time working with Amjad Khan. I am a singer as you would know. I did my graduation in music. Amjad ji was very fond of my singing and would ask me to sing every time we met. We used to have music sessions. I recall the time with great nostalgia. Though for Basu-da, I prefer my role in *Apne Paraye* more.
>
> *Chameli Ki Shaadi* was a Basu-da film that did well after quite some time. It had a decent run and could be classified as a big hit too. Today people are watching these films many times over. Most have lost count.

A little-known aspect remains that Prakash Mehra, despite being the director of completely mainstream films, admired artistic aspects as well. After a viewing of Satyajit Ray's *Shatranj Ke Khilari* (1977), he had expressed a desire to distribute the film in the Delhi-Uttar Pradesh circuit.[374]

* * *

Producer Prakash Mehra's say in the cast and crew was apparent. Advocate Harish (Amjad Khan), Charandas's guide and mentor, is the equivalent of Uncle Tom played by David in *Baton Baton Mein*. One can't help but 'see' David in the role of the friendly advocate—maybe he would have, had he not passed away in 1982. Apart from Amjad Khan who had played key roles in PMP Productions like *Muqaddar ka Sikandar* (1978) and *Lawaaris* (1981), Om Prakash, Ram Sethi, and composers Kalyanji-Anandji were three more of Prakash Mehra's regular team members who were drafted into the *CKS* team. None of these people had featured in a Basu Chatterji film before. But still, as far as the direction was concerned, Mehra appeared to have given Basu a free hand, as we see.

'Prakash Mehra was very cool during the film. He did not interfere, neither did he offer suggestions,' mentioned Basu to the author.[375]

* * *

By design, *CKS* was a parody of the outdated traditions of the north Indian caste Hindus who do not educate their female child and where marriage outside the *biradari* is taboo. Chameli had at least reached the eighth grade. Her father was a Class Six dropout. Her mother Champa was illiterate and could not even read Hindi. But Champa knows by instinct that erring daughters who aspire to marry outside their caste need to be slapped and locked up in their rooms. Despite his mouse-like timidity, Kallumal Koylewala (Pankaj Kapur) is the soft rebel, tentatively reasoning out with his wife in support of their daughter. And Chameli is the belligerent rebel—physically aggressive and stubborn in her decision to marry Charandas despite being incarcerated in her bedroom upstairs by her mother. Both the ladies put up an outstanding performance with Amrita Singh clearly showing the untapped acting potential in her—a potential that was realized decades later in films like *Two States* (2011) and *Badla* (2019).

Each actor played within his/her boundaries and contributed to the hilarity and wholesomeness, not the least being Annu Kapoor playing the drunk goonda Chaddam Lal.

Basu's small town in Bombay, in contrast to the small town near Delhi as in the story, was created completely in a studio set. It was a major change from what Basu would have done under normal circumstances. But Mehra, lenient with production costs, was willing to spend. As was Basu, to recreate the small-town kernel with props like the milkman, the bangle seller (something he had used in *Sara Aakash*), the transistor radio and the use of popular Hindi songs in the background. Rain too made an entry in a Basu film after some time, as one of the 'wait for it' moments in the song 'Tu Jahan Bhi Chalega Chalungi'.

CKS is probably the only Basu comedy that had a few fight sequences. The fight with Chaddamm was shot in a bar near Caesar Palace hotel in Khar.[376] Today, neither the hotel nor the bar exists. The film continues to fascinate viewers.

* * *

CKS, released in Bombay on 21 February 1986, remained Basu's last hit. The later part of the 1980s was mostly a tryst with the small screen. It included the political satire *Kakaji Kahin* with Om Puri in and as a corrupt politician. Initially titled *Netaji Kahin*, the name was probably altered to avoid references to someone famous. Basu also had plans of casting the three Gangoly brothers but was unable to translate the idea into action as Kishore Kumar was unwilling. In Kishore's absence, Basu went ahead with Ashok and Anoop and named the serial *Bhim Bhavani*, which was aired on TV in the late 1980s. Incidentally, both the brothers were shooting at Esel Studio, Trombay, for the serial, when the news of Kishore Kumar's death reached them on 13 October 1987.

Death of a Girl

The 1990s started on a low note for Basu. In late 1989, *Kamla ki Maut,* which got certification on 31 August 1989, was rejected by the Regional Committee set up to select films for screening at the Calcutta Film Festival, which was held from 10 January to 20 January 1990. Basu had based the film on *Mrityur Pore*, a Bengali story by Swaraj Bandopadhyay about the impact the suicide of an unmarried but pregnant girl had on her neighbours. He had come across the Hindi translation of the story in *Sarika* around the early 1970s. It was a subject after his heart. Toying with the idea of making a film on the resultant ramifications, Basu had approached B.R. Chopra in 1974, only to settle with *Chhoti Si Baat.* After a gap of 15 years, Basu had gone ahead with the theme. It was topical in 1974. It was topical in 1989 as well. Only that the producers in the late 1980s were demanding more and more of the Shakti Kapoor-Kader Khan variety of comedy. Even B.R. Chopra, who shared Basu's vision inasmuch as his recording studio at 20th Road, Khar was like Basu's second home, had shifted to TV serials. His *Mahabharat* (1988) united families.

In the absence of the kind of cash flow Basu was used to in the 1970s, he had fallen back on NFDC. K.K. Mahajan no longer worked for him. Neither did Narinder Singh. Bansi Chandragupta was long dead. Basu's films did not have the finesse of a *Swami.* Or the visual delight of *Chitchor.* The screenplay was his strength, and Basu had given *Kamla ki Maut* his best shot. Only to find it being shunted out of film festivals.

Instances of films being called back for review were not new. Rabindra Dharmaraj's *Chakra* (1981) and Mani Kaul's *Satah Se Uthata Aadmi* (1980) were precedents, films that were approved for exhibition by the committee after being rejected in the first stage of assessment. As part of the Central Committee, Basu too had called back Buddhadev Dasgupta's *Andhi Gali* (1984) once, but the jury vetoed the film during the re-evaluation phase.

Unfortunately, a refutation at the regional level implied that there was no second opportunity. Any recommendation by the Central Committee was possible only when the film was shortlisted by the regional committee. Basu was not the only well-known film-maker who faced rejection. He was part of the elite list that included Mani Kaul (*Siddheshwari*), G. Aravindan (*Marattam*) and Girish Kasaravalli (*Bannada Vesha*). The reaction to the film by Dolly Thakore, TV host, theatre actress, and noted newsreader, who was part of the panel was: 'A total atrocity, and Basu has missed an excellent opportunity as it had a strong script. The treatment was out of depth.' There were also pointers like lack of attention to detail, which resulted in anachronism in the form of a Maruti car being shown on the road in the early 1960s.[377]

Basu had to take the blame. His focus on cinema as a visual medium had certainly lessened starting from the late 1970s. His emphasis on mid-shots synched more with television. However, *Kamla ki Maut* had probably been made with the television in mind, though it was certified as a feature film produced by NFDC. Basu, realizing that small theatres in India would remain a pipe dream at least in his lifetime, had found his audience in the television viewers and would try and exploit that format where the emphasis would naturally move to more and more mid shots. Or close-ups.

The film was facing release-related issues as well. The initial release at Chaplin Theatre in Calcutta did not augur well for the film. Subsequently, Basu had to arrange special shows for some friends in the media to showcase his latest effort. As a result, the film reached a particular fraternity that voiced their opinion. And to his relief, most of the lot had views that were contrarian to that of the regional panel. Veteran journalist Iqbal Masud mentioned: 'I enjoyed this film thoroughly. It is a well-cast movie.' He felt that the rejection was most unjustified and showed only the incapacity and insensitiveness of the panel members to good cinema. He added, 'Who are these members to judge films of Aravindan, Kaul, Basu or Girish? It is an insult to these film-makers.'[378]

The panel for the Western region was headed by veteran journalist Bikram Singh, and included film-maker Sudhir Mishra, actor Ramesh Deo, producer and lyricist Amit Khanna, and journalist Vinod Tiwari, apart from Dolly Thakore. Point to note, Amit Khanna and Basu were friends who had worked together and would work together again. Basu was the Chairperson of the central committee the previous year when Amit Khanna's *Shesh* (1988) and Sudhir Mishra's *Main Zinda Hoon* (1988) had been rejected.[379]

★ ★ ★

A year later, Basu decided to take the institution head-on. And this happened during the 38th National Film Awards, for the best of Indian cinema of 1990. Representing a group called Forum for Better Cinema, Basu had made a candid statement questioning the process of juror selection.[380]

The incident happened when Basu was in New Delhi during the first quarter of 1991. Incidentally, he was at Ashoka Hotel, where the jury too had put up. His arrival almost coincided with his film *Hamari Shadi* (1990) being shown to the jury headed by Ashok Kumar. It was during this visit that he questioned the capability of a few jurors. This resulted in his longest opinion piece in the *Times of India*'s Bombay edition dated 2 May 1991. Titled 'We Beg Your Pardon Too', it was a rejoinder to juror Kalpana Lajmi's article 'I Beg Your Pardon' on 18 April 1991 in the same publication. It was a strong response articulating how Lajmi's defence held no water and was only helping the 'profiteers of big-budget cinema'.[381] Basu's riposte proved uncannily prescient, in the sense that commercial cinema started gaining a foothold in the domain of National Film Awards in the years to come. Incidentally, the DFFI awarded Basu his second and last National Award the following year. For *Durga* (1991), a film that did not have even a proper commercial release. Sukanya Kulkarni, who played the title character, recalls a few stories of her association with the film:[382]

> Basu-da probably saw me act in a Marathi play, as I had a theatre background. For *Durga*, we had to go to the location in Chhattisgarh. Basu-da sponsored my first flight from Bombay to Nagpur from where we drove down to the location. My mother accompanied me on the trip. We were put up comfortably, in a three-star hotel. My role was of a poor daily wage earner, who cleans utensils for a living. I do not have many memories of the film, but remember that Basu-da took me to a shop and asked, 'Do you have a VCR?' What's that, I asked him. He gifted me a VCR, which, at the time, cost him Rs 16,000. This was his way of appreciating my work. It happened after the National Award.

Durga won the National Award in the category 'Best Film on Family Welfare'. The prints of the film are not in the public domain. Neither did the film have a commercial release. *Kamla Ki Maut,* on the contrary, became famous with time. It had a theme never tried before, about how the unwanted pregnancy of a twenty-year-old resulting in her suicide takes a neighbouring family back in time, to seedy moments of their unsavoury past, and finally questioning the rigid morality of the lower middle class. Aided by excellent acting, especially by Pankaj Kapur, the film also found the use of outdoors after a long time in a Basu Chatterji film. Basu went back to his tried and trusted supports as well. Panchgani, its lake, and the viewpoint which had served as the location for 'Jab Deep Jale Aana' in *Chitchor* (1976) were back. The name Prabha was back too, this time for someone who was never shown on the screen. Probably sensing that Chameli was a lucky mascot, going by the popularity of his last hit *Chameli ki Shaadi* (1986), one of the characters was given the name Chameli. The film is also an important milestone in the sense that it marked the debut of four actors in Hindi cinema, of which one is regarded as among the best of the twenty-first century. Irfan Khan.

A major grouse Basu nursed was the censor board, then headed by Moreshwar Vanmali, granting the film an Adults Only certificate, which not only laid restrictions on viewership but would also lead to reduced attendance during TV broadcasts. This came with an added disadvantage. In India, films with 'Adult Certification' would normally attract an all-male viewership. In pre-Google days, in the absence of easily available Internet porn, young male viewers would flock to the theatres expecting erotic sequences.

Basu's film was targeted at families, especially couples and young women. It had nothing to do with sexual desires. Unfortunately, the film was taken off theatres before the target audience had a clue about such a film being exhibited in their city.

The popularity of the film spiralled after NFDC came out with a DVD set in 2013, though the majority of the critics had been quite effusive in their praise when the film was released for press shows in 1989 and 1990.

Talking of popularity, one that achieved it rather instantly was a serial Basu would make when checking back on a film made by Satyajit Ray.

The Super Sleuth

The idea came to him while revisiting Satyajit Ray's *Chiriyakhana* (1967), says Gautam Banerjee.[383]

Ray has gone on record declaring *Chiriyakhana* as one of his weakest films, though his statement has not been backed up by relevant data, apart from the fact that he expressed dissatisfaction with the whodunit genre. Saradindu Banerjee, the author on whose work the film was based, was not too fond of the film either, but his reasons were different, as there were major changes to the story made by Ray. His statement that Byomkesh [Bakshi] never wore glasses was also proven to be an incorrect assessment.[384] Notwithstanding the opinions of the author and the film-maker, *Chiriyakhana*, with its noir-like treatment supplemented with some exemplary acting by Uttam Kumar, Sushil Mazumdar, Chinmoy Roy, Jahar Ganguly, Subhendu Chatterjee and Shyamal Ghoshal, has a dedicated following even fifty years later. Basu Chatterji had enjoyed it immensely, prompting him to read up the complete collection of Byomkesh stories, following it up with translating the stories into Hindi. All thirty-three of them. Conceived in late 1990, the translation took over two years.

Consequently, Basu wasted little time in sending an application to Mandi House.

The turnaround for approving the serial format was fast. DD approved the first thirteen stories, the assumption being that the success of the same would determine the action for the remaining ones. That Pune-based Sanu Banerjee—Saradindu's son—was Basu's friend, helped. There was one more point for the rapidity with which things were processed. Basu had, in his words, found the perfect face to play Byomkesh. He did not want to waste time. Thirteen stories were aired in 1993, and the remaining twenty in 1997.

Quixotically, in an act of contradiction, Ray did a whodunit a decade later, called *Joy Baba Felunath* (1979).

★ ★ ★

Rajit Kapur, the perfect Byomkesh according to Basu, was no rookie, having appeared on television first when he was in Class VI of Cathedral and John Connon School, Bombay. He was a regular after graduating from Sydenham College of Commerce and Economics, Bombay, in 1985. However, he was not yet in the bracket reserved for the famous. In a chat with the author, he goes back in time, talking about his association with Basu:[385]

> Writer Sujit Sen had put across a word to Basu-da who I believe was on the lookout for actors for his serial *Byomkesh*

Bakshi. I went to meet Basu-da at Natraj Studios. We spoke for around ten minutes. And that was it. He asked me what I was doing then, whether I was free, how comfortable I was with Hindi, etc. Assured that I had time to spare for his work, he said, 'Okay, I have all the scripts ready. When you come the next time, I will give you a copy of all the scripts.' I am not sure if I was the only actor interviewed for the role. He never mentioned anything about that. I knew that he was looking for actors to play Byomkesh and Ajit. I think he had already met K.K. Raina. I was mildly surprised when I was told that Ajit will be played by him, as K.K. Raina was an NSD grad and many years my senior. I was expecting to play Ajit to K.K. Raina's Byomkesh.

During our next meet, Basu-da gave me the full set of stories. He had already taken the trouble of getting them all translated. He told me, 'My Hindi may not be so good, so if the Hindi has to be corrected, please do so. Make your notes. If you have any questions, ask me before the shoot. Let us not have discussions on the sets.'

Most of the indoor shoots happened in Bombay. It was a long stretch, spread over three to four months. We started with all the houses of Byomkesh, something which was done at Seven Bungalows, Versova, at Kapoor Bungalow, close to Nana Nani Park. The bungalow does not exist anymore. This was opposite a shop named Sancha Ice Cream. I remember the shooting happening in May, times when it was very hot. During lunch, I used to cross over and have ice cream.

Basu-da had a house nearby.

The series was not shot in sequence. It was shot like a film. The shooting was planned based on the location and not episode-wise.

Being shot in the manner of a cinema came with its limitations. Maintaining continuity was one, as, in the day's shoot, Byomkesh could be twenty-five years old for the first two hours, forty-four for the next two, and thirty-six for the rest of the day's shoot. Both Basu and the team had kept this aspect in mind, and the makeup would change accordingly. A pair of glasses were part of the detective's attire from the eleventh episode, 'Tasveer Chor'. Initially titled 'Photograph' by Basu, this and 'Raste ka Kanta' were stories that had Rajit completely foxed.

White boot polish was used as the hair whitener. Starting with 'Chiriya Ghar' in Season One, this was used regularly for Season Two which had the next twenty stories.

* * *

It was almost fifteen years after *Apne Paraye* that Basu travelled to Calcutta for a shoot, post the Bombay spree for Season One. The unit was put up at Lytton Hotel on Sudder Street. The Calcutta team joined him there.[386] Keshto Mitra, the production manager, knew many of the high officials, and it was he who arranged the shoots at landmarks like the Howrah station, High Court, etc.

There were two more reasons for the Calcutta shoots. Veterans Utpal Dutt and Robi Ghosh were both based out of Calcutta. Utpal Dutt had a major role in the third story 'Seemant Heera'. This was one of Dutt's last works, and his last shoot for Basu. Robi Ghosh was wasted in an inconsequential role as Badridas Marwari in the story 'Amrit ki Maut', which was shot in 1996 as part of the second season.

Talking of characters, the three main ones in the serial were Byomkesh, Ajit and Satyavati, the wife of Byomkesh. Satyavati came later, in the fifth episode of Season One, 'Wasiyat'. She was not there in most, and if at all there, poor thing, she was just relegated to making tea.

Sukanya Kulkarni, who played Satyavati, has no regrets though and recollects her association with the serial with fondness:[387]

> I was staying in Dadar. Basu-da would travel from Santa Cruz. He had a Premier car. For the shoot, I used to go to his house, and he would take me to Seven Bungalows. During the return trip, he used to drop me at Mahim, from where I used to take a taxi back home. He used to give us conveyance also, Rs 100 or 200 per day, even though he was dropping me back. He said, 'Keep it as pocket money.' The shooting followed by the travel implied that I was not getting an opportunity to see the serial, as, by the time I used to be back home, it would be over on TV. He gifted me the VCR to record the episodes.
>
> He was very fatherly. You might have noticed me repeating a yellow saree in the serial. I love Bengali sarees, and he said, 'You like it? Take it.'
>
> Today, two and a half decades later, I still have that saree.

The occasional gift notwithstanding, the atmosphere during the shoot was thoroughly professional. Mentions Rajit Kapur:[388]

> He knew the economies of scale. He was also the producer. Wasting time was a strict no-no. For a 9 a.m. shift, the rolling would start at 9.20. If the cameraman—Ajay Prabhakar—was tired, Basu-da would operate the camera himself. We would also shoot carefully so that dubbing could be minimal. A word or two, if needed, would be changed during the edit only if there was a reference in an earlier story or if some character had said something and a correction was needed. These would happen in Khar where BR Studios had a setup. It was a five-minute drive from Basu-da's house in Santa Cruz.

There was only one deviation to the shooting schedule, and that too due to a force majeure, mentions assistant director Ravindra Singh.[389]

> We had a 9 a.m. to 6 p.m. schedule. We would also have a 2 p.m. to 10 p.m. schedule at times. Basu-da was very strict

about completing the work on time, and I do not remember a single delay. Except one, during the episode, 'Kile Ka Rahasya', when there was a city-wide power cut. I was staying in Bhayandar in Thane at that time which had no bus connection to the main city. Local trains were not running due to the power grid failure. I did not have a phone either. The only option left for me was to walk, which I did up to Borivali. From there I took a bus to Andheri, and then, another bus to Andheri East, managing to reach the location at 2 p.m. Apprehending a verbal thrashing, I discovered that the shoot was postponed for want of a generator which was finally received around 5 p.m. The shoot ended at 3 a.m.

The allotted time per episode was forty-five minutes. Dada's calculation and perception were extremely good. He knew exactly where to cut. You need to see the shot breakdown. Cut to Cut. He knew where he had cut, and where the next shot would begin. The average time per episode was around three days only.

★ ★ ★

The success of *Byomkesh Bakshi* was unprecedented. Basu used the golden rule of sticking to the original plot. The serial, though, had issues like the occasional anachronism, sloppy production values, a drab and insipid colour scheme and pedestrian acting from a few of the supporting cast. The tension so essential to detective stories was missing too. Basu also made minimal use of the background score, which could have enhanced the dramatic quotient of the mysteries. But Anand Shankar, working with Basu for the only time, created a very catchy title score. Title scores had become DD's trademark; most of its serials from *Hum Log*, *Yeh Jo Hai Zindagi* to *Chunauti* or *Subah* had title scores that stood out. Basu had no desire to be an exception. The title song of *Rajani*, sung by Asha Bhosle and composed by rhythm guitarist Bhanu Gupta, is fondly remembered and hummed even today. As there is nostalgia for Salil Chowdhury's instrumental title for *Darpan*. And the fusion-based title of *Byomkesh Bakshi*.

But the main reason behind the spectacular success of *Byomkesh Bakshi* was Rajit Kapur. People, especially Bengalis, had started to identify with him as the real Byomkesh, the private eye as created by Saradindu. As they were extremely happy with the faithful recounting of the plots, something Ray had circumvented in his version of a Byomkesh story. Nonagenarian Shantanu Bandopadhyay, the youngest son of Saradindu, in an exclusive interview with scribe Pallab Chattopadhyay, mentions as such.[390]

> Initially, I was not enthused by the Hindi serial of Basu Chatterji. However, after seeing the other productions (which include the entire repertoire of Bengali films made later on the titular character, and Dibakar Banerjee's 2015 Hindi feature *Detective Byomkesh Bakshi!)*, I felt it was much better than the others. Especially Rajit Kapur in the role of Byomkesh was a perfect fit.

★ ★ ★

On 27 March 1986, a few years before Basu would hobnob with a fictional detective, there was an armed robbery at his place. A gang of four young Turks, on the pretext of presenting him a bouquet for *Rajani*, entered his flat one afternoon and made way with whatever cash and jewellery they could find. Basu was not at this house then.[391]

Basu recalls: 'Ironically, the thieves used the loot to launch a film, as per the detection masterminded by Shakti Samanta. Incidentally, the launch of that film happened at Natraj Studio, and we were witnesses without having a clue.' (Natraj Studio was the office of both Samanta and Basu.)[392]

Failed Dreams

'For after all, the best thing one can do
when it's raining is to let it rain.'
—Henry Wadsworth Longfellow

The 1990s . . . and Later

Bombay

Humour, romance and music, at times in isolation, and generally as elements of the same set made for the cinema of Basu in the 1970s. Unfortunately, the 1980s Bombay panorama was mostly about hamming and pelvic thrusts, which left the likes of Hrishikesh, Gulzar and Basu confused. The 1990s struck the death knell for their kind of cinema. Hrishikesh bid adieu to the rat race. Gulzar was marginalized till he hung up his boots. Curiously, Basu, who had crossed sixty in the late 1980s, kept on making films, while deeply identifying with the dilemma faced by the troika. In an interview with Sanjeev Verma, on being asked if his cinema was being phased out, he said:[393]

> So it would appear. Not just me. All of us—Gulzar, Hrishikesh Mukherjee—are finding existence as film-makers increasingly difficult. The audience is simply not there. The whole thing is going from bad to worse.

It is at this cusp that Basu seriously thought of shifting to television. His Bombay chapter had started in 1985 with *Rajani*;

the Calcutta one (talked about later in the book) began in 1988. But the balancing act between cinema and TV, something Basu had managed well in the mid-1980s, was seriously upset in the years to come. The dividing line between the two genres had fundamentally blurred. Basu's relationship with visuals was gradually veering towards close-ups and mid shots.

The failure of *Kamla ki Maut* made him go back to a tried and tested formula: comedy. And thus, was born *Hamari Shadi*, a feature for television. Receiving its film certification on 12 October 1990, a shot of the leads Ajit Pal and Indrani Halder adorned the cover of the now-defunct NFDC magazine *Cinema in India*. Unfortunately, this remained its only claim to fame. The film was lost in the maze that was 1990s cinema, where simplicity was no longer a status symbol. Binod Pradhan's stylized cinematography with high crane shots, low-angle tracking shots, and complex points of view—especially in Vidhu Vinod Chopra's *Parinda* (1989)—was branded as a game-changer. As was Santosh Sivan's artificially created, deeply saturated colours in Mani Ratnam's *Roja* (1992). The bottom line was that in an era where film-makers were moving towards new techniques of shot-taking, handheld cameras and static shots with the zoom was passé. *Hamari Shadi*, for all its naiveté, was like an extension of a DD TV serial, which needed multiple 'happening' episodes to hold the interest of the viewers. Today, prints of the film are not available in the public domain.

NFDC is also partly to be blamed for its policy of distribution, mentions Indrani Halder:[394]

> I had just appeared for my higher secondary examination when the request came to me from the boom man of *Mondira* (1990), which was my first film as a lead. The shooting for *Mondira* was happening in Bombay, and I was stationed there for a month. The boom man also used to work for Basu-uncle, and it was with some trepidation that he approached me through my mother, mentioning that Basu Chatterji was looking for a new girl for a film. In a few days, I was taken

> to meet Basu uncle, where it was 'approval at first sight'. All the members of the family also joined in the endorsement process. Basu uncle just said, in a voice that was a mix of a grin and that of an affectionate father—'*Khub bhalo, khub bhalo, korbe tumi*? [Very good, very good, would you do the role],' to which I said, why not?
>
> The shopping for the costumes was done jointly by me and Tinku (Rupali). Part of the shopping I did on my own at Fab India in Delhi where I was there for some work. Basu uncle had just mentioned his budget for costumes and given me the liberty to choose what I thought was fit for my character. The glasses were mine too. I also stayed with Basu uncle's family during the shooting phase.
>
> I am not sure if the film had a commercial release at all. I think it was released at Nandan, which was the case for most films produced by NFDC. That's about it. How I wish I could see the film sometime.
>
> I must say that Basu uncle was one of a kind. It is difficult to find someone of his level of intellect and brilliance.

The genesis of the film happened much before though. Rupali mentions that in a discussion with Basu, I.K. Bahl had talked about the roadblocks to his marriage and how he had to circumvent the same. Basu loved the conflict angle. 'Surely a film can be made on this?' was his reaction.[395]

However, the crystallization happened later. The story development was the result of a separate discussion, as reported:[396]

> The story of *Hamari Shaadi* was conceived in the *Times of India* building at the Filmfare office. 'Bikram Singh and Umesh Kalbagh (both journalists working with Filmfare) developed this idea of two teenagers struggling to get married in a big city like Bombay.' The copyright of the story was purchased by Basu-da and he wrote the screenplay for Doordarshan's approval. Doordarshan accepted the film idea without any

fuss. After that, Basu-da shot the film in twenty-one days in Bombay on a shoestring budget.

Budget was indeed an issue, mentions Sanjoy Chowdhury to the author. 'I was paid only Rs 5000 for composing.'[397]

In this context, it could be mentioned that Sanjoy's father Salil Chowdhury had received Rs 10,000 for the music of Basu's first film *Sara Aakash*. Twenty years later, when the price of gold had gone up by eighteen times (ten grams of 24-carat gold was Rs 176 in 1969, whereas it was Rs 3140 in 1989), the music director was paid half the amount.

Sanjoy also mentions an amusing incident that took place during the song sitting. After hearing the compositions, Kumar Sanu, the singer, blurted out, 'Why are the tunes so complicated? Who do you think you are? Salil Chowdhury?', not knowing that he was talking to his son.[398]

The music of the film was Sanjoy's, though Basu used portions of the background score previously composed by his father. Both were credited in the film. Few would take notice, as marketing efforts for his joint venture between Basu and DD was zilch.

Basu went on record expressing concern over the film's success at the theatre, admitting that it would be very optimistic to hope that the film would run for over three weeks. But he was hopeful that it would be seen by more than a million people on TV.[399]

That never happened.

★ ★ ★

The failure of *Hamari Shaadi* probably made Basu come out of his comfort zone. And attempt a satire on the exploitation of women, especially in and around the villages in central and northern India. *Durga* followed. Few remember a commercial release that should have been a natural successor to the censor clearance, which happened on 31 July 1991. Not losing heart, Basu gave a few interviews about *Triyacharitra*, his next film, which had rape of a most unusual kind as the central theme. Technically one of Basu's better works in terms of locale, dialect and night photography (by Ajay Prabhakar at a set put up at Kamalistan Studio), the film suffered from the syndrome which had become Basu's Achilles' heel: production values. And immature acting by some of the supporting cast, inasmuch as bigwigs Naseeruddin Shah and Om Puri failed to elevate the film beyond the ordinary. In his effort to control the budget, Basu landed in a penny-wise pound-foolish situation. He did not create authentic, elaborate sets needed for the story. 'He would focus only on the content. His reliance on zoom during the outdoor shoot at Allahabad was at the cost of the 'Block lens' which he had ordered. Prabhakar wanted to use the same, but Basu-da continued the trend of zoom in and zoom out,' mentioned Deepak Qazir to the author, and continued, 'At the end, he was a content-based director. The story is good, and it touches you, right? Let's take it ahead.'[400] The shot compositions, bereft of depth gave the work a telefilm-like quality—which it was partly, a joint venture of NFDC and DD—sans the arresting flow a telefilm was supposed to have. *Triyacharitra* was no *Sadgati* (1981). Neither was it an *Aadmi Aur Aurat* (1984). Or a *Tamas* (1988).

This was Basu's last work for NFDC. While Basu would often blame NFDC for the lack of strategic foresight in building small theatres for art films, in his heart of hearts he surely knew that good cinema eventually did well. Contemporaries like Shyam Benegal made *Suraj ka Satvan Ghoda* (1993), *Mammo* (1994) and *Sardaari Begum* (1996) around the same time. These films enjoyed critical acclaim. They still do.

But the worst was still to come.

★ ★ ★

Amit Khanna, in an interview with the author, goes back in time:[401]

I produced Basu-da's *Gudgudee* (1997). He had great expectations for the film. And was very confident about its success. Before the release, he did something unusual. He wanted a press show followed by a dinner, and subsequently, we had a screening and a dinner for 30–40 people at Ritz Hotel at Churchgate. The failure of the film disappointed him. Badly.

The disappointment was not without genuine reason. *Gudgudee* was a project after Basu's heart, where he tried to redo Billy Wilder's *The Seven Year Itch* (1955). This was something he had in mind for two decades. His initial choice of the female lead was Manisha Koirala followed by Juhi Chawla, but date issues led him to check out Pratibha Sinha.[402] Subsequently, the build-up to the film was meticulously planned. Six songs had been composed, and the music had been popularized through Plus Music, the sister company of Amit Khanna's Plus Films. The initial sales were promising. A surprise element of seeing Shahrukh Khan introducing the film was also there. A deal had been worked out with Rajshri for the release at the theatres. To top it all, it was Basu's costliest film ever. The budget was Rs 75 lakh.

This was a rare occasion when Basu was not glorious in failure. Contrary to his near genial take on rejections, he blamed Anupam Kher, the lead, for the flop.[403]

Calcutta

Basu's return to the big screen with *Gudgudee* was like a diversion from the world of television. One of the reasons for the same was the failure of the sequel of *Rajani,* which happened during the period 1993-95 where different people directed different episodes. Unfortunately, the charm of Season One was no longer dominant ten years later. Neither were the viewers seriously bothered about the failure of the government machinery. They had better things to do, and satellite television was one of them. A major chunk of the Hindi viewers had shifted to sitcoms on Star/Zee TV. DD serials were on the verge of being passé, one of the last serials of note being Jaspal Bhatti's *Flop Show* (1989), which redefined satire on the small screen. The sitcoms that continued on DD, like

Chandrakanta (1994) were juvenile, catering to the small towner and villages where colour TV was still a luxury and cable TV out of reach.

Another reason was probably his failure to establish himself in Calcutta, though his debut had interested many. It all started in 1988 when Washington DC-based Shankar Basu had come down to India and floated the idea of producing a TV serial. Shankar Basu was well connected with people like Hrishikesh Mukherjee; he was also a member of NFDC and DFFI for some time, mentions Gautam Banerjee, and continues:[404]

> Anil Dey, a man from the theatre world, had collected a few stories, mostly inspired from the west, and had submitted them to DD Calcutta. Shankar and I liked the concept. Shankar had the necessary contacts, and we decided to take the concept ahead and approached Basu-da. The series was named *Jodi Emon Hoto* (Had it happened). It had twenty-six stories: all 'What if' situations.
>
> My relationship with Basu-da goes long back. He used to call me every time he used to come to Cal. Probably because I did not drink, and often had to escort people back home. Many Cal-based luminaries would join our evening *addas*. It included Salil Chowdhury, Prabodh Maitra (the administrator of Nandan then), Mriganka Shekhar Roy (writer–director), Arun Pramanik (connected with the Calcutta chapter of FTII), Gautam Ghosh (director), Mrinal Sen, and his wife Shobha Sen, et at. Basu Bhattacharya too was an occasional visitor. Prabodh Mitra was a good friend of Basu-da, so when Basu Bhattacharya would come, Basu-da would say, 'Prabodh, you won't get an opportunity to open your mouth. Basu-da (Bhattacharya, who had the gift of the gab, would do most of the talking) is here.'

This was not Basu's first invitation to the world of cinema in Bengal. He had offers from bigwigs as well, including one from

Dilip Sircar, son of B.N. Sircar, and had also thought of a role for Uttam Kumar in a Hindi film. None of these transpired though. Basu's first shoot in Calcutta happened much later, in August 1988, at the Chandra Guest House at Gariahat in South Calcutta. In an interview,[405] Basu had also discussed the serials happening in Bombay at that time, including *Udaan* (1988), which he loved, *Ramayan* (1987), which he found absurd, and *Adalat*, which in his eyes belonged to the same ridiculous category as *Ramayan* and understandably, had been granted an extension by Mandi House. Basu's sardonic sense of humour had not deserted him even when he was struggling to cope with the unprofessional standards of Calcutta, where the first day's work had begun late.

Jodi Emon Hoto received a lukewarm response, forcing Basu to temporarily quit Calcutta. But he had to return, chasing someone who had stolen a Moviola from his Bombay office. Gautam Banerjee accompanied him to the police headquarters at Lalbazaar to get the machine back. Banerjee knew a flat owner near the place, and it was through his help that Basu bought his first tangible property in the city. A residential flat in Ballygunge, it would become the hub for some great conversations with a portrait of Satyajit Ray in the background. This happened in 1993. Soon, he was back in the city with the thought of producing Bengali films, and, along with producer Debesh Ghosh, he bought a single-storeyed house opposite NT2 Studio Cooperative on Prince Anwar Shah Road, with plans of converting it into an editing unit.[406] Basu had, by then, become the owner of three cameras. Two Arriflex 2C models and an Arriflex 3. Discussions for film production were on with film-maker Rituparna Ghosh, who was being hailed as the successor to Satyajit Ray then, and the idea for *Sob Choritra Kalponik* [later made by Ghosh in 2009] was being crystallized in mid-1996.[407] The plan did not work out and Basu shifted to making a film himself. In Bengali.

Thus started his collaboration with Bangladeshi actor Ferdous Ahmed. Starting with *Hathat Brishti* (1998), which propelled the actor to stardom, Basu went on to make four films with him, his last being *Hothat Sedin* in 2012, almost a line-by-line translation of *Rajnigandha* (1974). In between, he made *Chupi Chupi* (2001), recreating *Hamari Shaadi,* and improved upon the original, following it up with *Tak Jhaal Misti* (2002). However, except for the taut scripts, moderately good acting by a few, the recurrence of the name Deepa (ode to *Rajnigandha*), the introduction of a character named Sriman Barua as the hero's co-traveller (as a dedication to his friend, played by FTII grad Kalyan Chatterjee) in *Hathat Brishti*, and a near naturally filmed rain[408] in the climax of the aforementioned film,[409] the work added little value to Basu's oeuvre. It seems Basu, now over seventy, was in a hurry to tell his stories. Often the same ones; just that the language was different.

The final nail in Basu's filmmaking journey had already been hammered in the coffin by *Trishanku* (2009). Based on a short story which Mannu Bhandari had modelled on her daughter Rachana's adolescent love affair, not only was this Ashok Surana production calamitous, it also pushed an entire generation of Basu lovers to feel let down. Film critic Shoma A. Chatterji, one of the very few who saw the film, sums it up thus. 'Ideally, one should not draw comparisons between the literary source and its celluloid representation. Even so, *Trishanku*, briefly summed up, is a disaster, never mind its literary origins.'[410] Chatterji was perhaps not aware of Basu's earlier attempt at presenting Ajoy Kar's Bengali classic *Saptapadi* (1960) as *Prateeksha* (2006), his last completed Hindi feature. It was a film Basu should have avoided.

By that time, Mandi House had severed its relationship with Basu. This happened in late 2005 when Basu was 78 years young and eager to work even more. Unfortunately, his last work for DD, *Ek Prem Katha*, a selection of twenty-six love stories collected from various languages of the country, failed to inject any enthusiasm in the minds of the viewers who had been sold on cable TV. Basu also repeated a basic mistake, translating period pieces into contemporary stories. The two did not gel.

> Basu tipped his hat to Ray once again in *Ek Prem Katha*. 'Abhinetri', the Bengali story by Narendranath Mitra, had been used as one of the stories in the series Satyajit Ray presented too.

By that time, Basu had moved to Calcutta, and most of the shoot was interim. He was the honorary chairman of the Satyajit Ray Film and Television Institute.

Pack Up

It was a soggy morning on 4 June 2020 when Basu Chatterji, suffering from old-age ailments, passed away in the early hours. He was ninety-three. Fit, both physically and mentally almost up to the age of 88, the last five to six years had taken a toll on his health, especially his memory. He would fail to recall his later films. Memories of a *Hamari Shaadi* or a *Lakhon ki Baat* were completely missing. *Chakravyuha?* 'Was it something I made?' was his response, though funnily, he remembered that he had worked with Rajesh Khanna. And had good words to say about Neetu Singh.

Majorly, people loved Basu. Madhuchhanda, his first heroine, would mark him as a nervous man who did the impossible. Zarina Wahab, whose stardom began with *Chitchor*, recalled him as a sweet man under whom work was fun. This was a point of view echoed by most who worked with Basu. Film-maker Vinay Shukla, gold medallist in Film Direction at FTII, 1971 batch, who disapproved of the quality of his post-late 1970s work, mentioned that Basu Chatterji knew cinema well and could have done better by remaining focussed and doing fewer films.[411] One film a year till the age of sixty and then gradually cut down on work? Maybe, as a thumb rule, used by most great film-makers. Hitchcock, Wilder, Ray, Basu's gurus all, no one was above this rule.

The problem with Basu was that he refused to live without making films. He was completely obsessed with cinema. There would be a time when he was doing three shifts a day—7 a.m. to 2 p.m., 2 p.m. to 10 p.m., and 10 p.m. to 6 a.m. He used to view cinema from the point of view of the producer, mentions Putul Guha, actor, and son of film-maker Dulal Guha, also related to Basu through his brother Pintu's marriage with Rupali.

> Every producer wanted to be like him. He believed that the onus was on the director to ensure that the producer does not lose money, and he planned it out in detail. During the first day of the shooting of *Sheesha*, Basu Chatterji sat down to pay the crew himself. The accountant was sitting on his side, watching. During that time, Sarla, actress Laxmi Chhaya's sister, was Moon Moon Sen's hairdresser. She was a star hairdresser and would ask for a rate much higher than what was the market norm. Basu Chatterji refused to budge an inch and paid her per the rate agreed with the association. Sarla was later compensated by Moon Moon Sen.[412]

Unlike hyperboles attributed to the deceased, this testimonial to Basu's control at the lowest level is not apocryphal. He would place equal importance on the economics of filmmaking, something ignored by directors and left to production managers and controllers. This was a reason why producers placed a lot of confidence in Basu handling their money. And yet, Basu would side with his team when they were deprived of their legitimate dues. K.K. Mahajan, the rebel superstar, once stopped the shoot when the producer of a mid-1970s film did not pay his crew on time. Basu sided with him. A contract needs to be honoured, was the way he used to look at things. Unfortunately, Basu often signed contracts cheap, and honouring them could be difficult with the quality of technicians he loved to work with. Attrition was a normal consequence. In the tug-of-war between art and commerce, the former suffered. Basu could not extricate himself from the middle-class syndrome of refusing to take financial risks. But at the end of the day, if not frequenting a film festival, he would go back to his best film: *Sara Aakash*. Or the film after his heart, *Jeena Yahan*. The artist in him was very much alive. Just that it was misplaced in a commercial outlet like the film industry. This continued to be with him till his last days. Says Rupali:[413]

> A few years back when Bapi (father) had pretty much stopped communicating and had begun to forget things I decided to watch a film with him via the inimitable firestick. We started the film, and I kept looking at him as the film progressed, wondering if he's grasping anything. He seemed interested. The film got over. Mom was dying to catch up on *Rani Rashmoni* [a Bengali serial] and insisted I change channels when he surprised us all and asked, 'Who was the director of this film?' 'What was the name of the film?' 'Who was the actor?' It was a moment of immense joy and pride for me as I witnessed a glimpse of the man who breathed cinema. I bow to director Rajat Kapoor and actor Sanjay Mishra for their immensely poignant *Ankhon Dekhi* (2013).

★ ★ ★

A point often ignored in connection with Basu Chatterji is his catering to the have nots, recalls actor Akhil Mishra, and continues[414]

> Basu-da was my inspiration when I wrote *Dhat Tere Ki* (1983). He came into my life when someone brought him to see one of my plays in 1979. It was a comedy based on a play by Carlo Goldoni for which I had received a National Award from the Critics Circle of India. He must have liked it, as he later used to come and watch my plays. He would sit at the back and meet us after the play was over. He was a fatherly figure. Protective. When he was angry, it was like a father scolding his son. We enjoyed the camaraderie and used to eat together on the sets. The 'we' included veterans like Ashok Kumar (on the sets of *Bhim Bhavani*), Om Puri (during *Kakaji Kahin*), et al. There was no ego in him.

He was very protective of his actors. During my first shoot with him, the cameraman was upset as I must have gone out of the frame. He said, 'What are you doing?' in a manner which sounded aggressive. Dada (Basu) snubbed him. 'He is my actor. He'll do whatever he feels is right, he will improvise based on his expertise. It is your job to capture him.'

If he saw somebody was uncomfortable, he would ask about the problem. I have this issue with hay fever which results in a lot of sneezing. Once, I had to take an anti-allergic which makes you very drowsy. Basu-da stood by me and helped me complete the shoot.

A similar point of view was expressed by Pradip Acharya, who had worked as a production manager with Basu:[415]

Basu-da joined SRFTI as an Honorary Chairman in 2004 or 2005. After going there, it was brought to his notice that there was a three-year backlog for diploma films, something which soon snowballed into a major issue leading to a student strike. Apprehensive that they were losing three precious years of their careers, the students demanded that the institute brings to the board a professional production chief, as the person in charge of production then had a degree in film direction from FTII but was not aware of the nitty-gritty of production. Aware of my expertise in the area, Basu-da invited me to join SRFTI in that role. This was in 2005 November, when I was involved with work for BBC at Jaipur. Basu-da was my godfather, who had guided me all along during my journey in cinema. I could not say no to him, and I came down to Calcutta and joined SRFTI on 1 December 2005. By April 2006 I closed the backlogs. That was my guru dakshina to him.

The role of the chairman at SRFTI was something Basu performed with all seriousness. Despite being in an honorary position, he was extremely active during his tenure of five years. He had been offered a guest house accommodation which he gently refused, only to buy a small flat opposite the institute. The funds for the same he generated by selling his Prince Anwar Shah Road flat. And also, some of his equipment, including an Arri which he sold to the SRFTI. He would also take classes, confirms Samik Kumar Rakshit, a graduate of the institute.[416]

Like Mishra and Acharya, many admitted to having benefitted by Basu. One does not have to try hard for prominent names. Few knew Amol Palekar and Vidya Sinha before *Rajnigandha*. Or Zarina Wahab and Vijayendra Ghatge before *Chitchor*. For that matter, Rakesh Pandey and Suresh Chatwal's stock value increased only after they appeared in *Sara Aakash* and *Piya ka Ghar* respectively. Thanks to Basu, the mother and son pair of Pearl Padamsee and Ranjit Chowdhry, despite their immense talent, became characters etched in our memories only after *Khatta Meetha* and *Baton Baton Mein*. Ashalata, Bharti Achrekar, Kiran Vairale, all of them debuted under Basu before moving on to do other or better-known acts in cinema. Basu was all for junior artistes being given their due. One might recall a tall gent as Ashok Kumar's secretary in *Chhoti Si Baat*. R.S. Chopra, a junior artiste originally from Patna, became a regular with Basu from 1975 to 2005. Despite having single-shot appearances in most, he is remembered due to the nature of his roles. Basu acted as an enabler for his actors, allowing them to shine even when their presence on the screen was limited to a few minutes.

The feel for people was not limited to his cast and crew. Basu had no inhibitions in initiating conversations with the passer-by, cab drivers, milkmen or for that matter anyone he encountered in his day-to-day life. His character was devoid of snob value. Anybody was welcome to discuss cinema. The established template for film people did not work in his case. His interest level would multiply manifold if the person was a native of Uttar Pradesh. He remained someone who never forgot his humble roots.

* * *

Be it good health, or simply God's will, Basu outlived most of his contemporaries. The list includes Pratibha Dixit, the real-life character on whom his first heroine Prabha was modelled. Pratibha passed away on 9 February 1995. She was sixty-five. Prakash Dixit, her husband, is probably the only person from that generation who managed to outlive Basu.

Basu's death happened without any associated histrionics. There was no twenty-four-hour media coverage flashing news of his health condition. Like his true-to-life scripts, his passing away was uneventful. Due to the restrictions on account of COVID then, shooting was already stalled at major studios. The few which were on were not called off. Basu must have been happy on his last journey. Had shootings been called off officially, he might have risen inside the hearse and called out—'Come on, are you guys serious? Wasting a full day's shoot for me?'

Notes

Morning

1 Interview with Basu Chatterji in April 2015.
2 Apurba Chattopadhyay, 'Flashback', *Saptahik Bartaman*, 15 July 1995.
3 Interview with Kajol Majumdar, Basu Chatterji's niece.
4 Ibid.
5 Interview with Basu Chatterji by the author in 2014.
6 Apurba Chattopadhyay, 'Flashback', *Saptahik Bartaman*, 15 July 1995.
7 'Morphology of Middle Class', *Patriot*, 12 December 1982.
8 Interview with Basu Chatterji by the author in 2015, and also *Guftagoo with Basu Chatterji* on Rajya Sabha TV.
9 Deepa Gahlot, 'The Middle Class Mandarin', *Cinema in India*, September 1990. Gahlot mentions that Kishore Kumar was the hero, but it is incorrect.
10 H.N. Narahari Rao, *The Film Society Movement in India*, Asian Film Foundation Mumbai, 2009.
11 Interview with Basu Chatterji in April 2015.
12 Ibid.
13 Interview with Banya Barua in April 2021.
14 'Morphology of Middle Class', *Patriot*, 12 December 1982.
15 Interview with Jayanta Gupta in November 2019.
16 Apurba Chattopadhyay, 'Flashback', *Saptahik Bartaman*, 22 July 1995.
17 Information courtesy Vivek Kumar, Film Aficionado.
18 Information courtesy Dinesh Shankar Shailendra.
19 Ibid.
20 Information courtesy Praba Mahajan, then a member of *Anandam*.
21 Email exchange with Kumar Shahani on 10 April 2021.
22 Interview with Basu Chatterji in April 2015.
23 Interview with Narinder Singh in April 2021.
24 V.K. Cherian, *India's Film Society Movement*, SAGE Publications, 2017, pp. 62–63.

25 Interview with Indraneel Kaul in March 2021.
26 Khalid Mohamed, 'Smiles to Go: Remembering Basu Chatterjee, Champion of Middle-Class Cinema', *Mumbai Mirror*, 5 June 2020.
27 Information courtesy Jayanta Gupta in April 2021.
28 Cherian, SAGE Publications, 2017, p. 156.
29 Interview with Narinder Singh in April 2021.
30 Cherian, SAGE publications, 2017, p. 156.
31 Information courtesy Sonal Pandya in April 2021; also, an interview with Basu Chatterji in April 2015.
32 Information courtesy Dinesh Shankar Shailendra; and interview with Basu Chatterji in April 2015.
33 Apurba Chattopadhyay, 'Flashback', *Saptahik Bartaman*, 15 July 1995.

The Variegated Sky

34 Interview with Basu Chatterji in April 2015.
35 Interview with Rachana Yadav in June 2020.
36 Interview with Rupali Guha in April 2021.
37 Interview with Kajol Majumdar in April 2021.
38 B.K. Adarsh, *Film History of India*, 1963. Reproduction courtesy Cinemaazi.
39 B.K. Karanjia, *Counting My Blessings*, Viking, 2005.
40 Details courtesy Praba Mahajan.
41 Mrinal Sen, *Always Being Born,* Stellar Publications, 2006.
42 Anirudha Bhattacharjee and Amitava Chatterjee, *Amitabh Bachchan: The Book of Lists*, Big Ideas, 1992.
43 Satyajit Ray, *An Indian New Wave—Our Films Their Films,* Orient Longman Limited, 1976.
44 Interview with Basu Chatterji in Kolkata, April 2015.
45 Preface to *Sara Aakash* by Rajendra Yadav.
46 Interview with Viraj Dixit, son of Prakash and Pratibha Dixit, in July 2020.
47 Interview with Basu Chatterji in April 2015 at Calcutta.
48 Interview with Viraj Dixit in July 2020.
49 Ibid.
50 Interview with Rakesh Pandey in July 2020.
51 Ibid.
52 Ibid.
53 Interview with Madhuchhanda Chakrabarty during June and July 2020.
54 Interview with Nandita Thakur in July 2020. [There is another line of thought, though. The cast and crew of *Teesri Kasam* were in Bina (a border town between Uttar Pradesh and Madhya Pradesh) during the outdoor

shoot, and many were guests at the house of Satyabrata Ghosh, who was a lecturer at a college there. Basu Chatterji was there as part of the crew. He had probably seen and remembered Nandita—the daughter of Satyabrata Ghosh—years before the *Eve's Weekly* issue.]

55 Interview with Basu Chatterji in April 2015.

56 Interview with Madhuchhanda Chakrabarty during June and July 2020.

57 Details sourced from the preface to *Sara Aakash Patkatha*, Rajkamal Prakashan, 2007.

58 Interviews with Rakesh Pandey, Madhuchhanda Chakrabarty, Nandita Thakur, Biswajit Mitra and others.

59 Interview with Narinder Singh in June 2020.

60 Interview with Dilip Raghuvanshi, son of Rajendra Raghuvanshi, Agra, in March 2020. Also, interview with Basu Chatterji in 2014.

61 Interview with Nandita Thakur in July 2020.

62 Interview with Madhuchhanda Chakrabarty in June 2020.

63 K.K. Mahajan, *The History and Practice of Cinematography in India*, Raqs Media Collective, December 1996.

64 Interview with Narinder Singh in June 2020.

65 Interview with Rachana Yadav in July 2020.

66 Preface to *Sara Aakash Patkatha,* Rajkamal Prakashan, 2007.

67 Interview with Nandita Thakur in July 2020.

68 Interview with Narinder Singh in June 2020.

69 Interview with Madhuchhanda Chakrabarty in June 2020.

70 Ibid.

71 Interview with Kajol Majumdar in April 2021.

72 Interview with Basu Chatterji in 2015.

73 Interview with Narinder Singh in June 2020.

74 Preface to *Sara Aakash* by Rajendra Yadav, Radhakrishna Prakashan.

75 Interview with Madhuchhanda Chakrabarty in June 2020.

76 Ibid.

77 Interview with Kajol Majumdar in April 2021.

78 Interview with Dilip Raghuvanshi in March 2021.

79 Interview with Madhuchhanda Chakrabarty in July 2020.

80 Interview with Rupali Guha in May 2021.

81 Names from the Censor certificate number 60087, https://www.cbfcindia.gov.in/main/list-of-chairpersons.html

82 The *Sunday Standard*, 27 September 1970.

83 Interview with Yasir Abbasi in May 2021.

84 Interview with Ramesh Gupta on 11 September 2021.

85 A report in *Filmfare*, 1 July 1960.

86 Interview with Basu Chatterji in April 2015.
87 Preface to *Sara Aakash Patkatha*, Rajkamal Prakashan, 2007.
88 Gautam Kaul, *The New Middle-Class Cinema*, *The Hindu*, 5 October 1990.
89 Poster of *Sara Aakash* from the National Film Archives of India, Pune.

Basu's Bombay

90 Naseeruddin Shah, *And Then One Day: A Memoir*, Penguin India, 2014.
91 Interview with Arunaraje Patil in July 2021.
92 Interview with Vikas Desai in July 2021.
93 Tête-à-tête with Rupali Guha in May 2021.
94 Interview with Basu Chatterji in April 2015. Basu seeing the original version in the editing room at the FTII was described by Vikas Desai.
95 Interview with Anil Dhawan on 12 September 2020.
96 Interview with Madhuchhanda Chakrabarty in July 2020.
97 Interview with Narinder Singh in June 2020.
98 Interview with Anil Dhawan on 12 September 2020.
99 Ibid.
100 Interview with Ajay Prabhakar in June 2020.
101 Interview with Anil Dhawan on 12 September 2020.
102 Ibid.
103 A YouTube link tells us that the song was probably composed in A major, https://www.youtube.com/watch?v=iqLRsJfQ3k8
104 Interview with Anil Dhawan on 12 September 2020.

The Common Man

105 Interview with Rachana Yadav in June 2020.
106 Mannu Bhandari, *Ek Kahani Yeh Bhi,* Radhakrishan Prakashan, sixth edition, 2019.
107 Interview with Suresh Jindal on 21 July 2020.
108 'Rajnigandha' producer Suresh Jindal, 'Basuda Lit the Path for Me to the Industry', *Outlook*, 8 June 2020.
109 Sulagna Biswas, 'Flashback Friday: Rajnigandha', *Telegraph*, Kolkata, 5 September 2019.
110 Ibid.
111 Interview with Basu Chatterji in 2014.
112 Interview with Rakesh Pandey on 5 July 2020.
113 Interview with Basu Chatterji in 2014.
114 Interview with Amol Palekar conducted by Balaji Vittal in 2018.

115 Interview with Preeta Mathur Thakur on 14 June 2021.
116 Interview with Basu Chatterji in 2015.
117 Roshmila Bhattacharya, 'This Week, That Year: Memories of Rajnigandha and Vidya Sinha', *Mumbai Mirror*, 28 September 2017, https://mumbaimirror.indiatimes.com/entertainment/bollywood/this-week-that-year-memories-of-rajnigandha-and-vidya-sinha/articleshow/60505699.cms
118 Tête-à-tête with Praba Mahajan in June 2020.
119 Interview with Nandita Thakur in July 2020.
120 Tête-à-tête with Rupali Guha in June 2021.
121 Tête-à-tête with Praba Mahajan in June 2020.
122 Tête-à-tête with Rupali Guha in June 2021.
123 Interview with Basu Chatterji in April 2015.
124 Tete-a-tete with Rupali Guha in June 2021.
125 Ibid.
126 Interview with Basu Chatterji in 2014.
127 Multiple interviews with Yogesh from 2009 to 2015.
128 Interview with Preeta Mathur Thakur on 14 June 2021.
129 Interview with Basu Chatterji in 2014.
130 Multiple interviews with Yogesh from 2009 to 2015.
131 Suresh Jindal, *My Adventures with Satyajit Ray*, Harper Collins, 2018, notes section.
132 Ibid., p. 53.
133 Interview with Suresh Jindal after the film was released in 1974, published in leading magazines. Also: '"Rajnigandha" producer Suresh Jindal: Basuda lit the path for me to the industry (FIRST PERSON),' *Outlook*, 8 June 2020.
134 Interview with Suresh Jindal on 21 July 2020.
135 Jindal, Harper Collins, notes section.
136 Interview with Suresh Jindal on 21 July 2020.
137 Tête-à-tête with Roshmila Bhattacharya in June 2021. The details shared were told to her by Dinesh Thakur during an interview.
138 Interview with Preeta Mathur Thakur on 14 June 2021.
139 '"Rajnigandha" producer Suresh Jindal: Basuda lit the path for me to the industry (FIRST PERSON),' *Outlook*, 8 June 2020.
140 Interview with Basu Chatterji in 2014 by Balaji Vittal.
141 Page 141, Methuen in 2014
142 Interview with Basu Chatterji in 2014.
143 Interview with Narinder Singh in June–July 2020.
144 Interview with Nandita Thakur in July 2020.
145 Interview with Basu Chatterji in 2014.
146 Interview with Amol Palekar conducted by Balaji Vittal in 2018.

147 Interview with Ajay Prabhakar in June 2020.
148 Interview with Basu Chatterji in 2014.
149 Interview with Ajay Prabhakar in June 2020.
150 Interview with Nandita Thakur in June 2020.
151 Interview with Basu Chatterji in 2014.
152 Ibid.
153 Apurba Chattopadhyay, 'Flashback', *Saptahik Bartaman*, 15 July 1995.
154 Basu Chatterji's interview with Sourav Majumdar and Mahuya Paul, *Business Standard*, 29 August 1998.
155 Basu Chatterji's interview with Moushumi Biswas, *Asian Age*, 6 September 1996.
156 Information courtesy interaction with Rameshwari on 2 October 2020.
157 Interview with Bindiya Goswami on 5 July 2021.
158 Interview with Ajay Prabhakar in June 2020.
159 N. Bharathi, *Basu Chatterji—A Touch of Comedy.*
160 Shabana Azmi, 'Being FTII', Ministry of I&B, 2021.
161 Truncated except from Raaj Grover's *The Legends of Bollywood*, Jaico Publishing House, Kindle edition, Chapter 21.
162 Interview with Zarina Wahab on 20 July 2021.
163 Ibid.
164 In the actual recording, music director Rahul Dev Burman had artificially reproduced the sound.
165 Interview with Arup Gangoly in July 2020.
166 Interview with Zarina Wahab on 20 July 2021.
167 Nadeem Khan, 'The Boss and I', *Cinematography Art*. Shared by Praba Mahajan.
168 Interview with Ajay Prabhakar in March 2021.
169 Interview with Zarina Wahab on 20 July 2021.
170 Interview with Pandit Subir Chakrabarty on 12 March 2021.
171 Interview with Basu Chatterji in 2014.

The Misses

172 Interview with Basu Chatterji in April 2015. Also, Anirudha Bhattacharjee and Balaji Vittal, *S.D. Burman: The Prince-Musician*, Westland, 2018.
173 Interview with Ramesh Gupta on 11 September 2021.
174 Saptahik Bartaman, 15-22 July 1995.
175 Ibid.
176 Ibid.
177 Rishi Kapoor and Meena Iyer, *Khullam Khulla*, Harper Collins India, 2017.
178 Interview with Moushumi Chatterjee on 20 June 2021.

179 Interviews with Rupali Guha and Praba Mahajan, May 2021.
180 Interviews with Rupali Guha, May 2021.
181 Interview with Ramesh Gupta on 11 September 2021.
182 Interview with Basu Chatterji in 2014.
183 Multiple interviews with Yogesh in 2009, 2010, 2011 and 2014.
184 Interview with Moushumi Chatterjee on 20 June 2021.
185 Interview with Basu Chatterji in April 2015; Bhattacharjee & Balaji, Westland, 2018.
186 Basu Chatterji sang the phrase, *Hui*, during the interview in April 2015.
187 Interview of Basu Chatterji by N. Bharathi.
188 Sai Paranjpye, *A Patchwork Quilt: A Collage of My Creative Life,* Harper Collins Kindle Edition, 2019, p. 278.
189 Interview with Saikat Mitra in July 2020.
190 Not to be confused with the predominantly Bengali film actor Ashim Kumar who was given the pseudonym Manish in Hindi cinema.
191 Interview with Rana Bhattacharya and Rajeev Bhattacharya, sons of Ashim Kumar.
192 Interview with Arup Kr Gangoly.
193 Interview with Rana Bhattacharya.
194 *Filmfare*, dated 11–24 November 1977.
195 Interview with Arup Kr Gangoly in July 2020.
196 Interview with Basu Chatterji in April 2015.
197 Ibid.
198 Interview with Sabita Bose on 6 June 2021.
199 'Patalbabu Film Star' is a story by Satyajit Ray, first published in July 1963 in the magazine *Sandesh*.
200 Interview with Asha Sachdev on 18 May 2021.
201 Interview of Rakesh Roshan by Priyanka Bhatt on 22 June 2021.
202 http://www.sukanyaverma.com/2016/04/when-jeetu-neetu-played-newlyweds-in-basu-chatterjees-priyatama/
203 Interview with Arvind Haldipur on 29 September 2020.
204 Interview of Rakesh Roshan by Priyanka Bhatt on 22 June 2021.
205 Multiple interviews with Yogesh during the period 2009–2015 by Balaji Vittal.
206 Email correspondence with Rajesh Roshan on 11 October 2021.

And the Ones Which Rocked

207 Interview with Rita Mehta in July-August 202.
208 https://www.thecitizen.in/index.php/en/NewsDetail/index/2/16919/What-Bengal-is-Doing-Today-India-Should-Never-Do-Tomorrow--

209 Interview with Basu Chatterji in April 2015.
210 Report of the Working Journalists Wage Committee, https://indianculture.gov.in/report-working-journalists-wage-committee
211 Interview with Rita Mehta in July-August 2021.
212 Interview with Basu Chatterji in April 2015.
213 Interview with Rakesh Roshan by Priyanka Bhatt on 22 June 2021.
214 Interview with Bindiya Goswami on 5 July 2021.
215 Interview with Arup Kumar Gangoly in June 2020.
216 Interview with Dinesh Shankar Shailendra in June 2020.
217 Interview with Rakesh Roshan by Priyanka Bhatt on 22 June 2021.
218 Interview with Bindiya Goswami on 5 July 2021.
219 Ibid.
220 Godrej: The Archives Times Aug 2012, shared by Diptendu Bhattacharya, Senior General Manager at Godrej & Boyce Mfg. Co. Ltd.
221 Interview with Arup Kumar Gangoly in June 2020.
222 Interview with Dinesh Shankar Shailendra in June 2020.
223 Interview with Bindiya Goswami on 5 July 2021.
224 Interview with Arunaraje Patil on 1 July 2021.
225 Interview with Bindiya Goswami on 5 July 2021.
226 Interview with Arup Kumar Gangoly in June 2020.
227 Interview with A.K. Bir in August 2020.
228 Ibid.
229 Interview with Dinesh Shankar Shailendra in June 2020.
230 Interview with Arup Kumar Gangoly in June 2020.
231 Basu Chatterji's interview in Alokepath, May 1989.
232 Dayawanti Gurrung, *Star & Style*, 24 October 24–6 November 1986.
233 From a Facebook comment by Dara Kotwal to a post on *Khatta Meetha* by K.E. Eduljee on 10 June 2020, in the group 'Zoroastrian Heritage'.
234 Interview with Bindiya Goswami on 5 July 2021.
235 Email correspondence with Rajesh Roshan on 11 October 2021.

Bengal Stories

236 Mannu Bhandari, *Ek Kahani Yeh Bhi,* Radhakrishan Prakashan, sixth edition, 2019.
237 Interview with Shabana Azmi on 10 July 2021.
238 Interview with Vikram on 14 June 2020.
239 Interview with I.K. Bahl in January 2021.
240 Basu Chatterji interview with Deepa Gahlot, Cinema in India, September 1990.
241 Interview with Shabana Azmi on 10 July 2021.

242 Interview with I. K. Bahl in January 2021.
243 Girish Karnad, *This Life at Play*, Harper Collins, 2021.
244 Interview with I. K. Bahl in January 2021.
245 Interview with Dheeraj Kumar on 24 August 2021.
246 Ibid.
247 Interview with Vikram in June 2020.
248 Ibid.
249 Ibid.
250 Interview with I.K. Bahl in January 2021.
251 Interview with Shabana Azmi on 10 July 2021.
252 Email correspondence with Rajesh Roshan on 11 October 2021.
253 Interview with Banya Barua in April 2021.
254 Interview with Shabana Azmi on 10 July 2021.
255 Mannu Bhandari, *Ek Kahani Yeh Bhi,* Radhakrishnan Paperback, sixth edition, 2019.
256 Interview with Shabana Azmi on 10 July 2021.
257 Interview with Vikram in June 2020.
258 Interview with I.K. Bahl in January 2021.
259 Basu Chaterji's Interview with N. Bharathi.
260 https://dff.nic.in/images/Documents/92_25thNfacatalogue.pdf
261 Karnad, Harper Collins, 2021.
262 Interview with Samir Samanta in October 2020.
263 Interview with Shabana Azmi on 10 July 2021.
264 Interview with Bharti Archrekar on 26 June 2020.
265 Interview with Shabana Azmi on 10 July 2021.
266 Multiple interviews with Yogesh in 2009, 2010, 2011 & 2014.
267 The Pansi boat shown in the film is the 'Calcutta Pansi', used for pleasure trips. These boats are not generally oared. These are propelled by sculling (only steering oar used for plying). The other sailed boat(s) in the song is the Sultani, a boat of Nurpur, Patikhali, Bhangagara on the mouth of the Ganges. Information courtesy Swarup Bhattacharyya.
268 Shabana Azmi, 10 July 2021.
269 *Screen*, 1 August 1980.
270 *Screen*, 5 September 1980.
271 *Star & Style*, 24 October–6 November 1986.

Failure with Superstars

272 Interview with Moushumi Chatterjee on 20 June 2021.

273 Based on interviews with Basu Chatterji (in April 2015), Moushumi Chatterjee (in June & August 2021), Rakesh Pandey (in July 2020), and Rupali Guha (in June 2021).
274 Interview with Moushumi Chatterjee on 20 June 2021.
275 WhatsApp chat with Praba Mahajan in April 2021.
276 Interview with Ajay Prabhakar in June 2020.
277 Interview with Basu Chatterji in April 2015.
278 Interview with Dinesh Shankar Shailendra in June 2020.
279 Interview with Dinesh Shankar Shailendra in June 2020.
280 Interview with Arup Ganguly in July 2020.
281 Interview with Mrs Sabita Bose in July 2020.
282 Interview with Arup Gangoly in July 2020.
283 Discussion with Yasser Usman in August 2021.
284 Interview with Ajay Prabhakar in June 2020.
285 Interview with Ajay Prabhakar in June 2020 & Arup Gangoly in July 2020.
286 Ibid.
287 Ibid.
288 Interview with Arup Gangoly in July 2020.
289 Interview with Narinder Singh in July 2020.
290 Interview with Siraj Syed on 8 June 2021.
291 Interview with Dinesh Shankar Shailendra in June 2020.
292 Interview with N. Bharathi.
293 Super, October 1981.
294 Pearl Padamsee, 'The New Generation, 1960-1980', (*Film India*, 1981, published by the Directorate of Film Festivals of India).
295 Interview with Amit Khanna on 26 September 2020.
296 Interview with Amit Khanna on 26 September 2020.
297 Ibid.
298 Ibid.
299 Interview with Vikas Desai on 21 September 2021.
300 Interview with Amit Khanna on 26 September 2020.
301 Ibid.
302 Ibid.
303 Email correspondence with Rajesh Roshan on 11 October 2021.
304 Interview with Basu Chatterji in April 2015.
305 Interview with Basu Chatterji in April 2015.
306 Interview with Praba Mahajan in June 2020.
307 Interview with Basu Chatterji in April 2015.

Finding Oneself

308 Interview with Basu Chatterji in April 2015.
309 Interview with Arup Gangoly in July 2020.
310 Interview with Uday Chandra on 28 June 2021. The Helen Cottage outside which Henry would often be waiting for Nancy is Helen Haven apartments today.
311 Interview with Arup Gangoly in July 2020.
312 Interview with Saikat Mitra in July 2020.
313 Email correspondence with Rajesh Roshan on 11 October 2021, where he mentions that Pearl Padamsee sang the part featured on Leela Mishra.
314 Interview with Amit Khanna on 26 September 2020.
315 Anirudha Bhattacharjee & Balaji Vittal, *R.D. Burman: The Man the Music*, Harper Collins, 2011.
316 Interview with Uday Chandra on 28 June 2021.
317 Interview with Kiran Vairale on 29 October 2021.
318 https://www.moneycontrol.com/news/business/did-george-fernandes-drive-coca-cola-out-from-india-in-the-70s-3447791.html
319 Interview with Kiran Vairale on 29 October 2021.
320 Interview with Shabana Azmi on 10 July 2021.
321 Mannu Bhandari, *Ek Kahani Yeh Bhi,* Radhakrishan Prakashan, sixth edition, 2019.
322 Interview with A.K. Bir in August 2020.
323 Girish Karnad, *This Life at Play*, Harper Collins, 2021. Karnad makes a slip; the place was Mysore and not Khajuraho.
324
325 Interview with Basu Chatterji in April 2015.
326 Interview with D.N. Joshi on 23 April 2022.
327 Email correspondence with Rajesh Roshan on 11 October 2021.
328 Interview with Bindiya Goswami on 5 July 2021.

Middle-of-the-Road Cinema . . . or End-of-the-Road?

329 Javed Akhtar in a tête-à-tête with the author at the Kolkata Literary Meet in January 2016.
330 Gautam Banerjee in an interview with the author in June 2020.
331 Interview with Tinnu Anand on 30 June 2021.
332 Ibid.
333 Interview with Dinesh Shankar Shailendra and Ajay Prabhakar in June–July 2020.

334 Ibid.
335 Facebook post of Rupali Guha on 6 June 2020.
336 Interview with Ramesh Gupta on 11 September 2021.
337 Interview with Gautam Banerjee in June 2020.
338 Interview with I.K. Bahl in January 2021.
339 Interview with Ajay Prabhakar in June 2020.
340 Interview with Samir Samanta in October 2020.
341 *Screen*, 23 April 1982.
342 Interview with Dharmanand Joshi on 6 July 2021.
343 The figure as per interview with I.K. Bahl in January 2021.
344 Interview with Ajay Prabhakar in June 2020.
345 Chirashree Bhattacharya was married to the Mitra couple's son Raja Mitra. Not to be confused with the film director of the same name.
346 Interview with Yogesh by Balaji Vittal in 2009.
347 Information courtesy of Ajay Prabhakar in June 2020.
348 Interview of Basu by Dayawanti Gurrung, *Star & Style*, 24 October–6 November 1986.
349 Interview with Deepak Qazir Kejriwal on 19 December 2021.
350 Interview with Archana Shourie on 30 October 2021.
351 Interview with Rakesh Pandey in July 2020.
352 Interview with Tariq Khan on 6 July 2020.

His Last Hurrah

353 Interview with Sabita Bose on 10 November 2021.
354 Ananth Mahadevan, *Once Upon a Prime Time*, Embassy Book Distributors, Kindle edition, 2020, p. 30.
355 Ibid.
356 Mannu Bhandari, *Ek Kahani Yeh Bhi,* Radhakrishan Prakashan, sixth edition, 2019.
357 Ibid.
358 Interview with Bharti Archrekar on 26 June 2020.
359 Ibid., p. 151.
360 https://www.indiatoday.in/magazine/special-report/story/19850831-basu-chatterjis-rajani-on-doordarshan-becomes-a-movement-801935-2014-01-03, accessed on 13 November 2021.
361 Interview with I.K. Bahl on 31 July 2021.
362 Bhandari, Radhakrishan Prakashan, 2019.
363 Ibid., p. 151.

364 Interview with I.K. Bahl on 31 July 2021.
365 Interview with Ranjit Kapoor on 18 December 2021.
366 Ibid.
367 Interview with Deepak Qazir Kejriwal on 19 December 2021.
368 Ranjit Kapoor, 18 December 2021.
369 Ibid.
370 Ibid.
371 Transliterated dialogues from *Dharkanein* by Om Prakash Sharma.
372 https://www.rachanakar.org/2006/01/blog-post_10.html, accessed on 6 November 2021.
373 Interview with Bharti Archrekar on 26 June 2020.
374 Suresh Jindal, *My Adventures with Satyajit Ray*, Harper Collins, 2018.
375 Interview with Basu Chatterjee in April 2015.
376 Interview with Ajay Prabhakar on 17 June 2020.
377 Sriprakash Menon, 'Rejection of Basu's film criticised', *The Independent*, 1 December 1989.
378 Ibid.
379 Ibid.
380 Basu Chatterji, 'We Beg Your Pardon Too', *Times of India*, Bombay, 2 May 1991.
381 Ibid.
382 Interview with Sukanya Kulkarni on 17 May 2021.
383 Interview with Gautam Banerjee on 17 November 2021.
384 The story 'Adwitiyo' published in the periodical *Desh* in 1961 has an illustration where Byomkesh is bespectacled. Information courtesy of Sarbajit Mitra.
385 Interview with Rajit Kapur on 22 August 2021.
386 Gautam Banerjee, 17 November 2021.
387 Interview with Sukanya Kulkarni on 17 May 2021.
388 Rajit Kapur, 22 August 2021.
389 Interview with Ravindra Singh on 6 July 2021.
390 Interview with Shantanu Bandopadhyay by Pallab Chattopadhyay as part of the book *Chirayato Saradindu*, edited by Bhaskar Bose, Café Table Publications, 2020.
391 *Telegraph*, 28 March 1986.
392 Anandalok, 9 June 1991, Apurba Chattopadhyay, 'Flashback', *Saptahik Bartaman*, 22 July 1995.

Failed Dreams

393 *Sunday Observer*, 4–10 November 1990.
394 Interview with Indrani Halder on 6 December 2021.
395 Telephonic conversation with Rupali Guha on 30 October 2021.
396 Sriprakash Menon in the *Independent*, 10 October 1990.
397 Interview with Sanjoy Chowdhury on 7 September 2020.
398 Ibid.
399 A.L. Chougule in Newstime, 17 February 1991.
400 Interview with Deepak Qazir Kejriwal on 19 December 2021.
401 Interview with Amit Khanna on 26 September 2020.
402 Basu Chatterji, in an interview with Chaya R.B., published on 11 March 1997.
403 https://timesofindia.indiatimes.com/bangalore-times/basus-back-in-bollywood-with-pratiksha/articleshow/28362.cms, accessed on 5 December 2021. Interview of Basu by Nayare Ali.
404 Interview with Gautam Banerjee on 17 November 2021.
405 Pritha Sarbadhikari, *Saptahik Bartaman*, 3 September 1988.
406 Gautam Banerjee, 17 November 2021.
407 Mousumi Biswas, 'I Never Expected Much From Life', *Asian Age*, 6 September 1996.
408 Ferdous, in an interview with the author, clarifies. 'We shot mainly in Ballygunge for the film. And Basu-da used to wait for the rain to happen, after which he would use the rain-gun for the actual shoot. This added to the realism he wanted to depict, as the wet look of the actors would mesh well with the surroundings.'
409 Interview with Ferdous on 15 December 2021.
410 http://archive.indianexpress.com/news/trishanku/888189/0, accessed on 15 December 2021.

Pack Up

411 Interview with Vinay Shukla on 27 July 2021.
412 Interview with Putul Guha on 30 September 2020.
413 WhatsApp conversation with Rupali Guha on 30 October 2021.
414 Interview with Akhil Mishra on 4 July 2021.
415 Interview with Pradip Acharya on 17 November 2021.
416 Conversation with Samik K. Rakshit on 16 December 2021.

Index